# Category Management Principles

Dr. Russell J. Zwanka

Dr. Brian F. Harris

ISBN-13: 978-1533452498

ISBN-10: 1533452490

Thanks to Tucker, Cooper, and Lily!  Thank you for your support, and always being there for me, as we work through this thing called life.


A special thanks to Dr. Brian Harris, founder of the original step-by-step process we call Category Management.  Your imparting of knowledge and skills has been invaluable.  It is through your energy and enthusiasm that we will use this information to train the next generation in this great industry!

It is with expressed written permission that multiple content sources for this text have come from Dr. Brian Harris, The Partnering Group, and ECR Europe. Roland Berger was also an original contributor to the ECR Europe study and content.

# *About Dr. Zwanka*

Dr. Russell J. Zwanka serves as Director of the Food Marketing Program, and Professor of Category Management and Food Marketing, at Western Michigan University, one of the top Food Marketing programs in the world. Delivering high quality curriculum and applied food marketing skills, Western Michigan University endeavors to work with the food industry to provide real-time solutions, while also helping educate the future leaders of the food industry. The WMU Food Marketing program delivers an incredible 100% employment rate from the major! Zwanka has previously taught Marketing Research, Personal Selling, Marketing Strategy, Food Marketing, Business Strategy, Global Business, Cannabis Marketing, and Marketing Principles.

Having spent a career in the food industry before teaching, Dr. Z conceptualized and formed the Food Marketing Concentration at Siena College; as well as the Food Marketing Track at the State University of New York at New Paltz.

Dr. Z has led the merchandising, marketing, advertising, procurement, and all customer engagement areas for multiple food retail companies domestically and internationally.

Zwanka holds a Doctorate in International Business from ISM in Paris, France. He also holds a Master of Science in Management from Southern Wesleyan University, and a Bachelor of Science in Psychology from the University of South Carolina. Zwanka's 28 books are sold globally, and cover topics from doing business in Cuba to food marketing to public speaking. Dr. Zwanka was named a Top Retail Expert in 2024, by ReThink Retail, and has contributed to over 250 media publications and conferences.

# About Dr. Harris

Dr. Brian F. Harris is a former Marketing Professor at the University of Southern California, and is the originator of the practice called Category Management. Originally from Australia, Dr. Harris earned a BA in Economics from the University of Queensland, an MBA from Lehigh University, and a PhD in Marketing from Michigan State University. While teaching in the University of Southern California's Graduate School of Business Administration, Harris became the Director of the Food Industry Management Program, where he co-founded the Quaker Oats Buying Skills Seminar.

While Harris was a professor, he developed a software program called Apollo Space Management System that could calculate the optimal level of space for products on a store shelf per category of product. The first in-store testing, and use of the program resulted in the test store becoming the dominant shop in the region. The product was developed in conjunction with an organization called ABA Groups, which Harris founded.

In the late 1980s Harris originated the concept of Category Management. The concept has evolved over time; however, the most used Category Management model today was developed into an eight-step procedure by Harris in 1997 and is called the Brian Harris Model. The basis of category management, according to Harris models, is to: force consumer focus during retail decisions; create strategy for differentiation and competition; provide a model for collaboration; promote information sharing for the sake of better decision-making; provide strategic logic when developing tactical decisions; clarify decisions when it comes to asset allocation; and clarify employee responsibilities.

In 1990, Harris founded a category management consultation services firm called The Partnering Group. The Partnering Group became known for establishing best practice policies for collaborations between retailers and suppliers. Harris still serves as founder and chairman of The Partnering Group.

# *Foreword*

I am delighted that you have chosen to study the topic of Category Management. In the 25 years since I first introduced this management concept it has become a global business practice used across all segments of the consumer packaged goods industry including retailers, manufacturers, wholesalers and a wide range firms that support the process of Category Management. Its continuing appeal over all these years is based upon the simple fact that it continues to deliver better business results for all parties that use it. In the dynamic business that is retail marketing and merchandising, it is rare that a business practice retains its popularity and use for over a quarter of a century. The fact that the principles of Category Management have retained their meaningfulness, and the business process of Category Management has continued to successfully adapt to the many changes that occur in this industry, is testimony to the practicality and value of Category Management.

As students, the knowledge you will gain from this course in Category Management will serve you well in several areas. First, it will clearly provide an important and differentiating element for your resume as you move into the job market. To be able to tell a potential employer that you understand the principles and business process of Category Management will give you a distinct advantage, as you will have valuable knowledge and some important foundational skills to use in whatever sector of the retail marketing and merchandising field you chose to enter. There are only a few universities and colleges in the United States that teach Category Management, and the fact that you have this opportunity will be a plus for you as you enter this next phase of your career.

Secondly, what you learn in this course will start you on a solid foundation of new knowledge and skills that are now essential for success in any part of the consumer packaged and retail marketing world. Regardless of whether you choose a career in the retail or the manufacturing sector, in sales, merchandising or marketing, Category Management is an essential component of the foundation for success.

I know you will learn much from this course. Enjoy it and gain the maximum advantage from the time you spend on this course in Category Management. Dr. Z was one of the first "students" of Category Management in the US, and I am trusting he will be an excellent steward of this information for the next generation. Good luck in your studies of my favorite subject!

Dr. Brian Harris
Founder and Chairman, The Partnering Group

# Works by Zwanka

*Trends, Tips, and Tactics for Today's Grocery Industry*

*Today's Store Walk*

*The ABC's of THC and CBD*

*The Store Walk: A Walk Through a Grocery Store in Today's Environment*

*Magic Mushrooms: Future Trend or One-Time Trip?*

*A Post Pandemic Store Walk*

*Pandemic Positivity: Turning a Pandemic into a Roadmap for a Positive Life*

*Food Forethought: 48 Healthy Food Tips for Navigating the Grocery Store*

*Simple Solutions to Make Customers Feel Like Your Supermarket is Their Supermarket*

*Ties That Bind: Inside the Extraordinary (sometimes knotty) Food Marketing Continuum*

*CBD Reality*

*A note from your professor*

*CBD Dreams*

*Public Speaking for Everyone*

*So, how do I do this Marketing thing?*

*Marketing in Today's Cuba*

*A Store Walk*

*Dr. Z's Guide to Grocery and Cooking and Cool Stuff Like That*

*Successfully Succinct Stage Speaking*

*A Marketing Manual for the Millennium*

*Category Management Principles*

*Customer Connectivity in Global Brands and Retailers*

*Requisite Reading for the Renaissance Retailer*

*Operating in the New Cuba*

*Food Retail Management Strategic Cases*

*Would You Shop Here if You Didn't Work Here?*

*Customers First. Profits Second.*

# *Table of Contents*

# *Overview*

It is an exciting time to be in the food industry! Not only are the customers more informed than ever, but the demands they place on their retailers of choice include personalization, buying trait identification, and a strict adherence to data as the driver of the relationship. When will they run out of their favorite product? When do their demands change throughout their lives? When do they want you to help them, and when do they want you to back off? All are questions at the top of every food retailer's mind. In this text, we will take the reader from the origin of the science we call Category Management, through to the best practices and Category Management's impact for the future. You will learn how the Category Business Plan has evolved over time. And you will also learn how the basics have never changed. The customer of today, as did the customer of yesterday, places his or her trust, loyalty and confidence in their retailers of choice. The best retailers are the ones who work to earn that trust every day! Category Management will help you along the journey.

The effort to document the retailer/ supplier relationship with the customer started with **Efficient Consumer Response (ECR).** ECR was an attempt to clearly define the relationship between those activities performed by retailers and suppliers, and those demands placed upon the retailers by their customer. The function called ECR consists of four strategies of supplier-retailer cooperation that create superior value for the consumer at a lower cost. The four ECR strategies are:

---

**Efficient Replenishment** links the consumer, retail store, retailer distribution center, and supplier into an integrated system. Accurate information flows quickly through Electronic Data Interchange (EDI) linkages between trading partners, while products flow with less handling and fewer out of stocks from the supplier's production line into the consumer's basket.

**Efficient Promotion** refocuses suppliers' promotion activities away from retailer-sponsoring to selling through the consumer. A key aspect of Efficient Promotion is better matching of the promotional product flow to the demand of the consumer, yielding substantial benefits in operations with much less inventory in the system. Another aspect is developing the best mix of consumer-oriented promotions within categories.

**Efficient Store Assortment** focuses on offering the right assortment to the target consumers. This activity provides the essential starting point for optimum use of store and shelf space. This is the critical link to the consumer. Adopting an effective assortment management approach improves turnover and profit returns per unit of space. The ultimate goal of Efficient Store Assortment is to determine the optimal product offering that achieves target consumer fulfillment and enhanced business results for retailers and suppliers.

**Efficient Product Introduction** addresses the processes of developing and introducing new products that offer a solution to an unfulfilled or only partially fulfilled consumer need. The goal is for suppliers and retailers to develop more consumer-oriented products at lower costs through more cooperative efforts.

---

It has become clear that the development and management of highly competitive replenishment processes and promotion systems can significantly enhance a retailer's and a supplier's likelihood of success in its marketplace through cost reductions and higher consumer service levels. Despite these efficiency improvements, however, sustainable competitive advantage will also depend upon their ability to market products and services that meet the complex and ever-changing demands of the consumer more effectively. This opportunity is at the heart of Category Management.

Many retailers and suppliers focus their ECR programs only on efficiency improvements (the E of the ECR), where Category Management also integrates the other three more consumer-oriented strategies of ECR. Category Management provides a working process to realize the benefits of each of the four ECR strategies for a category in a framework of supplier-retailer cooperation. Only when Category Management is successfully applied to this extent will retailers and suppliers benefit fully from the promising opportunities of ECR.

Moreover, Category Management's demand-side aspects can enable a retailer and its suppliers to deal with the fact that, when all is said and done, consumers will have a hard time recognizing efficiency changes between trading partners. They will, however, continue to reward those who better meet their shopping needs. This is not to downplay efficiency improvements on the product-supply side. Rather, it acknowledges that, once achieved, these efficiencies will inevitably become the norm for the industry, not a substantial basis for creating competitive advantage in the marketplace.

Category Management is, therefore, a key component for ECR success since it can be a catalyst to changes that enhance both cost savings as well as turnover, profit, and market share growth. Category Management allows a retailer and its suppliers to move concurrently towards capturing important cost savings, while at the same time focusing on more effective, consumer-oriented marketing and merchandising practices. Experience shows that practitioners of Category Management find their greatest benefits in creating **consumer demand**.

Every component of Category Management described in this text is being practiced today. Few, if any, however, are being practiced to the level described in this report, although they are within the capabilities of all retailers and suppliers today.

---

**Definition of a Category** - Distinct, manageable group of products/services that consumers perceive to be interrelated and/or substitutable in meeting a consumer need.

**Definition of Category Management** - Category Management is a retailer/supplier process of managing categories as strategic business units, producing enhanced business results by focusing on delivering consumer value.

**Definition of Consumer Demand** – Economic principle that describes a consumer's willingness to pay a price for a product or service, holding all other factors constant.

---

The objectives of this text are to provide:

- A standard Category Management approach, including a methodology, specific definitions, and work processes for use by the industry.
- Sufficient details and insights to allow a company to evaluate the potential adoption of

Category Management practices to improve its competitiveness in the marketplace and its business results.

This text defines the process and describes techniques for Category Management. It is published with the intent of advancing grocery retailers' and manufacturers' understanding of this process. It is not intended to suggest that there is only one way to perform Category Management or to recommend that any company should implement Category Management. As was true with every aspect of the Efficient Consumer Response initiative, each company should evaluate whether Category Management provides benefits in the context of its own business objective.

# 1- Introduction: Why Category Management?

The growing worldwide interest among retailers and suppliers in Category Management has been the result of a set of business conditions that have increasingly challenged many traditional management methods. These conditions have mandated the adoption of, and transition to, more effective and efficient business processes. Increasingly, it is being recognized that many traditional management practices have not produced the desired results. First, some of these practices have impeded the focus on enhancing consumer value as the ultimate basis of profitability and competitive advantage. Second, traditional practices have been based on a view of competition and competitive behavior that has increasingly lost its relevance in today's changing competitive environment.

The business environment that exists today has created a need, as well as an enormous opportunity, for innovative new management approaches. Companies that quickly recognize and act upon the need to change their organizations will emerge as the leaders of the next century. While these realities are present for all industries, they seem particularly relevant for the retailing and consumer goods industries. These industries have always been characterized by rapid change and disastrous outcomes for those organizations that are slow to change. It is encouraging that there appears to be a growing recognition of the need to re-evaluate traditional methods. The willingness to replace these traditional processes with new ideas and approaches is high on the agenda of many of the world's leading retailers and suppliers. Among these ideas and processes is Category Management.

The purpose of this opening chapter is to firmly establish why Category Management presents a highly viable approach, and one that is emerging as a core strategy to meet today's changing business conditions.

## Industry Trends Driving Category Management

A few specific industry trends are driving the emergence of Category Management:

- Consumer Changes
- Competitive Pressures
- Economic and Efficiency Considerations
- Information Technology Advancement

## Consumer Changes

Category Management represents a method for managing the complex changes that are occurring in consumer needs and shopping behavior. Consumer needs and lifestyles have changed dramatically over the past decade. With technology at the forefront of the changes, the customers have almost complete transparency in pricing and information. In addition, population growth rates have declined, and consumer spending power continues to shrink, impacting at-home food spending. Given these challenges, retailers and suppliers must intensify their efforts to better understand consumer needs and to meet those needs more effectively. Many retailers and suppliers have a growing interest in understanding the composition of their "loyal consumer base" and in defining the purchasing behavior of loyal consumers. An awareness is growing that failure to recognize and reward customer loyalty can be costly. For retailers, research consistently shows that while the loyal consumer may only account for 20-30% of consumer traffic, this shopper base can account for 60% or more of a retailer's turnover and profit. A similar scenario exists for many manufacturers' brands.

At the core of the Category Management concept is a focus on a better understanding of consumer needs as the basis for retailers' and suppliers' strategies, goals, and work processes. This focus causes a re-evaluation of many current business practices, which have impeded a greater understanding of consumer needs and opportunities. Take two such practices:

⇒ How categories are described.

⇒ How categories are managed in a fragmented manner across departments.

The re-evaluation can be as simple as reviewing the terms that have been used to describe categories. Category descriptors, such as analgesics, cereals and oral care, for example, may have agricultural or manufacturing process significance; but may not have meaning to consumers as they relate these items to their needs. Consumers shop to satisfy needs, which are more likely to be defined in terms such as pain relief, breakfast food, fresh breath, etc. The use of category descriptors that do not relate in direct ways to how consumers define their needs can cause a lack of connection between how consumers shop and how retailers and suppliers merchandise, market, or promote in attempts to meet consumer needs. Category Management helps identify this lack of connection by emphasizing that **consumer-defined needs** and their solutions should be at the heart of decisions on how products and categories are marketed.

Among other management practices that have created a gap between consumer needs and how these needs can best be met is the "department" separation of categories. Take the "pizza" category as an example. Traditionally, most retailers have managed this category in several departments. Frozen pizzas are managed as part of the frozen food departments; fresh pizzas are managed as part of the "deli" department and ingredients to "make your own pizza" are part of the grocery department. The starting point for managing any category is to clearly understand the nature of consumer needs in that category. Do consumers define their needs for pizza as "'total pizza", or do they separate needs for frozen vs. fresh vs. make your own pizza? If the consumer need is more at the total pizza category, managing this category as three separate businesses, in many cases managed by three different people, will diminish the retailer's ability to meet the consumer's needs through an integrated pizza offering. Evidence also suggests that when a single category is managed across numerous departments, sales are often traded among the competing components. Increased sales of frozen pizza because of a promotion, for example, could merely switch sales away from a retailer's fresh pizzas and "make your own pizza" ingredients.

Category Management draws attention to these kinds of unproductive departmental separations by emphasizing that *categories should be defined first and foremost by consumer need and not by departmental separations*. Traditional approaches have created some obvious competitive disadvantages for retailers. For example, the current need of supermarket retailers to compete more effectively against the inroads of "home meal replacement" providers is exacerbated by the barriers that departmentalization has created. Effective responses to these competitive threats require cross-departmental planning. By focusing on consumer needs and solutions, Category Management provides an approach for addressing these issues.

## Competitive Pressures

New approaches are also necessary to meet the challenges of today's intense and varied forms of competition. The traditional focus on similar format competition is inadequate to understand and to respond effectively to the emergence of competition from successful alternative formats. New formats employing different methods of competition have seriously eroded the competitive positions of many traditional retailers. The success of these alternative retailer formats, such as hard discounters, specialty "category killers", online-only, and convenience stores has been felt by most traditional retailers. Of the greatest concern is how these formats compete. Their methods are new and require different responses by traditional retailers.

Take the specialty "category killers" as a case in point. This format has successfully entered categories as diverse as coffee, pet food, and supplies, cigarettes, and tobacco, non-alcoholic beverages, bath and personal care products, baby care and prepared meals. Success has come predominantly at the expense of traditional retail formats. This type of competitor focuses on a category, not at a total store level. Specialty retailers identify a category opportunity and exploit it by offering superior consumer value in that category. There is no attempt to compete across a broader base of categories. In some of these categories, the negative impact on the sales of the traditional retailers has been dramatic.

The key point to learn is that management approaches that only focus on competitive differentiation at a total store level, or even a department level, have not been and will not be successful response strategies to this new form of retail competition. Focus must shift to the "category" level and strategies must be carefully devised at that level. It has not proven effective, for example, to compete against pet care specialty "category killers" through the traditional emphasis on one-stop-shopping convenience of large supermarkets, or on lower overall prices. To compete effectively against these new forms of competition, carefully devised and implemented strategies at the category level are essential. This strategy is the essence of the Category Management process. It provides the necessary competitive perspectives, management methods, and tools to meet the challenges of these new category-focused competitive formats.

Suppliers as well are faced with increasing competitive pressures. In addition to the intense competition among manufacturers in increasingly mature categories, the emergence of high-quality retailer private label programs has put further pressure on brand market shares. Concurrently, many suppliers are experiencing unprecedented new product failures. It is estimated that 95 percent of all new items introduced each year will fail within twelve months of introduction. As a result, like retailers who are overstocked, many parts of the industry have surplus capacity especially in the utilization of production facilities.

Traditional sources of competitive advantage for suppliers, such as new product development, consumer advertising and trade promotions, have lost impact as supplier competition is increasingly among more equally resourced companies. New forms of differentiation are needed. These include superior consumer knowledge and expertise and co-marketing programs with trade consumers. Category Management can, and is, providing the platform for the implementation of these new competitive advantage opportunities.

## Economic and Efficiency Considerations

Various economic factors also influence the need to adopt new management approaches. The slow-growth economy in recent years, along with low interest rates, have eliminated turnover and profit growth attributed to inflation. Additionally, the stock markets have pressured many companies to improve their financial performance and have heavily scrutinized transactions ranging from leveraged buyouts to new acquisitions to capital requests for additional production facilities or store capacity. To respond effectively to these economic conditions, retailers and suppliers must operate more efficiently. The birth of the ECR movement has been a direct response to an industry-wide initiative to reduce costs. These initiatives are revealing opportunities and are developing new, more efficient approaches in both supply chain management (efficient replenishment) and demand management areas (efficient assortments, promotions and new product instructions). Category Management can provide the work processes and organizational designs to achieve greater efficiencies in an integrated manner across both demand and supply-side management.

An important outcome of these economic conditions has been, and will continue to be, increasing consolidation in all segments of the industry. The advantages of size, balanced with local connection, can now be leveraged more effectively through the improved technological capabilities that are now possible in areas such as centralized purchasing and direct marketing. The search for improved efficiencies and lower costs will continue and will probably accelerate the trend towards consolidation. Similar trends will continue in the supplier sector. Globalization of brands and marketing programs, as well as the global expansion of customers, such as Carrefour, Ahold, and Walmart, will promote further supplier consolidation and management focus on opportunities that transcend traditional market boundaries. Management methods that can be applied in a consistent and therefore more productive manner, across broader retailer/supplier geographies will be needed to support this new business environment. The processes and disciplines of Category Management are proving to be an important component of this capability.

## Information Technology Advancements

Information Technology Advancements now make it possible for retailers and suppliers to share information and change collective business practices in ways that would have been unrealistic in the recent past. The growing availability of syndicated markets, consumer panel data, and the move to open systems and client/server technologies has greatly facilitated the adoption of new management approaches in the areas of ECR and Category Management. These advances are significantly increasing the capabilities of retailers and suppliers to obtain, organize, access, analyze and act upon the data required for effective Category Management. These systems, along with the closing of skill gaps that have traditionally existed across suppliers and retailers, are creating a "common language" based on complementary information.   Category Management provides the business processes for effective deployment of these new skills and information sources without neglecting to provide the necessary firewall systems to protect proprietary data and information (especially regarding prices).

The net impact of all these and other changes has been to enable many within the industry to do more with current resources and to refocus on meeting consumer needs for value, variety, and service, as the basis for creating competitive differentiation. Category Management provides a powerful yet "back to basics" approach for meeting these changes in a marketplace, which is more competitive and less forgiving of mistakes than it was in the past. The principles and disciplines of Category Management are a logical step in the evolution of management approaches to confront these challenges. These are not revolutionary new principles or methods. By focusing on a superior understanding of consumer needs, Category Management provides renewed opportunities for meeting consumer needs; and, at the same time, for achieving competitive advantage as well as lower costs through greater work process efficiencies.

# Chapter 1 Discussion Questions

1. Name and discuss the four basic ECR strategies.

2. Discuss how the ECR focus on logistics has transitioned to what we call Category Management.

3. Define consumer demand.

4. Define a category.

5. Define category management.

6. What consumer trends are driving the emergence of Category Management?

7. Categories should be defined, first and foremost, by what?

8. Pick a category and discuss how your buying habits have changed in that category in the last four years.

9. Why is it important to introduce new items onto the grocery shelves as quickly as possible?

10. With technology in every customer's hands, why has the focus moved away from pricing as a key differentiator?

# 2- Category Management in the United States and Europe

Category Management has been in existence in the US retail and consumer goods industry for many years. Thanks to the facilitation and promotion by the Joint Industry Project on Efficient Consumer Response (ECR USA), Category Management has become the preferred way of doing business for several major retailers and suppliers. The standard US industry model for Category Management describes what it is and how it is carried out and implemented. Although the European model for Category Management consists of the same six interrelated components, the contents of each of the components is different to address the specific problems and requirements of the European Model for Category Management and it describes the European differences that have an impact on each of its components.

**The ECR Europe Best Practices Category Management Model**

The ECR Europe Best Practices Category Management Model consists of six interrelated components depicted here.

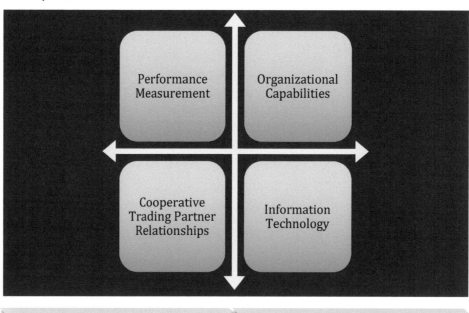

Two of these components are critical and are therefore named the "core" Category Management components:

- Strategy
- Business Process

   The other four components are called "enabling" Category Management components and are vital to support the strategy and the business process:

- Performance Measurement
- Information Technology
- Organizational Capabilities
- Cooperative Trading Partner Relationships

Each of these components has a clear purpose and is described below:

## Core Component: Strategy

The core component Strategy describes the strategic linkages between a company's overall mission, goals and strategies and the management of category level strategic business units. It provides the umbrella for the Category Management Business Process. These linkages are required in both the retailer and the supplier organizations to implement Category Management effectively. Given the essential and generic nature of this core component, very little difference exists between Europe and the U.S. This component is a fundamental requirement of any strategic management approach regardless of the operating environment. Retailers and suppliers must answer strategic questions before starting the category management business process. Amongst these are:

| |
|---|
| • What is the company's overall purpose/mission?<br>• What is the basis of competitive positioning?<br>• What are the key corporate goals?<br>• Who are the core/target consumers?<br>• What are the key strategies (regarding pricing, assortment, promotion, customer service, product supply, etc.)?<br>• What is the present relationship between the retailer and the supplier? |

The answers to these questions must provide key strategic directions and a strategic framework for consistent category level management decisions.

## Core Component: Business Process

The second core component Business Process guides the retailer and the supplier step by step through the cooperative work required to develop, implement and monitor a category business plan. The fundamental Category Management business process is Category Business Planning. This is a structured, measured set of activities designed to produce a specified output: the development and implementation of a written Category Business Plan. It implies a strong emphasis on how work is done within and across the retailer and supplier organizations, in contrast to only focusing on what is done. It is a specific ordering of activities across time and place, with a beginning, and end and clearly identified inputs and outputs within the category.

The output, a Category Business Plan, provides the blueprint for action within the category. The diagram below shows the 8-step Category Business process for Best Practices Category Management in Europe:

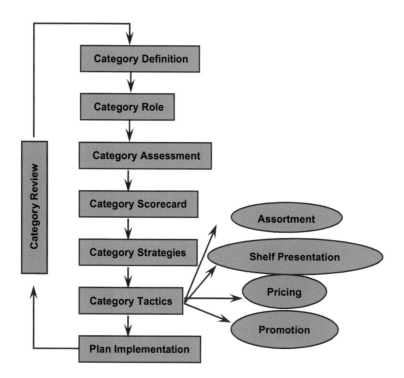

Experience to date has shown that this business process, which is the same as in the US-model, applies very well to Europe but needs special attention to accommodate the following European conditions:

- Less availability of advanced consumer and market data to modify the approach for category definition, role and assessment.
- Alternative approaches for retailers and wholesalers are to be developed given extensive wholesale sectors in Italy, Sweden, etc.
- The process must be applied both at headquarters (centralized) and stores (decentralized) due to operating characteristics of hypermarkets (France, Spain) and the predominant role of co-operatives (Germany, Switzerland).
- Each of the steps is adapted to meet a generally lower level of resources (# of support people, technology, etc.) both on the retailer and supplier sides.
- European process incorporates more supply-side processes than the US model because of the higher level of supply-side readiness of some European firms (especially in the Netherlands, Great Britain).
- Tactical business process steps need to address greater stock-keeping unit (SKU) complexity (e.g. regionality of the assortments) and will need to put greater emphasis on price-only purchasing and selling in Europe. SKUs are a distinct type of item for sale, such as a product or service, and all attributes associated with the item type that distinguish it from other item types.

**Enabling Component: Performance Measurement**

The Performance Measurement, or Category Scorecarding, component provides the capability to measure the results of the Category Management business process in a retailer and supplier organization against mutually established business objectives at the category level. The concept of measuring results against established objectives is fundamental in any effective business organization, regardless of whether the operating environment is in US or Europe. Nevertheless, the Performance Measurement component in the European model must address the following constraints:

- Lack of adequate data for a balanced scorecard (e.g. consumer, market, asset productivity and causal data).
- More emphasis on team versus individual basis of performance measurement in some countries.

**Enabling Component: Organizational Capabilities**

The purpose of this enabling component is to design an organizational structure with clearly defined job roles and performance measures that enable Category Management to be implemented effectively and efficiently. While the basic organizational design principles also apply to Europe, they were redesigned to address the following European specifics:

- Greater decentralized merchandising decision making in hypermarkets.
- Higher penetration of wholesalers in some countries (both retailer and wholesaler organizational designs will be needed).
- European market structures are generally more concentrated (fewer, large companies).
- In some cases, large European retailers have more developed internal marketing capabilities than US counterparts.
- Transition work is required to guide companies from organizational designs based upon hard price bargaining and adversarial work processes to more cooperative processes.
- More emphasis on integrating product supply/logistics work processes within the Category Management processes will also impact the organizational design.
- Less emphasis on individual level accountability, for example defined scorecards.
- European Manufacturers need to work cross-culturally, whereas US manufacturers work in a relatively homogenous market environment.

**Enabling Component: Information technology**

Systems, databases and analytical tools are needed to support Category Management effectively. The development, implementation and performance monitoring of category business plans make up the third enabling component of Category Management, Information Technology (IT). Within Europe, IT infrastructures differ significantly compared to the US and even country-by-country. Although the basic elements of IT infrastructure exist in Europe (POS scanning data, IRI/Nielsen Market Data, consumer panel data, analytical and application tool such as spaceman, etc.), the degree of development is generally lower than in the US.

Therefore, the aim of the European model is to provide the industry with:

- A definition of minimum IT requirements.
- An identification and assessment of currently available sources of data and systems.
- A road map to guide IT strategies and decisions of both retailers and suppliers from current IT levels to Category Management capability levels.

### Enabling Component: Cooperative Relationships

The enabling component Cooperative Relationships defines the principles of relationship management that guide the cooperative Category Management work between a retailer and a supplier. This relationship includes the responsibilities, commitments, and policies that are needed to guide the conduct of interactions (e.g. policies for data sharing, confidentiality, etc.) Although the basic principles of cooperative relationships are the same (e.g. trust, objectivity, mutual benefit, etc.), the following Europe-specific inhibitors must be addressed:

- Stronger traditions in adversarial hard price bargaining-based relationships have created higher levels of mutual suspicion and barriers to information sharing.
- Less history/experience with information sharing between retailers and suppliers
- Traditional performance measures and job descriptions have not been conducive to cooperative relationships

The European model for cooperative relationships has been adapted to fit the European management culture. A set of relationship models has been developed along a continuum of profiles, moving from lower to higher levels of cooperation. The European model enables a gradual formation of mutually beneficial relationships over time.

### Category Management Benefits

The key benefits that will result from an implementation of the Category Management approach are:

- Higher levels of consumer satisfaction and value from more consumer-focused procurement, marketing and merchandising programs.
- Reduced system and marketing costs from more productive and less adversarial business processes.

### Conclusion

Category Management represents a significant and results-proven opportunity to achieve substantial business improvements, both for retailers and suppliers. It requires that each trading partner modify strategies, structures, work processes and systems. To make this commitment, top management must understand the potential contribution of Category Management, recognize the scope of change required and personally lead their company through these changes. Changing the organization means developing both the core and enabling components. It should be emphasized that, of the tasks required to implement Category Management in your organization, *only 20% relate to the Business Process; but 80% relate to the enabling components.*

In essence, the Category Management process is used to bring forward three major success factors: differentiation, collaboration, and organizational excellence. The development of the enabling components requires strict project management to guide the organizational change. A retailer and a supplier will usually need 2 to 3 years for full implementation of Category Management. Effective change management skills will be vital in this period. When the implementation is professionally structured, some Category Management benefits can be realized within 6 months.

Today, only a few retailers and suppliers can claim to be executing the total integrated Category Management practices described in this report. Taking a passive "wait and see" position on Category Management, however, is not likely to be a good strategic decision for retailers or suppliers of any size or type. Experience has already shown that companies, which lead the way in this transition, achieve unique sustainable competitive benefits. While lead times do shorten somewhat as industry experience grows, early adopters reap a larger share of the benefits and can diminish response options of follower companies.

Chapters 3 and 4 describe the core components while chapter 5 describes all four enabling components as they appear in a Category Management company environment. We invite the reader to benchmark the level of development of these components in his own company environment against the ones described in this report. From the comparison, readers should understand how their company needs to change. How to manage and organize the implementation of this change is then described in chapter 6.

# Chapter 2 Discussion Questions

1. Name and define the two core components of the Category Management model.

2. Name and define the four enabling components of the Category Management model.

3. Pick a category and a nearby retailer (choose wisely, we will be using this category for questions throughout the text). How do you think this category fits into the strategic vision of the retailer?

4. From your knowledge right now, what do you think the Category Management process is?

5. What would be the purpose of performance management scorecards? Name one measure you think would be a key measure.

6. What is a SKU?

7. In what way do you think retailers and suppliers have had adversarial relationships in the past?

8. On what measures do you think retailers and suppliers can collaborate where both can mutually benefit?

9. Define gross profits.

10. What is an efficient assortment? Why is it important?

# 3- The Core Component: Strategy

Category Management, which began as a tactical bottom-up approach between buyers and sellers, has evolved into a significant top-down strategic business practice between trading partners. As a result, Category Management has, in the past few years, gained the attention of the industry's top managers and has become a critical component of their vision for the future.

> The core component "strategy" refers to the strategic choice to organize, lead, and manage the business from a foundation of strategic business units based on category. It is the overall framework to guide decision-making in the business process.

## Introduction

The core component of "strategy" involves two issues in relation to Category Management:

> - Top management commitment and leadership.
> - Corporate strategies and their links to category strategies.

## Top management commitment and leadership

Among several leading **retailers**, Category Management has become (or is becoming) a "way of life," a primary way of doing business. Marking the change to Category Management requires leadership from top management. Most importantly, it requires management to *abandon old principles such as organizing around aisles, vendors, or functions and to organize multi-functionally around categories.* This is fundamental, but not easy. Only top management can make these decisions and then provide the resources and leadership to make them operational.

Experience suggests that it takes retailers two to three years to successfully deploy all the components of Category Management described in this report. While significant attention is currently placed on the buying and merchandising functions, Category Management will impact every function within a retailer's organization. Category Management will impact every function within the retailer's organization. Finally, Category Management is as much a cultural change as it is a change in business practices and systems. Category Management forces the entire organization to think and act in a more consumer-focused manner. Strong leadership is necessary to ensure that Category Management is successfully deployed without destroying the positive cultural aspects of the organization.

**Suppliers** considering Category Management need to align their thinking, their organizations, and their business processes around categories. Historically, suppliers have thought "brands." Their organizations are structured to sell "brands" and all business processes and policies are brand-oriented or, at the very least, not category-oriented. Even suppliers who have multiple brands in a category have seldom developed an integrated strategic architecture for the category.

Effective supplier Category Management will also require senior management intervention. Moving from brand orientation to category orientation is too multi-faceted and too complex to expect it to be created by well-meaning subordinates. Many supplier organizations may have to reinvent and re-design themselves to compete effectively in the new environment. As it is for retailers, the time frame for successful transition to Category Management by suppliers is two to three years.

## Corporate Strategies and their links to Category Strategies

As Category Management drives decision-making and accountability down to the front-line implementers, a strategic framework to guide their decision-making is important for both retailer and suppliers. Trading partners will have difficulty developing or implementing sound Category Business Plans without strategic guidance from top management.

It follows that a well-developed corporate strategic framework is a prerequisite for an effective Category Management business process. A sufficiently robust corporate strategy should include a company mission statement, financial goals and strategies for marketing, product supply and other functional areas. Given the importance of this strategic framework for Category Management, the following section describes the elements of this framework and how this framework should look for the retailer and the supplier.

## Retailer Strategy Linkages

The strategic framework of a retailer consists of the mission, the financial and marketing objectives, the overall marketing strategy, the product supply strategy, and the supplier relationship strategy. Once these variables are defined on a corporate level, they are translated into departmental strategies that support the overall corporate strategies. These departmental strategies will then guide the strategic management of the categories within these departments.

As seen in the previous exhibit, the most effective structure will involve a flow with a full integration from the company strategy through to the Category Business Plans. A more detailed description of the elements that are part of this strategic framework follows.

*Company Mission*

The company's overall mission is the fundamental reason for why the company is in business. It typically states how the retailer wants to be perceived in the marketplace, how it will satisfy consumers and how it will differentiate itself from competitors.

*Financial and Marketing Objectives*

These are the most important financial and marketing objectives, which the company wants to achieve through its buying, merchandising, marketing, replenishment and store operations programs.

*Marketing Strategy*

A retailer's overall marketing strategy consists of a definition of its target/core consumer, the key points of competitive differentiation and specific statements for the key marketing strategies that that retailer will implement in the areas of store formats, customer service, assortment, pricing, advertising, promotion and shelf presentation.

*Product Supply Strategy*

A retailer's product supply strategies define what will be implemented by the retailer in the areas of product ordering, procurement, and distribution to ensure maximum consumer value is achieved at the point of sale.

*Supplier Relationship Strategy*

An essential element of Category Management strategy is a statement that clearly defines the commitment the retailer makes to its suppliers and the expectations it has of its suppliers, from cooperative-based Category Management business processes. Such a strategy statement is needed to ensure that these expectations are consistently understood and implemented. It is especially important in an environment in which retailer-supplier relationships have been traditionally narrow in scope and often adversarial in nature.

*Retailer Department Strategies*

These corporate level strategies are translated into parallel department level (grocery, HBC/General Merchandise, perishables, etc.) strategies. In the grocery department, for example, any differences to the corporate strategies for target consumer, competitive positioning, or specific marketing strategies (e.g. assortment, pricing, etc.) are clearly specified and stated to be consistent with corporate-level strategies. This linking of corporate-to-department strategies provides the necessary strategic framework for linking category level strategies to these higher-level strategies through Category Business Plans.

## Supplier Strategy Linkages

Similarly, suppliers must also recognize the strategic linkages between their mission, goals, and strategies and those of their retail customers and ultimately through to the consumer. The exhibit below shows the links between company mission and the retailer relationships.

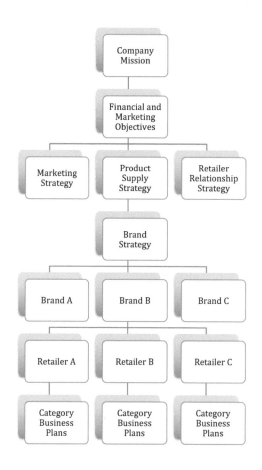

## Summary

Category management is an ongoing strategic management process. It becomes a key element in how a retailer or a supplier "goes to market" to achieve superior consumer value. As such, logical linkages must be created between corporate division/department/brand and category level strategies. These links become the essential strategic connections through which consistency of decision-making and asset allocation occur. For Category Management to be successful, top management must lead and supervise the creation of these linkages. The role of decision makers at the category level, brands and SKUs are managed in conjunction with these overall strategic guidelines. Category Management as an ongoing strategic management process simply will only be effective when these higher-level linkages are put into place.

# Chapter 3 Discussion Questions

1. Strategy involves two issues in relation to Category Management. What are they? Define them.
2. For the retailer you chose last chapter, please find and list their mission statement.
3. How are a company's mission and strategic plan related?
4. What is a target market?
5. Name four different food retail formats, and describe how they are different

   (You will need to research retail formats using alternate sources from the text.).
6. Describe how those same four formats are similar.
7. Why would a retailer establish a supplier strategy? Name one.
8. Why would a supplier establish a retailer strategy? Name one.
9. How is assortment related to the company's strategy?
10. Of your chosen retailer, how does their strategy show up in the store, in the ad, online?

# 4- The Core Component: Business Process

The Category Management business process is a structured, measured set of activities designed to produce a specified output for the trading patterns and their consumers. It implies a strong emphasis on how work is done within and between organizations, in contrast to a singular and exclusive focus on the specific products or services delivered to the consumer.

The Category Management business process is therefore a specific ordering of work activities across time and place, with a beginning, an end, and clearly identified inputs and outputs. It is structure for action. Unless the participants (i.e., retailer and suppliers) can agree on the way work should be structured, it is very difficult to systematically improve, or "operationalize," that work into routine practices within which trading partners do business.

Successful suppliers and retailers must, of course, offer quality products and/or services, and employ productive business processes for producing and selling them. However, cooperative retailer-supplier marketing, product supply and administrative work processes represent major opportunities for improvement. The Category Management process creates a balance between product and process investments, with attention to work activities throughout the total system, from supplier to retailer to consumer.

Finally, although supplier and retailer have separate organizations, different skills and varying roles to play within the Category Management environment, the process itself is and should be the same for both trading partners. Without a common process, the parties seldom develop optimal Category Business Plans. The process becomes both a common language and road map permitting both partners to contribute their unique capabilities for mutual advantage.

There are several distinct characteristics of the best practice Category Management business process. These are:

1. The Category Management business process adopts the consumer's point of view. It is the structure by which a supplier and retailer do what is necessary to produce value for their consumers. As the consumers are the final arbiters of work process design and ongoing performance, they are represented throughout all phases of the Category Management business process.
2. The Category Management business process also has clearly defined "process owners", i.e. individuals with clearly assigned responsibility for design and execution, and for ensuring that consumer, supplier and retailer needs are met.
3. The business process provides a common format and language for both the retailer and the supplier. If suppliers and retailers follow significantly different processes, much of the value is lost. The process is a powerful form of common language, which links the supplier's and retailer's business objectives for enhanced results and consumer value.
4. As emphasized in the previous section, the business process is directed by the retailer's and supplier's corporate and departmental/divisional strategies. These strategies guide the decisions required to complete the Category Management business process.
5. The business process strongly supports both the development and implementation of

Category Business Plans. Well-developed business plans, which are poorly executed, do not deliver either consumer value or enhanced business results.

6. The business process provides the platform for leveraging supplier and retailer expertise/resources.

7. The business process stimulates continuous improvement through the repetitive refinement of category data and plans. The output of the business process (e.g. the formal, written Category Business Plan) is measured, monitored and refined on a periodic basis.

The eight steps of the Category Business Planning process are illustrated in the following chart.

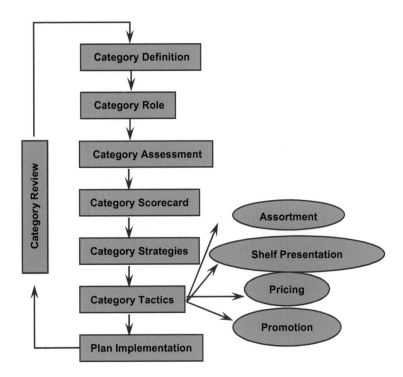

The next section of this report describes each of these eight steps in detail. The purpose for doing each step and the work involved in its completion are explained. Examples of the output of each step are also provided.

# Chapter 4 Discussion Questions

1. Name and describe two characteristics of the Category Management process.

2. What is the difference between a Category Business Process and the Category Business Plan?

3. List and briefly describe the eight steps of the Category Business Process.

4. How do the retailers and suppliers work together inside the Category Business Process? Why do they work together?

5. Which part of the process can be called the "continuous improvement" part?

# 4.1- Category Definition

Category Definition is the first and most essential step in the category business planning process. How the category business unit is defined has a significant influence on all the steps that follow. There are two purposes for this step. First, it defines the selection of the specific SKUs that will comprise the category. Second, it defines the structure, or segmentation, within the category. Agreeing on the appropriate definition and structure for a category is fundamental to Category Management.

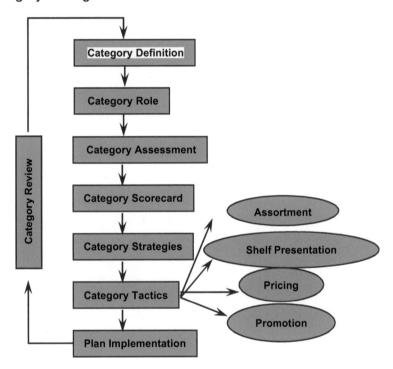

Some key benefits are described below:

1. Better retailer/supplier alignment with the consumer
   a. Historically, the definition of many categories was driven by distribution systems (e.g. direct store delivery, warehouse, refrigerated, etc.), or third-party data definitions. Under Category Management, the appropriate basis for a category definition starts with the consumer: "How would consumers define the category, subcategories and segments based on their needs, and how do they make purchase decisions within this category?"
2. Better retailer-supplier alignment
   a. Co-defining the category based on consumer dynamics helps retailers and suppliers arrive at a common definition, which serves as the foundation for cooperative business planning.

3. New Perspectives
   a. Experience has shown that suppliers and retailers often gain significant new perspectives of the category upon completion of the category definition work. This important phase of the process can highlight unnoticed competitors or other opportunities that have been overlooked in the past.

Before beginning the process of category definition, the retailer and supplier should agree on a definition of the word "category". The "best practices" definition of a category is:

**A distinct, manageable group of products/services that consumers perceive to be interrelated and/or substitutable in meeting a consumer need.**

## Defining the Category

The work involved in the category definition is usually completed by the retailer Category Manager and the supplier representative participating in the category business planning process. The supplier's marketing research department plays a significant role in providing consumer information to support the selected category definition. The category should be approved by the retailer's department manager.

The supplier's category expertise and consumer knowledge generally play a key role in developing the appropriate definition and segmentation/structure of the category. The supplier's consumer research is often the primary source of this information. Most suppliers have invested heavily in research to understand consumer usage habits, needs and desires. This gives suppliers a unique perspective in understanding the consumer's definition of the category and its structure (i.e., the way consumers organize product forms, flavors, price options, sizes, etc., when they buy and use the category). As suppliers often have this data, they can bring it to the table and present the retailer with their vision of the way the consumer defines and organizes (structures and segments) the category.

The diagram below illustrates the process and criteria used to select SKUs that are combined to determine an appropriate category definition. It provides an example of the use of this process in defining the pet care category.

   ✓ Starting with the need of the consumer, all the products/product groups that provide a solution to this need are determined.

   ✓ In the next step, consumer research is carried out to find out what the consumer sees as interrelated products and substitutable products in meeting his or her need for pet care.

   ✓ In the next step, the retailer defines what it can manage together. In the original structure of the retailer, pet treats, bedding, food, and toys were managed in different departments. As this category definition process was done in an early category management implementation stage, the retailer decided not to combine these products into one category and still treat them in separate departments. Nevertheless, he or she was aware of the opportunities and the need for a different organizational structure based on more consumer-oriented category definitions.

✓ In the next step of the definition funnel process, the retailer and the manufacturer check whether the remaining products comprised in the category are measurable and manageable. In practice, they check whether the information needed for Category Management can be retrieved from their current information systems or from the syndicated data suppliers. The products passing this last check constitute the category. Typically, the result of this definition process consists of a list of SKUs or product groups that are part of the category and a list of products that are not.

There is no single standard definition for any category. A category may be narrowly defined or very broadly defined, depending upon many factors. The following example illustrates many different possible category definitions for pet care. Defined very narrowly the pet care category might include only pet food. At its broadest definition it might include housing and travel accessories. The outcome of the category definition process is to decide what is included in the category and what is not. The key factor to be considered in deciding what should or should not be included in a category is the consumer's perspective: When making a purchase decision to meet a need, what options are in the consumer's decision set?

Ultimately, the retailer is responsible for managing the defined category. The retailer brings two important pieces of information:

1. How it currently defines the category (e.g. planogram, item codes, buyer/category manager responsibility, etc.).
2. What is feasible/manageable.

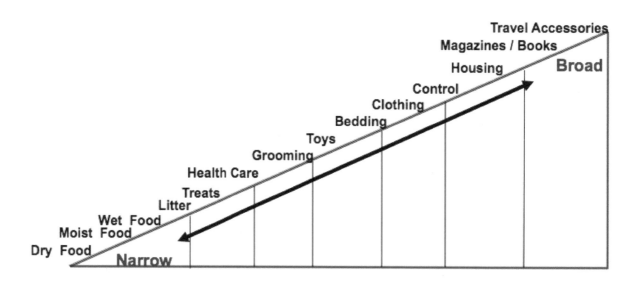

While the current definitions of many categories may not be adequate, making changes to category definitions must offer more benefits than costs. While category management does not imply managing more than SKUs, suppliers or brands, it does not recommend managing a "category that is not manageable". Through the application of this methodology, category definitions are changing. Some examples are the pet care category above, which combines pet food and pet accessories; and the baby care category, which comprises baby foods, diapers, baby formula, and baby accessories.

## Category Structure - The Consumer Decision Tree

The following diagram illustrates an example of the Category Structure, which is the identification of the category's key sub-categories, segments and sub-segments. Work done to date suggests there are several ways to determine the category structure. Every category is different. In some categories, sub-categories will be made up of different product forms (e.g., roll-ons, sticks, spray, deodorants); in other categories a sub-category could be an end-user (e.g. dogs vs. cats), in other categories a sub-category may be ingredient driven (caffeine vs. decaffeinated; light or sugar, etc..). Similarly, segment and sub-segment relations vary from category to category. Many suppliers have conducted very sophisticated research, perceptual and/or substitutability maps that help them understand the category's structure. The key is that the structure of a category reflects as closely as possible how a consumer makes a decision when a purchasing within the category. A category structure is map of the "consumer decision tree", or how a customer runs through his or her options when deciding to purchase a certain category.

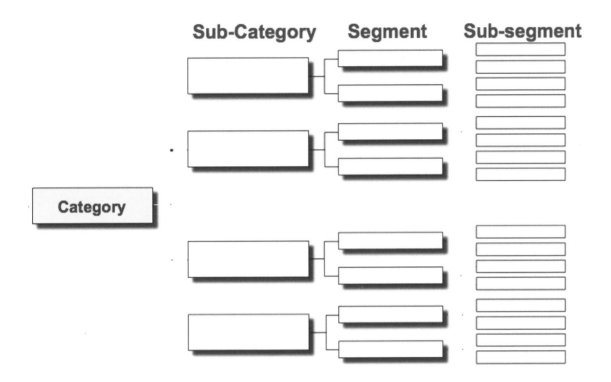

The following diagram shows how Category Management can change the "classical" structure of a category into a consumer-oriented definition. Previously, most retailers would have considered pet care to be separated by pet food and pet supplies. At these retailers, consumers would typically find all pet food located in the grocery department and all pet supplies and litter in the general merchandise department. Clearly, the two categories were managed completely separately. Consumers that have pets do not think like that and the consumer decision tree does not look like that. By defining the category in this way, the retailer may overlook some segments, even sub-categories. He or she also does not profit from cross-merchandising opportunities between food and supplies, which can be a highly effective way of increasing overall category gross margins and average transaction sizes.

A retailer using Category Management would define the category and its structure differently. A partial Consumer Decision Tree for the "Pet Care" category is shown in the following diagram. Now pet food, pet supplies, and litter are managed as one category because the consumer sees supplies and litter as interrelated with pet food in addressing his or her need to take care of the pet. Therefore, the name of the category is "Pet Care". What is now the first step in the consumer decision tree? Consumer research has shown that the type of animal is the first and dominant purchasing decision factor in the decision process.

The next decision factor proved to be the kind of care the consumer wants to give to his pet. For dogs, this means food, health accessories or treats. Only then came the differentiation among wet, dry and moist food. The diagram also shows that the classical definition and structure of the category omitted birds, small animals and fish. As these parts of the categories are located at the very top of the consumer tree, this retailer could have lost consumers that have these pets because they could not offer a one-stop-shopping experience. Clearly, the

Category Management definition and structure of Pet Care shown below is much more consumer oriented. Managing pet care as one category also brings new opportunities such as cross-merchandising food and supplies, where supplies have much high gross margins.

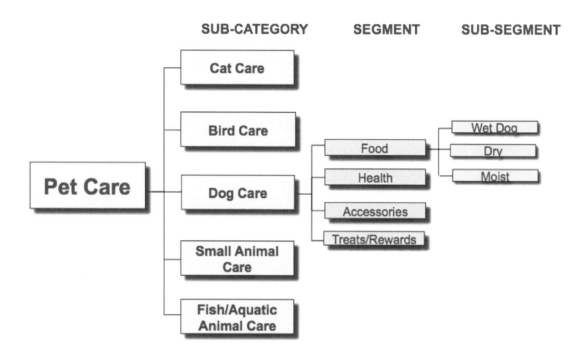

## Category Definition Outcome

The outcome of this first step of the Category Business Planning process is the following:

1. A specific name for the category relating to the benefit or solution the category provides to consumers.
2. A definition of the products and SKUs that constitute the category.
3. The category's structure/segmentation (e.g. sub-categories, segments, etc.) that reflects how consumers typically make purchasing decisions within the category (the "consumer decision tree").

Examples of the Category Decision Tree (CDT) formation are as follows in the next three diagrams.

Once the retailer and supplier have decided upon the categories and sub-categories, the data must be used to determine a "walk" or "switch" level of substitution. This level of substitution will be the beginning of your SKU rationalization, as well as help in deciding shelving and promotion activities.

**Walk:** The level within the CDT at which, unless the consumer's need is met, the consumer will not make a purchase in the category. That is, the consumer will "walk" out of the store without making a purchase.

**Switch:** The level within the CDT at which the consumer will switch between products on the shelf without walking out of the store.

Here is an example of a finalized CDT for Fresh Bread.

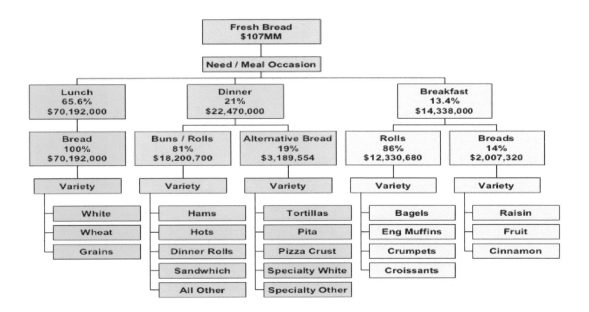

# Chapter 4.1 Discussion Questions

1. Which two areas of the category business unit are defined in the category definition?

2. Why define a category?  Define the category you chose previously.

3. How would you define that same category if you were a manufacturer of products in that category, as opposed to being a retailer?

4. Define the word "category".

5. The definition of any category starts with who in mind?

6. Using the response to question 5, define your category differently than you did in question 2.

7. What is a Consumer Decision Tree?  Describe the CDT for the category you chose.

8. Would the CDT differ between the retailer and the supplier?  Explain your answer.

9. What is the difference between Pet Care and Pet Food?  Explain your answer.

10. Change one thing about your chosen category, based upon your new definition.

# 4.2- Category Role

The second step in the Category Business Planning process is the assignment of the Category Role. The role establishes the priority and importance of different categories in the retailer's overall business, and the resource allocation among categories.

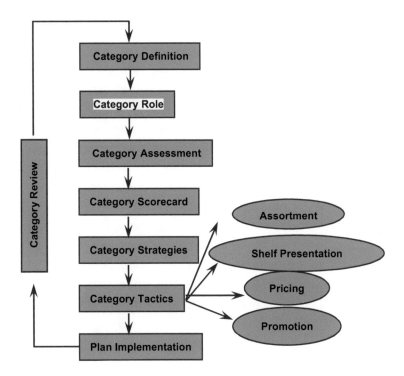

The Category Role development process involves completion of the following steps:

1. The determination of company-wide category roles to be used
2. The assignment of category roles to each category
3. The allocation of resources among categories based on these roles.

The assignment of roles to categories is one of the retailer's most important decisions. This process provides the basis for competitive differentiation and resource allocation among the retailer's strategic business units. The discipline of category role assignment is *one of the most important benefits to be achieved from Category Management.*

**The determination of company-wide category roles to be used**
In a retailer's store there can be from 150 to 400 categories, depending upon the format. In a typical supermarket, there are normally 150 to 200+ categories. In a hypermarket format there can be as many as 400 categories. Each category plays a significant, but varying, role in

delivering the retailer's mission, goals, and strategies. Top management within a retailer's organization should develop the list of overall category roles that will be used company wide.

To develop category roles, a retailer should use the following guiding principles:

- Category role should describe the *desired state*. This means that the category roles define what the retailer wants to accomplish with each category. Category roles then provide the category manager and suppliers with the framework for managing each category.
- Category roles should be *consumer oriented*. They should help the retailer and suppliers maintain an outward focus on better meeting consumer needs.
- Category roles should be *coordinated*. The typical supermarket manages 150 to 200+ categories that can range in diversity from perishable foods to motor oil to greeting cards. The balance of roles assigned across these categories should provide the retailer with a competitive advantage. Defining requires both internal and external coordination. First, roles ensure that decisions made at the category level are consistent with the broader, internal strategic goals of the organization. Second, roles should be designed and coordinated to maximize external opportunities among the consumer, competition and suppliers. Category roles should enable the retailer to better capitalize on the consumer's total "shopping occasion" behavior, which is typically comprised of purchases from multiple categories. Category roles should be coordinated so the way the retailer manages its mix of categories makes the total experience more rewarding for the consumer. Roles also need to be assigned based on competitive realities, such as what roles the retailer's competitors are using for their categories.
- The category roles should be *understandable*. The retailer's organization and its suppliers must be able to understand roles and be able to link their category and tactical decisions to these roles.

The four most common Category Role are Destination, Preferred, Occasional/ Seasonal, and Convenience. The characteristics of each are described below.

The role of the **Destination** category (only 5-7% of all categories) is:

- To be the primary provider of these product to the target consumer.
- To help define the profile of the retailer in the eyes of the target consumer
- To deliver consistently superior value to the target consumer
- To lead all (retailer) categories in the areas of turnover, market share, consumer satisfaction, service level and operating expense management.
- To lead the retailer's people, systems and technological development towards achieving the corporate mission, goals and strategies.

The role of a **Preferred** category (55-60% of all categories) is:

- To be the *preferred* provider of these products to the target consumer.
- To help *build* the target consumer's image of the retailer.
- To deliver *consistent, competitive* value to the target consumer.
- To play a *primary* role in delivering profit, cash flow and Return on Assets (ROA).

The role of an *Occasional/Seasonal* category (15-20% of all categories) is:

- To be a *major* provider of these products to the target consumer.
- To help *reinforce* the target consumer's image to the target consumer
- To deliver *frequent, competitive* value to the target consumer
- To play a *secondary* role in delivering profit, cash flow and ROA.

The role of a *Convenience* category (15-20% of all categories) is:

- To help *reinforce* the target consumer's image of the retailer as the place for one-stop shopping.
- To deliver *good, everyday* value to the target consumer.
- To play an *important* role in profit generation and margin enhancement

Category roles must be developed with the consumer in mind and must reflect typical consumer shopping behavior. Additionally, these roles provide a logical framework for the allocation of the retailer's resources based on its mission, goals, and strategies and on the competitive market situation. Lastly, the key result of this step is a balanced set of roles across all categories. Some retailers focus only on Destination category roles and fail to recognize the need for a coordinated balance of roles among categories. Each category plays a critical part in achieving the retailer's overall corporate objectives, and therefore, should be managed as part of an integrated whole.

## The Assignment of Category Roles to each Category

The selection of the appropriate role for a category is a key determining factor for how the category will be managed by the retailer and its trading partners. It has a major impact on the selection of performance measures, strategies, and tactics for the Category Business Plan. There are several benefits associated with assigning the appropriate role for the category:

1. It helps the retailer deliver better consumer value. Since categories are not equally important in the mind of the consumer, category roles should reflect these different priorities within the retailer's stores and whole organization.
2. It maximizes the retailer's and supplier's return on resources invested by directing the appropriate level of resource allocation among categories.

The technique for determining the role of a category is cross-category analysis, which compares the targeted category to a group of similar categories (e.g. categories within the same department, aisle, etc.). The cross-category analysis is a quantitative and qualitative analysis, which uses various types of consumer, retailer and market data to answer four key questions:

- How important is the category to the retailer's **target consumer?**
- How important is the category to the **retailer?**
- How important is the category to the retailer's **competitors?**
- What is the category's outlook within the retailer's **market?**

As a cross-category analysis requires data for several categories, and suppliers normally only have data for their categories, it is mainly a task for the retailer. Nevertheless, the supplier can provide some analysis to influence the role decision of the retailer. The next four diagrams show examples of a cross-category analysis using one measure in each of these four areas.

## How important is the Category to the Target Consumer?

| Diapers Category Criteria | Rank* Amongst All Categories | | | |
|---|---|---|---|---|
| | Actual | H | M | L |
| Consumer Annual Expenditures (HH $ All Channels) | $395 | | X | |
| Consumer Annual Expenditures (HH $ Grocery) | $257 | | X | |
| Consumer Household Penetration (% All Channels) | 14% | | | X |
| Consumer Household Penetration (% Grocery) | 12% | | X | |
| Annual Purchase per Buyer (# All Channels) | 42 | X | | |
| Annual Purchase per Buyer (# Grocery) | 39 | X | | |
| Middle Household Income** | 50% | X | | |
| Household Size 1 or 2** | 8% | | | X |
| Household Size 3 or More** | 92% | X | | |
| Household Buyer Age Under 35** | 71% | X | | |
| Household Buyer Age Under 35-54** | 27% | | X | |
| Household Buyer Age Under Over 54** | 2% | | | X |

*Rank  H=Top 20%  M=Middle 60%  L=Bottom 20%                    **Percent of Category Sales

The diagram above shows that Diapers are most important for households with more than 3 members (92%), household buyers under 35 (71%), and the category is purchased 39 times per year by each household buyer in grocery and 42 times per year per buyer in all channels. With high percentile ranks like these, Diapers could qualify as a Destination category. Similar target consumer development analysis can be made for the other characteristics of the target characteristics. The necessary data for this kind of analysis can be sourced in different ways. Household panel data is one source. Some retailers will explore the possibility of linking consumer loyalty cards to scanning data for this kind of analysis.

The next diagram shows the gross margins of the Diapers category. It shows that Diapers have a relatively high gross margin % compared to the retailer's overall grocery gross margin, but low overall gross margin $. The high Market Basket number ($18.40) is a good clue that the retailer may want to have a high focus on the Diaper category, but it may not have enough household penetration to be considered Destination. Retailer Profit per Cubic Foot, at $13.67, reflects the high cube and floor space that must be dedicated to the Diaper category. The high cube will also point the retailer away from designating Diapers as a Destination category.

# How important is the Category to the Retailer?

| Diapers Category Criteria | Rank* Amongst All Categories | | | |
|---|---|---|---|---|
| | Actual | H | M | L |
| Retailer Sales $ | $40.5M | | X | |
| Market Sales $ (Grocery) | $240.0M | | X | |
| Market Sales $ ( All Channels) | $410.0M | | X | |
| Retailer Market Basket $ | $21.50 | X | | |
| Market Basket $ (Grocery) | $18.40 | X | | |
| Annual Purchase per Buyer (# Grocery) | $576.00 | | X | |
| Retailer Gross Profit $ | $4.4M | | | X |
| Retailer Gross Profit % | 10.9% | X | | |
| Retailer Loyalty (%Share of Cons. Req.) | 29.0% | | | X |
| Retailer Buyer Conversion Rate % | 75.0% | | X | |
| Retailer Sales/Cubic Foot | $125.40 | | X | |
| Retailer Profit/Cubic Foot | $13.67 | | | X |
| Retailer Sales/Transaction $ | $6.10 | X | | |
| Market Sales/Transaction $ (Grocery) | $5.80 | X | | |
| Market Sales/Transaction $ (All) | $6.30 | X | | |

*Rank  H=Top 20%  M=Middle 60%  L=Bottom 20%

The next diagram depicts the 5-year projected market growth of the Diaper category. This analysis shows that Diapers face medium growth in the coming years of 7-8%. This growth will not be robust enough to be a Destination category, but Diapers could be Preferred based upon the relative importance of an "early family growth" category to future retailer loyalty

# What is the Category outlook in the Marketplace?

| Diapers Category Criteria | Rank* Amongst Relevant Categories | | | |
|---|---|---|---|---|
| | Actual | H | M | L |
| Retailer Market Share Index (Cat Share/Mkt Avlblty - Grocery) | 92 | | X | |
| Retailer Market Share Index (Cat Share/Mkt Avlblty - All Channels) | 104 | | X | |
| Projected Growth  2017-2022 % | 7 to 8 | | X | |
| Competitive Shelf Space index  (Retailer Space ft/Comp Space ft) | 94 | | X | |
| Competitive Category Assrtmt Index  (Rtlr # of Skus/Comp # of Skus) | 107 | | X | |

*Rank  H=Top 20%  M=Middle 60%  L=Bottom 20%

The following qualitative analysis of the Diaper category consists of a set of qualitative questions about the importance of the category for the consumer, the retailer, the market and the supplier. The results of both analyses in the example of Diapers supports a Preferred role.

| DIAPERS CATEGORY | | |
|---|---|---|
| CONSUMER-BASED EVALUATION | YES | NO |
| Are the category sales affected by major consumer lifestyle changes? | X | |
| Does the category have a high level of personal importance? | X | |
| Is the category likely to grow in importance in the near future? | | X |
| Is there a significant consequence when the category is not used? (Is it a non-discretionary purchase?) | X | |
| | | |
| RETAILER-BASED EVALUATION | | |
| Does this category, with a particular role, provide a source of differentiation for the Retailer? | X | |
| Can the category, with a particular role, help build store loyalty among target consumers? | X | |
| Can the primary demand for the category expand easily? | | X |
| Does the category, with a particular role, leverage the Retailer's strengths? | | X |
| Does the category, with a particular role, align with the Corporate strategies? | X | |
| | | |
| MARKET-BASED EVALUATION | | |
| Has competition underestimated the importance of the category? | | X |
| Would the category with a particular role trigger an unfavorable competitive response? | X | |
| Does the Retailer have a good chance of capturing an unrealized market opportunity? | | X |
| | | |
| SUPPLIER-BASED EVALUATION | | |
| Are the suppliers in this category capable of supporting a particular role? | X | |
| Are the suppliers willing to support a particular role? | X | |

The next diagram below shows a summary cross-category Quantitative Analysis Grid, which shows how a targeted category (e.g. Diapers) might compare to other categories on a series of relevant measures. It shows that overall Diapers rank about medium in importance. This would suggest a Preferred role. This quantitative analysis combined with qualitative analysis based on experience and intuition assists retailers in assigning the appropriate roles for their categories.

**Category:** **Diapers**
**Role:** **Preferred Routine**

| Quantitative Analysis | Category Ranking (Among All Categories) | |
|---|---|---|
| Consumer-Based Evaluation | High | |
| Retailer-Based Evaluation | Medium | |
| Market-Based Evaluation | Medium | |

| Qualitative Analysis | Response | |
|---|---|---|
| | YES | NO |
| Consumer - Impact by Lifestyle Changes | X | |
| Consumer - High Level of Personal Importance | X | |
| Consumer - Emerging Growth | | X |
| Consumer - Non-Discretionary Purchase/Usage | X | |
| Retailer - Source of Differentiation | X | |
| Retailer - Build Target Consumer Loyalty | X | |
| Retailer - Primary Demand Expansion | | X |
| Retailer - Leverages Strengths | | X |
| Retailer - Aligns to Corporate Strategies | X | |
| Market - Underestimated by Competition | | X |
| Market - Triggers Unfavorable Competitive Response | X | |
| Market - Significant Market Opportunity | | X |
| Supplier - Willing to Support a Particular Role | X | |
| Supplier - Capable of Supporting a Destination Role | X | |

While the decisions on category roles will be the retailer's, a supplier can provide important data and perspectives to ensure the right role is chosen. To contribute, a supplier should attempt to provide the consumer with the necessary knowledge to assist in the cross-category analysis. Second, knowledge of the market, and the future of the category is vital. Finally, a supplier needs to communicate its willingness and capability of supporting the role the retailer selects for its category. If a supplier cannot or will not support a particular role, one of its options is to try to convince the retailer to select an alternative mutually suitable role. The other option is to accept the retailer's role choice and conduct business with the retailer based on the role assigned.

The next diagram shows the result of the assignment of category roles for a major grocery chain. This retailer has assigned a balanced matrix of the four roles across all categories. In this example, Pasta Meals are used as a Destination role category, primarily because of their excellent fit to the retailer's target consumer (families with small children) and their significantly higher purchase frequency than the core, or Preferred role, categories of Soft Drinks. The store is "balanced" through using categories, such as Back to School with an Occasional/Seasonal role, and Floral as a Convenience role category. Such a balance of roles allows the retailer to achieve its corporate goals (mission and financial goals, and its competitive positioning strategies) as well as providing maximum value to its target consumer. These same categories would likely be given different roles by other retailers for these same reasons.

| Destination | Routine | Seasonal | Convenience |
|---|---|---|---|
| Pasta Meals | Soft Drinks | Back To School (D) | Motor Oil |
| Fresh Baked Breads | Salty Snacks | Garden | Home Fashion |
| Fresh Salads | Laundry | Sun Care | Floral |
| Fresh Beef | Prepared Foods * | Seasonal Candy | Apparel |
| Baby Care | Pet Care * | Ice / Snow | Video |
| Photo | Paper Towels | Flu / Cold | Hardware |
| Wine | Candy | Christmas | Toys |

*Preferred Routine          D = Seasonal Destination

## The allocation of resources among categories based on these roles

Managing categories strategically goes beyond the development and assignment of category roles. In fact, the category role often provides the guidelines for the allocation of a retailer's resources - ranging from inventory, shelf space and promotional/advertising investments to capital spending and management's time. As a result, the category role definition and assignment establish the priorities with which a retailer and its suppliers allocate resources.

As a retailer and its suppliers develop Category Business Plans designed to achieve the various category roles, they are recognizing the need for a formal resource reallocation process. These decisions typically take place during this part of the business process, and they address the discovery by category managers and suppliers that their category has an inappropriate level of dedicated resources. For example, a category manager and his suppliers may conclude that to achieve the Destination role for their category, they need to allocate more resources in the form of shelf space and promotion activities. On the other hand, another category manager and his supplier may conclude that they can achieve the role of Preferred for a particular category with fewer warehouse slots, retail shelf space and reduced display activity.

For a retailer, the resource allocation process takes place amongst and between the category managers and their department managers. Without this process, a retailer will have a difficult time managing its categories strategically and improving its return on assets. For suppliers, the resource allocation process takes place in several ways, most commonly among the account executive and their respective sales and/or product managers. Suppliers can allocate their promotional budgets more effectively among their different clients based on the role assigned for the categories they are in at those clients. A supplier will typically invest more in promotions at a retailer where his category is defined as Destination than at a client where his category has a Convenience role. In addition, his efforts on the different areas of Category Management can be tailored to the role. Much more detailed analysis will be done in the framework of Category Management when a category is Destination than when it is Convenience. More advanced Efficient Replenishment techniques will be applied to Destination categories rather than to Convenience categories, etc.

Category Management is thus a process not only to better respond to the consumer's need, but also to provide the guidelines to refocus the resources on investments that bring the highest return for both the retailer and the supplier.

# Chapter 4.2 Discussion Questions

1. What does the Category Role establish?

2. What three steps are involved in the Category Role completion?

3. Apply these steps to your chosen category.

4. Define a Destination category- name one in your chosen retailer. Why?

5. Define a Preferred category- Name one in your chosen retailer. Why?

6. Define an Occasional/ Seasonal category- Name one in your chosen retailer. Why?

7. Define a Convenience category- Name one in your chosen retailer. Why?

8. Name two benefits of assigning category roles.

9. Describe the steps of how you would proceed in assigning a Category Role.

10. Name four retailer resources that would be impacted by the Category Role.

# 4.3- Category Assessment

The purpose of the Category Assessment step of the Category Business Planning process is to obtain, organize and analyze the information necessary to clearly understand the current performance of the category and to identify the areas of greatest opportunity for improved results in turnover, profit, and return on assets in the category.

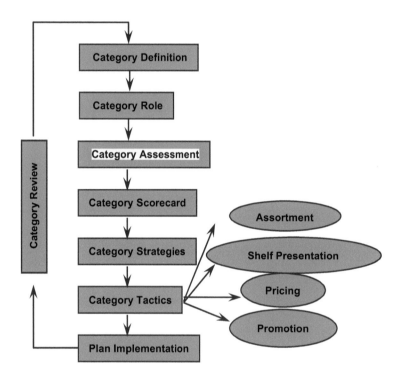

The category manager and the supplier need to assess the current performance of the category and its components (e.g., sub-categories, segments, brands, etc.) relative to the assigned role. The assessment step identifies the gap between current and desired state and uncovers the key business building opportunities within the category. A thorough assessment is essential for the development of category strategies and tactics.

The outcome of the category assessment step consists of an overall assessment of the category, which includes consumer, market, retailer and supplier assessments. The category assessment is a documented set of conclusions based upon these data with supporting charts and graphs. The conclusions focus on identifying where the biggest opportunities in the category currently exist for turnover, profit, and return on asset improvement. These opportunities provide the emphasis for the remaining steps of the Category Business Plan. In a sense, the category assessment is like a Strengths, Weaknesses, Opportunities, and Threats (SWOT) review for a company. All strategies and tactics will be driven from the resulting analysis.

## Characteristics of Category Assessment

Category assessment is a cooperative process; neither the retailer nor the supplier will have all the data or insights to perform this analysis effectively without the other. Thus, while the retailer and supplier may acquire and analyze some data separately, the conclusions flowing from that data need to be reached jointly.

Templates are essential to guide the assessment process in a logical, productive manner. Without well-structured templates, the assessment will lose its focus and much of analysis effort will be invested by both trading partners without producing the expected results. Some examples from a set of assessment templates are provided in this chapter.

The category manager and the supplier representative(s) have primary responsibility for the category assessment. They will need assistance, however, from their information systems departments, marketing/market research departments, and outside information companies. To complete a thorough category assessment, retailers will need supplier assistance in the areas of consumer data, market information, category trends, etc. The supplier's perspectives on the consumer and the category can be extremely valuable. To fulfill their role, suppliers should be prepared to provide category data (not just brand data) and have an excellent understanding of the category's consumer, based upon research they have completed.

On the retailer's side, turnover, profit, and current shelf space management data are, at a minimum, required for category assessment. In addition, retailers that have consumer loyalty card programs will begin to have access to highly valuable consumer purchase data. The following diagram demonstrates how data should be organized to support productive category assessment. Data in four areas is required (consumer data, market data, internal retailer data and external supplier data) and should be structured to enable analysis at category level as well as "drill down" levels (sub- category, segments., etc.) within the category.

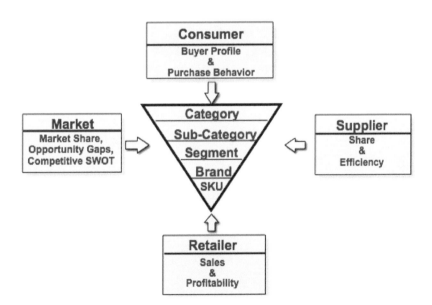

The assessment leads to more focused research and analysis, if needed. The assessment is not intended to answer every possible question about the category, but instead to answer the most important questions that identify the biggest opportunities through a logical, standardized approach. This focus tends to limit unproductive "fishing expeditions" and allows for additional, more directed analysis, while developing the category's strategies and tactics. Different categories will require different levels of analysis. Destination role categories warrant greater understanding and analysis than do Convenience role categories.

The critical elements of a productive category assessment include:

> ✓ Clear assignment of responsibilities between the retailer and the supplier partner(s).
>
> ✓ A standard assessment process guided by hard copy and/or electronic worksheets/templates.
>
> ✓ Information and technology tools to perform the assessment productively and objectively.
>
> ✓ A willingness, when appropriate, to share the necessary information and data between trading partners.

**Assessment Process**

The category assessment process can be a very time-consuming task unless productive methods are used. The key to making this process productive is to conduct the assessment in a logical sequence. The first area of assessment should be the consumer assessment, followed by the assessment of the market, the retailer, and the suppliers. These assessments provide the information needed for opportunity gap analyses. The final analyses focus on the key causal areas (assortment, pricing, promotion, shelf presentation, and product supply) that provide insights into why these opportunity gaps exist.

The analysis carried out in each part of the assessment is not done for the sake of analysis, as such. The analysis templates are designed to answer some key questions about the consumer, the retailer, the market and the suppliers. Below is an overview of the key questions retailers and suppliers attempt to answer in the assessment process and an example of an assessment template for one of the key questions of each part.

*1. Consumer Assessment*

Below is a list of key questions retailers and suppliers attempt to answer for the consumer assessment:

<u>Why</u> do consumers buy this category?
- ✓ What matters most? Second? Third?
- ✓ How important is the category to the consumer?

<u>Who</u> buys the category?
- ✓ What is their demographic profile? Where do they live?
- ✓ What is their psychographic profile? What is their lifestyle?
- ✓ What is the level of household penetration?
- ✓ What are the loyalty segments?

✓ Is there a difference between purchaser and user?

<u>When</u> do consumers buy the category?

✓ Is there seasonality? By year? By month? By week? (example shown below)

✓ What is the consumer's purchase frequency?

<u>How</u> do consumers buy the category?

✓ What is the purchase size?

✓ Are there related purchases?

✓ What is the market basket when consumers purchase the category?

✓ What is the type of shopping trip when they buy the category?

✓ Is the purchase planned or unplanned?

✓ How much is the purchase when the category is promoted?

✓ Are the consumers loyal?

✓ Are there store or brand switching patterns?

<u>Where</u> do consumers buy the category?

✓ Is the category usually purchased in a supermarket?

✓ In other retail formats?

✓ What are the purchase trends for the category among various retail format/channel options?

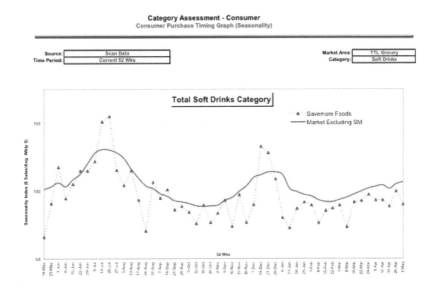

Once the consumer assessment is completed and the key findings are culled, the results are summarized as seen in this next diagram.

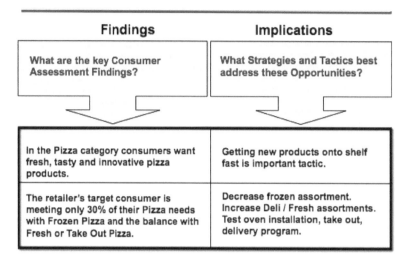

**Consumer Assessment Summary**

| Findings | Implications |
|---|---|
| What are the key Consumer Assessment Findings? | What Strategies and Tactics best address these Opportunities? |
| In the Pizza category consumers want fresh, tasty and innovative pizza products. | Getting new products onto shelf fast is important tactic. |
| The retailer's target consumer is meeting only 30% of their Pizza needs with Frozen Pizza and the balance with Fresh or Take Out Pizza. | Decrease frozen assortment. Increase Deli / Fresh assortments. Test oven installation, take out, delivery program. |

*2. Market Assessment*

Some of the key questions retailers and suppliers should attempt to answer to assess the current performance of the category in the market are:

- ✓ What are the sales and consumption trends of the category, sub-categories, segments, brands, etc. in the marketplace?
- ✓ What is the retailer's market share for the category? sub-categories, brands, etc.?
- ✓ Where are the retailer's biggest market share opportunity gaps in the category?
- ✓ How does the retailer's pricing compare to key competitors?
- ✓ How does the retailer's shelf presentation compare to key competitors?
- ✓ How does the retailer's assortment compare to key competitors?
- ✓ How does the retailer's promotion activity compared to key competitors?

The data from the questions above are then summarized, as we see in the next few diagrams.

# Competitive Assessment - Category Assortment

| Subcategory / Segments | No. of SKUs | | |
|---|---|---|---|
| Largest Opportunity Gaps | Retailer | Competitor A | Competitor B |
| 1. Potato Chips | 34 | 38 | 33 |
| 2. Tortilla Chips | 26 | 35 | 35 |

## Competitive Store SWOT Analysis
## Assortment and Pricing – *Refrigerated Juices*

| Subcategory Segments | No. of SKU's | | | | | | Key SKU Pricing | | | | | |
|---|---|---|---|---|---|---|---|---|---|---|---|---|
| Premium OJ | SV | B | C | D | E | F | SV | B | C | D | E | F |
| MMCOJ 64oz. | 12 | 10 | 10 | | | | 2.89 | 3.35 | 1.99 | | | |
| Simply Orange | 3 | 3 | 3 | | | | 2.99 | 3.49 | 2.59 | | | |
| Trop 64oz. | 15 | 15 | 12 | | | | 2.99 | 3.69 | 2.29 | | | |
| FN 64oz | 5 | 5 | 4 | | | | 2.59 | 2.95 | 2.04 | | | |
| MMCOJ 96oz. | 5 | 3 | 1 | | | | 3.99 | 4.19 | 4.19 | | | |
| Trop 96oz. | 6 | 4 | 4 | | | | 3.99 | 3.69 | 3.69 | | | |
| FN 96oz | 0 | 3 | 0 | | | | 0 | 3.99 | 0 | | | |
| MMCOJ 128oz. | 3 | 3 | 3 | | | | 4.99 | 5.69 | 3.99 | | | |
| Trop 128oz. | 3 | 3 | 0 | | | | 4.99 | 5.79 | 0 | | | |

# SWOT Summary - Refrigerated Juices

| Observations | Strategy | Tactic | Implications |
|---|---|---|---|
| Cub stocks less skus (Trop. 64oz) competition. Cub has lower EDRP. Utilize display end cap for sales, competition does not | Traffic Builder | Assortment and Pricing | No major implications. May have an opportunity to grab GP $s. |
| Cub clearly utilizes the transaction builders to grow category dollars. Stocks more SKUs, better EDRPs | Transaction Builder | Assortment and Pricing | No implication |
| Cub stocks more Economy OJ skus in then their competition. Including a regional brand. Comp. does not stock FC private Label | Profit Builder | Assortment | Possibly over sku'd verse competition. Regional brand maybe cannibalizing private label sales |
| Cub is the only retailer not to stock a private label in the Juice and Drink segment | Transaction Builder | Assortment | Opportunity to increase assortment, particularly in private label. |

The next diagram shows a market assessment template that organizes the market data in a way that identifies the market share opportunity gaps in the category.

## Where are the biggest Sales Opportunities?

| Category | Sales ($ mil) | % of Sales | Market Share | Annual Growth % in Market |
|---|---|---|---|---|
| Potato Chips | 8.22 | 24.5 | 17.3 | +5.5 |
| Tortilla Chips | 6.09 | 18.2 | 18.5 | +8.0 |
| Nuts | 4.51 | 13.5 | 21.2 | +3.8 |
| Better For You | 3.45 | 10.3 | 22.4 | +6.0 |
| Pretzels | 3.13 | 9.4 | 19.4 | (6.5) |
| Corn Chips | 2.30 | 6.9 | 22.6 | (3.2) |
| Cheese Snacks | 1.72 | 5.1 | 21.8 | (5.8) |
| Popcorn | 1.40 | 4.2 | 18.4 | (4.0) |
| Shelf Stable Dips | 1.35 | 4.0 | 21.0 | (2.0) |
| Misc. Snacks | 1.30 | 3.9 | 17.8 | (2.0) |
| TOTAL | $33.47 | 100.0 | 20.0 | 2.5 |

3. *Retailer Assessment*

Following is a list of key questions retailers and suppliers attempt to answer for the retailer assessment.

For this category and its components (i.e., sub- categories, segments, brands and SKUs):

✓ What are the retailer's sales trends?

✓ What are the profit trends?

✓ What are the trends in the product acquisition costs?

✓ What are the operating expenses for this category?

✓ How are the service levels?

✓ What are the returns on inventory and space assets for the category?

✓ What are the inventory turns and days of supply?

✓ How productive are the product supply (procurement and distribution) strategies?

✓ How productive is the current category assortment?

✓ How effective is the category shelf presentation?

✓ Are current pricing programs effective?

✓ How effective are the retailer's promotions?

An example of how the summary of market and retailer benefits will be shown is below.

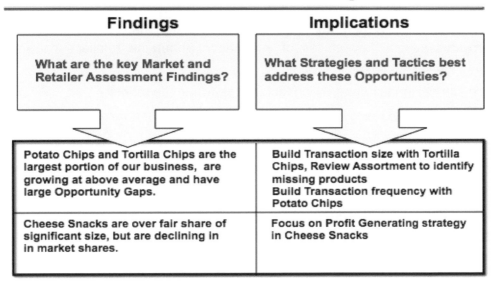

## Market / Retailer Assessment Summary

| Findings | Implications |
|---|---|
| What are the key Market and Retailer Assessment Findings? | What Strategies and Tactics best address these Opportunities? |
| Potato Chips and Tortilla Chips are the largest portion of our business, are growing at above average and have large Opportunity Gaps. | Build Transaction size with Tortilla Chips, Review Assortment to identify missing products<br>Build Transaction frequency with Potato Chips |
| Cheese Snacks are over fair share of significant size, but are declining in in market shares. | Focus on Profit Generating strategy in Cheese Snacks |

*4. Supplier Assessment*

Some of the key questions retailers and suppliers should attempt to answer to assess the current performance of suppliers in the category are:

✓ What are the sales and market share trends among suppliers in the category?

✓ How efficient are the category's suppliers?

> Are the supplier's information flows efficient?

> Are the supplier's physical flows efficient?

> Are the supplier's monetary flows efficient?

✓ Which supplier/ brands are most/ least profitable for the retailer?

✓ What replenishment (product supply) programs do the suppliers offer?

✓ Does the retailer take advantage of product supply programs?

✓ How reliable are the various suppliers in the category?

✓ What is the supplier's brand development at the retailer? In the market?

✓ Will the suppliers have any significant new products next year?

✓ Will the suppliers have any significant price changes next year?

✓ What are the suppliers upcoming promotions and what marketing funds are available?

**Opportunity Gaps and Quadrant Analysis**

The basic purpose for answering the key questions listed above is to identify where the biggest turnover, profit, and return on asset improvement opportunities exist in a category. That is, is there a gap between the chosen category role and the current performance level of the category? For example, if the category role of "Destination" demands a market share of 36%

and the current share is 28%, then there is an opportunity gap of 8%. A highly useful tool for showing opportunity gaps is Quadrant Analysis.

An example of a Salty Snacks quadrant analysis is below. Salty Snacks sub-categories are analyzed using two key performance measures: Market Share and Market Growth. This quadrant provides several key pieces of information about the retailer's current business performance in these categories:

✓ Which sub-categories are growing faster or slower in the market?

✓ Is the category role being delivered based upon current performance in the market?

✓ Does a gap exist between the category's performance and its role?

✓ Is the retailer receiving its "fair share" of a category's business?

✓ How important is each sub-category to the overall category?

Consider the Potato Chips sub-category, located in the Opportunity Gap quadrant below. This category is large (circle size) for the retailer and is experiencing better than average growth, but the retailer is not getting its "fair share" of the Potato Chips category.

# Market Share - Growth Quadrant

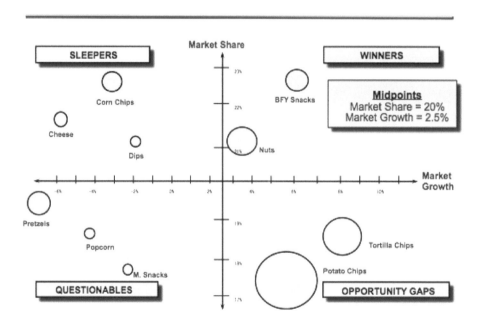

If, based on the role chosen for this category, the goal is to move this category into the "Winners" quadrant, what kinds of actions should the retailer take? The next diagram describes some of the appropriate actions that might be taken based upon the location of a category within a particular quadrant.

# Share / Growth Decision Matrix

| SLEEPERS | WINNERS |
|---|---|
| • Review product mix versus market<br>• Reallocate space to growth items?<br>• Reallocate promotion support?<br>• Increase margins? | • Continue current program<br>• Increase promotional support<br>• Review space management to ensure minimal out-of-stock potential<br>• Add good performing items not carried but available in the market |
| **QUESTIONABLES** | **OPPORTUNITY GAPS** |
| • Review assortment versus market<br>• Can prices be raised?<br>• Should promotion program be changed? | • Is the segment under-spaced?<br>• Review pricing mix - Is pricing of key items too high versus the market?<br>• Are category and key items under-promoted versus market?<br>• Review product mix - Is mix wrong for customer segments? Any new faster moving items not being carried? |

Similar Quadrant Analyses can also be used to identify profit and return on asset opportunities among categories, and within a category. Some of these additional applications include relating Turnover and Gross Margin, Inventory Turns and Gross Margin, Turnover per Cubic Metric and Gross Margin Unit Movement. The next diagrams are being used to show the profitability review of the Salty Snacks category.

# Category Profitability Assessment

| Category | Sales ($ mil) | % of Sales | Market Share | Annual Sales Growth % in Market | Gross Margin % | CTM |
|---|---|---|---|---|---|---|
| Potato Chips | 8.22 | 24.5 | 17.3 | +4.5 | 15.0 | 3.68 |
| Tortilla chips | 6.09 | 18.2 | 18.5 | +8.0 | 14.1 | 2.57 |
| Nuts | 4.51 | 13.5 | 21.2 | +1.8 | 18.0 | 2.43 |
| Better For You | 3.45 | 10.3 | 22.4 | +7.0 | 18.5 | 1.91 |
| Pretzels | 3.13 | 9.4 | 19.4 | (6.5) | 12.2 | 1.15 |
| Corn Chips | 2.30 | 6.9 | 22.6 | (3.2) | 13.5 | .93 |
| Cheese Snacks | 1.72 | 5.1 | 21.8 | (5.8) | 17.2 | .88 |
| Popcorn | 1.40 | 4.2 | 18.4 | (4.0) | 7.3 | .31 |
| Shelf Stable Dips | 1.35 | 4.0 | 21.0 | +1.0 | 18.3 | .73 |
| Misc. Snacks | 1.30 | 3.9 | 17.8 | +4.5 | 21.9 | .85 |
| Salty Snacks | $33.47 | 100 | 20.0 | 2.5 | 15.44 | 15.44 |

# Contribution to Margin Quadrant

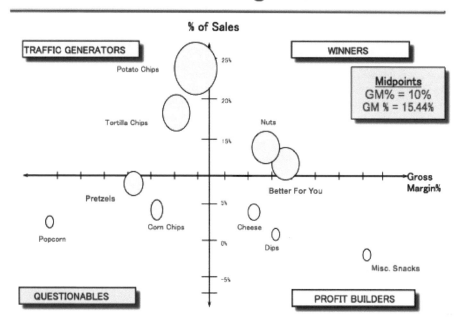

Based upon the profit analysis, the key findings can be summarized as such:

# Profit Decision Matrix

### TRAFFIC GENERATORS

▼ Increase margins where possible
▼ Shift sales distribution to higher margin sub-categories and items
▼ Reduce on-sale %, if feasible
▼ Increase on-sale gross margin

### WINNERS

▼ Reduce out-of-stocks
▼ Use signage to highlight sub-cats and items
▼ Improve shelf position
▼ Respond quickly to new item opportunities
▼ Promote profitable SKU's

### QUESTIONABLES

▼ Review assortment; delete poorest performers
▼ Reduce space, inventory levels
▼ Review gross margins/pricing
▼ Don't over-promote

### PROFIT BUILDERS

▼ Promotional tie-ins with Traffic Generators and Winners
▼ Look for share gaps
▼ Review shelf position
▼ Shift mix from traffic generators

As one last measure to use in understanding a category's return on inventory dollars invested, we then use a calculation called Gross Margin Return on Investment (GMROI). Before calculating GMROI, though, you must first calculate the category's Return on Assets (ROA). This result is calculated as follows:

# Category ROA Assessment (GMROI)

| Category | Sales ($ mil) | % of Issues Value | Market Share | Annual Growth % | Gross Margin % | CTM | Annual Turns | GMROI |
|---|---|---|---|---|---|---|---|---|
| Potato Chips | 8.72 | 24.5 | 17.3 | +4.5 | 15.0 | 3.68 | 33.8 | 5.96 |
| Tortilla Chips | 6.09 | 18.2 | 18.5 | +8.0 | 14.1 | 2.57 | 36.2 | 5.94 |
| Nuts | 4.51 | 13.5 | 21.2 | +1.8 | 18.0 | 2.43 | 16.0 | 3.51 |
| Better For You | 3.45 | 10.3 | 22.4 | +7.0 | 18.5 | 1.91 | 31.9 | 7.24 |
| Pretzels | 3.13 | 9.4 | 19.4 | (6.5) | 12.2 | 1.15 | 15.8 | 2.20 |
| Corn Chips | 2.30 | 6.9 | 22.6 | (3.2) | 13.5 | .93 | 39.2 | 6.11 |
| Cheese Snacks | 1.72 | 5.1 | 21.8 | (5.8) | 17.2 | .88 | 31.4 | 6.52 |
| Popcorn | 1.40 | 4.2 | 18.4 | (4.0) | 7.3 | .31 | 19.4 | 1.53 |
| Shelf Stable Dips | 1.35 | 4.0 | 21.0 | +1.0 | 18.3 | .73 | 13.1 | 2.93 |
| Misc. Snacks | 1.31 | 3.9 | 17.8 | +4.5 | 21.9 | .85 | 22.1 | 6.20 |
| TOTAL | $33.47 | 100 | 20.0 | 2.5 | 15.44 | 15.44 | 31.3 | 5.72 |

## Gross Margin Return On Investment

The amount of Gross Profit dollars generated on an annual basis for each dollar of inventory purchased.

**The formula:**

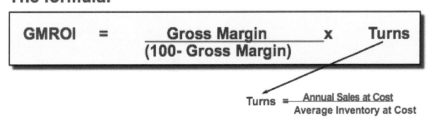

$$\text{GMROI} = \frac{\text{Gross Margin}}{(100 - \text{Gross Margin})} \times \text{Turns}$$

$$\text{Turns} = \frac{\text{Annual Sales at Cost}}{\text{Average Inventory at Cost}}$$

# Gross Margin Return on Investment

**Tortilla Chips**

$$\text{GMROI} = \frac{14.1}{(100 - 14.1)} \times 36.2 = 5.94$$

**Nuts**

$$\text{GMROI} = \frac{18}{(100 - 18)} \times 16 = 3.51$$

Once again, the results are placed into a Quadrant Analysis, as seen below.

# GMROI Quadrant

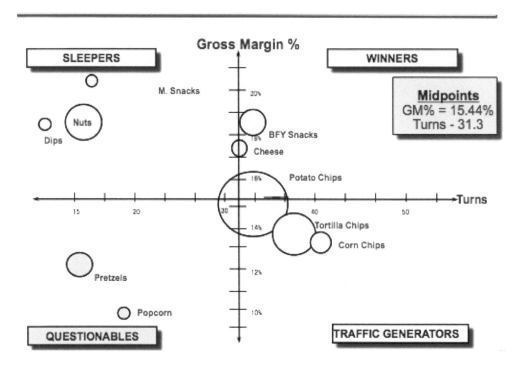

The resulting key findings are then summarized in a GMROI Decision Matrix (below).

# GMROI Decision Matrix

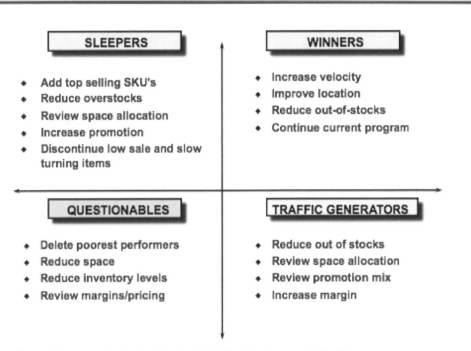

**SLEEPERS**
- Add top selling SKU's
- Reduce overstocks
- Review space allocation
- Increase promotion
- Discontinue low sale and slow turning items

**WINNERS**
- Increase velocity
- Improve location
- Reduce out-of-stocks
- Continue current program

**QUESTIONABLES**
- Delete poorest performers
- Reduce space
- Reduce inventory levels
- Review margins/pricing

**TRAFFIC GENERATORS**
- Reduce out of stocks
- Review space allocation
- Review promotion mix
- Increase margin

And, finally, all results are tabulated to lead to Strategies and Tactics.

# Category Opportunity Summary

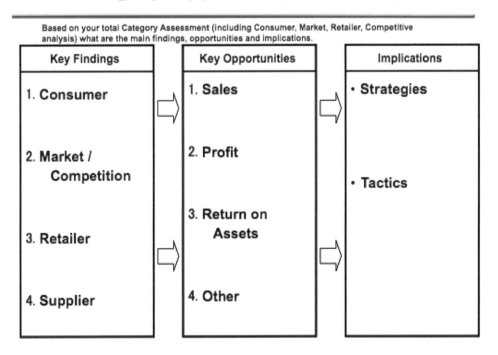

Based on your total Category Assessment (including Consumer, Market, Retailer, Competitive analysis) what are the main findings, opportunities and implications.

| Key Findings | Key Opportunities | Implications |
|---|---|---|
| 1. Consumer | 1. Sales | • Strategies |
| 2. Market / Competition | 2. Profit | |
| 3. Retailer | 3. Return on Assets | • Tactics |
| 4. Supplier | 4. Other | |

# Chapter 4.3 Discussion Questions

1. What is the purpose of the Category Assessment?

2. What are the minimum retailer requirements to start a Category Assessment?

3. How should data be sorted to provide a productive Category Assessment?

4. Name the four critical elements of a Category Assessment?

5. Define market share.

6. Perform a consumer assessment on your chosen category.

7. Perform a market assessment on your chosen category.

8. Perform a retailer assessment on your chosen category.

9. Perform a supplier assessment on your chosen category.

10. Define and explain the Share/ Growth Quadrant Analysis and Opportunity Gaps.

# 4.4- Category Scorecard

The Category Scorecard is used determine the target objectives that will be set by the retailer and supplier for achievement from implementation of the Category Business Plan. The target objectives are essentially the "hurdle rates" the category manager and the supplier(s) expect to achieve.

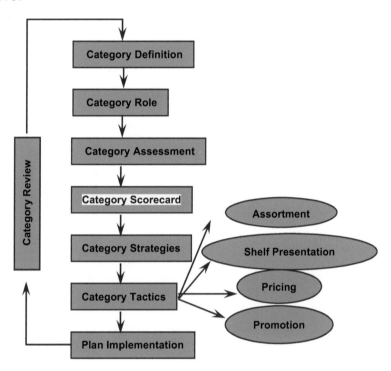

Target objectives must be consistent with the assigned category's role. For example, the target objectives of a Destination category may emphasize growth in turnover and market share while a Convenience role category is likely to place higher emphasis on profit performance measures. Developing appropriate target performance measures is an essential step because it allows the plan to be measured and monitored. Target objectives are typically developed on an annual basis with quarterly milestones for the purpose of business plan monitoring and modification.

The development of category performance measures involves setting the category's target objectives in a manner consistent with the category's role and the findings of the assessment step.

## Characteristics of Effective Scorecards

To measure the performance of Category Business Plans effectively, category performance measures should have the following characteristics:

- ✓ Balanced Architecture- Measures should be internal and external, and focused on both short and long-term results.

✓ Total System- Measures should allow results from all phases of a category's performance (production, procurement, distribution, and sales) to be measured.

✓ Allow for Comparison of Performance Over Time- Measures should be able to track actual results versus forecasts, budgets, and against results of previous periods.

✓ Timely, Accurate, Understandable Measures- Measures allow managers to make good decisions and should impact their behavior in a manner that is consistent with the overall company goals and strategies. Category measures should be able to be "rolled up" to higher-level financial measures.

A Balanced Category Scorecard is shown below.

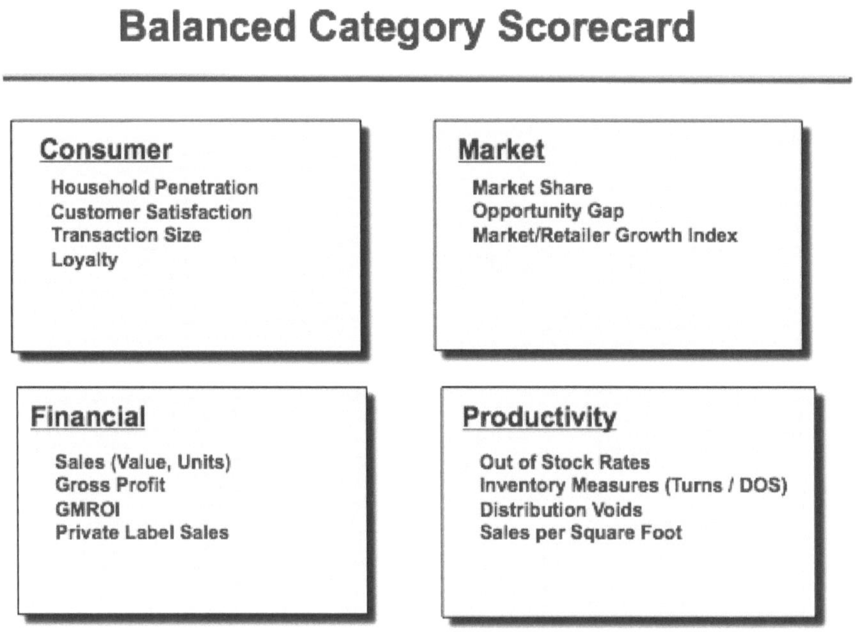

# Balanced Category Scorecard

### Consumer

Household Penetration
Customer Satisfaction
Transaction Size
Loyalty

### Market

Market Share
Opportunity Gap
Market/Retailer Growth Index

### Financial

Sales (Value, Units)
Gross Profit
GMROI
Private Label Sales

### Productivity

Out of Stock Rates
Inventory Measures (Turns / DOS)
Distribution Voids
Sales per Square Foot

*Retailer's Role*

The category manager and the supplier should evaluate whether the target goals are achievable as they develop the Category Business Plan. The conclusions from the assessment, and the expected outcome of the strategies and tactics may prove that the initial target objectives are too high or too low. It is the responsibility of the category manager to recommend appropriate target goals that are consistent with assigned category roles to higher-level management. The category manager should communicate target objectives to suppliers to enable them to provide programs, ideas, etc. that are consistent with these objectives.

*Supplier's Role*

The supplier should help evaluate the target objectives and either suggest a change or commit to working with the retailer to achieve these goals. The supplier's knowledge of key category trends, new item initiatives, product price increases and changes in category promotional funding are examples of useful information a supplier could provide to ensure that Category Business Plan measures and target objectives are realistic.

The outcome of this step is an agreed set of performance measures for the Category Business Plan and specific numerical targets for each measure. An example of a format used by one retailer is shown below.

Performance measures at the Category Business Plan level provide the basis for measuring, monitoring, and adjusting plans during the implementation phase. Most Category Business Plans set annual targets on these measures with quarterly milestones. Performance measures also provide the retailer with the capability of performing "bottom up" budgeting by "rolling up" Category Business Plan measures into department and company level financial budgets.

# Category Scorecard Example

|  | CURRENT | OBJECTIVE |
|---|---|---|
| **CONSUMER** | | |
| Consumer Service Level | 94.2% | 97.9% |
| Transaction Size | $2.31 | $2.37 |
| Penetration | 89.3% | 90.0% |
| | | |
| **MARKET** | | |
| Category Market Share | 36.5% | 38.9% |
| Opportunity Gap | (1.3%) | 0% |
| | | |
| **FINANCIAL** | | |
| Category Sales | $40,789 | $42,624 |
| Sales Growth | 2.3% | 4.5% |
| Gross Margin | 21.3% | 21.4% |
| Private Label Sales | $7536 | $7875 |
| GMROI | 4.71 | 6.62 |
| | | |
| **PRODUCTIVITY** | | |
| Inventory $ | $2347 | $1751 |
| Inventory Turns | 17.4 | 24.3 |
| Retail Service Level | 97.9% | 98.3% |
| Sales per Sq. Foot | $148 | $155 |

# Chapter 4.4 Discussion Questions

1. What is determined by the Category Performance Measures?

2. Category Performance Measures should have which characteristics?

3. What is the retailer's role in the Category Performance Measures?

4. What is the supplier's role in the Category Performance Measures?

5. What ten performance measures would you use for your chosen category? Why?

# *4.5- Category Strategies*

Category Strategy development is the step in the Category Business Planning process when strategies are developed to deliver the category role and the category performance targets.

At this point in the process, the retailer and supplier know the category role, have assessed the current performance of the category and have set preliminary targets for the category performance. The purpose of this step is for the retailer and supplier to develop strategies that capitalize on category opportunities through creative and efficient use of the resources that are available to the category.

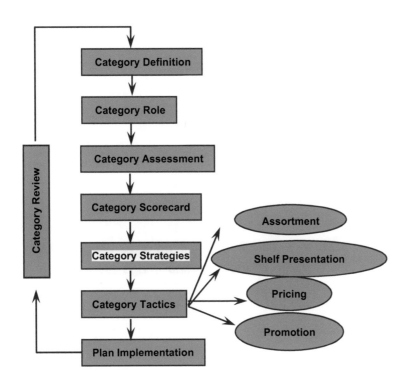

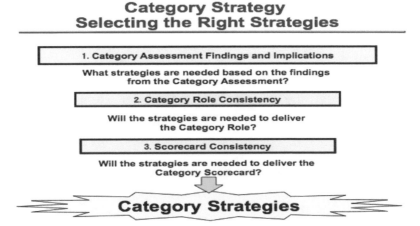

**Marketing and Product Supply Strategies**

Category Business Plans should specify strategies for both marketing and product supply areas. The strategies should cover how the retailer plans to purchase, distribute, market and service the category.

*Marketing Strategies*

A retailer's marketing strategies address the key question of how, working with its suppliers, it will market the category and its components (sub-category, segments, etc.) to achieve the category role and performance targets. The nine most typical category marketing strategies are:

Traffic Building- This strategy, when applied to a component of the category, focuses on drawing consumer traffic to the store and/or into the aisle and category.

Transaction Building- This strategy focuses on increasing the size of the average transaction in the category, aisle, or total store transaction (market basket).

Turf Protecting- This strategy aggressively positions certain parts of a category to protect the retailer's business in the category from targeted competitors.

Profit Generating- This strategy focuses on using parts of the category to generate profits.

Cash Generating- This strategy focuses on using parts of the category to generate cash flow for the retailer.

Excitement Creating- This strategy is used to communicate a sense of urgency or opportunity to the consumer.

Image Enhancing- This strategy is used in a category to help the retailer communicate its desired image to the consumer, in one or more of the following image areas: Price, Service, Quality, and Variety

*Product Supply Strategies*

Efficient product supply strategies are a key component of the overall goal of enhancing consumer value. Product supply strategies can, and should be, included in every Category Business Plan. Each product supply strategy is a combination of efficient replenishment techniques that improve the performance of the following four replenishment processes with suppliers and products:

Master Data Alignment- This process ensures the accurate exchange of product, price and promotional information between the supplier and the retailer. Realizing correct master data alignment results in fewer mistakes and therefore substantial cost savings in administrative work.

Ordering- This process ensures that the right deliveries are triggered at the right time. This can be done by means of sending orders or by means of Continuous Replenishment (CRP).

Physical Distribution- This process takes care of the physical product flow from the production plant to the shelf in the store. Improving performance of this process means working towards higher service levels, lower stock levels, lower handling and lower transportation costs.

Finance- This process takes care of the financial transaction between suppliers, retailers and their stores. Efficiency consists of error-free invoices and timely and correct payment via systems that use minimal human intervention.

Which techniques should be used depends heavily upon the current situation of the retailer, the role of the category and the characteristics of the SKU's that comprise the category.

## Selecting Category Strategies

The selection of the right mix of strategies within a category is one of the most important decisions the category manager and ·a supplier make in the Category Management process. The assignment of strategies to various components (sub-categories, segments, brands, SKUs) of the category provides the essential guidelines for which tactics (ranging, pricing, promotion, shelf presentation) will later be employed. The selection of appropriate strategies should be guided by the following:

✓ Strategies must be linked to category roles.

✓ Strategies are implied from category performance measures and targets.

✓ Certain characteristics of parts of the category suggest specific strategies.

### 1. Category Roles and Implied Strategies

Category roles are implemented through the right mix of strategies in a category. Certain strategies are implied by roles. The following diagram illustrates the type of marketing strategies that are most deployed to implement a category role. These strategies should be considered before other strategies.

## Category Roles Guide Category Strategies

| Category Role | Typical Strategies |
| --- | --- |
| Destination | Traffic Building<br>Turf Protecting<br>Transaction Building<br>Excitement Creation |
| Preferred Routine / Routine | Traffic Building<br>Transaction Building<br>Profit Generating |
| Convenience | Transaction Building<br>Profit Generating<br>Image Enhancing |
| Occasional / Seasonal | Traffic Building<br>Excitement Creation<br>Profit Generating |

*2. Matching Strategies with Product Characteristics*

The following diagram highlights some of the product characteristics that, for certain products, can help match the right marketing strategies to the right products.

## Assigning Products to Different Marketing Strategies

| Strategy | Product Characteristics |
|---|---|
| • Traffic Building | ⟶ Products with high share, high household penetration, frequent purchase, promotion sensitive. |
| • Transaction Building | ⟶ Products with larger transaction size, premium products. |
| • Profit Generating | ⟶ Products with higher margins, higher loyalty, less price sensitivity. |
| • Turf Protecting | ⟶ Known price value products, frequently promoted by target competitor. |
| • Excitement Creation | ⟶ New products, seasonal products, rapidly growing products. |
| • Image Enhancing | ⟶ Products that reinforce overall store strategy or theme (e.g. variety, quality, service etc.) |

**Outcome**

The major result of the category strategy step is the selection of the appropriate mix of strategies and how these strategies will be deployed against specific components of the category. These decisions then pave the way for the selection of the specific tactics to execute these strategies.

The most effective way to show these linkages is in the form of a "stratogram." An example is the diagram below, which shows the different strategies that a category manager has decided to deploy against various components of the Soft Drink category. Four marketing strategies have been selected. These strategies must be able to deliver the Preferred Routine role assigned to this category.

The final step in developing category strategies is to validate that the proposed strategies will deliver the desired financial results required by the Category Business Plan performance targets. This validation involves estimating the financial impact of each strategy. Validation of the likely impact of each strategy is an essential prerequisite to final approval of category strategies. Strategies that are not proven or validated by analysis should not become part of the Category Business Plan. The validation step establishes that the strategies can deliver increased benefits to the consumer, retailer, and supplier.

Marketing and product supply strategies must work well together. The best product supply and marketing strategies developed in isolation generally do not turn out to be the best strategies for an integrated Category Business Plan. Category managers and their supplier partners are typically responsible for defining the marketing strategies. Product supply strategies are usually developed by representatives from the retailer's and supplier's warehouse, logistics (suppliers) or operations functions. Finally, input from store retail operations managers has proven extremely valuable to ensure successful retail implementation of Category Business Plans.

# The Category Stratogram

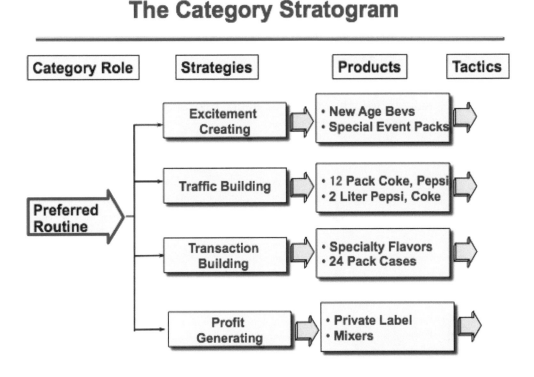

## Role of Suppliers

Many suppliers recognize that their ability to play a value-added role in assisting retailers develop category strategies is greatly enhanced when they develop strategies that are responsive to the differing category roles.

The same category could play a Destination role in one retailer and a Convenience role in another. Before engaging in the business process with retailers, a supplier should prepare category strategy recommendations for all appropriate category roles, and for all appropriate retailer formats (hypermarkets, supermarkets, etc.). These strategies include recommendations for marketing (traffic building, turf protecting, etc.), as well as product supply strategies. For example, a supplier of a health & beauty care category might develop strategy options for a supermarket choosing a Convenience role, a hyper market choosing a Preferred role, and a drug store choosing a Destination role.

These three options would generate different marketing and product supply strategies. As a result of this work, the supplier has a strategic plan it can use with individual retailers to help them develop appropriate category strategies. A supplier seeking to add value to category strategy development should be prepared to share relevant consumer and market data.

## Summary

The process of category strategy selection includes the following action steps:

- ✓ Determine marketing and product supply strategy options.
- ✓ Review category assessment findings.
- ✓ Select appropriate strategies to deliver category role and performance targets.
- ✓ Assign strategies to appropriate sub-categories, segments, brands, or SKU's.
- ✓ Validate strategies with analysis.

The end-result of this step should be a documented set of strategies (the "stratogram"), and category strategies validated to achieve the category role and provide direction for the next step- the development of specific tactics.

# Chapter 4.5 Discussion Questions

1. What is the purpose of the Category Strategy step?
2. Define and apply a Traffic Building strategy to your chosen category.
3. Define and apply a Transaction Building strategy to your chosen category.
4. Define and apply a Cash Generating strategy to your chosen category.
5. Define and apply a Profit Generating strategy to your chosen category.
6. Define and apply a Turf Defending strategy to your chosen category.
7. Define and apply an Excitement Creating strategy to your chosen category.
8. Define and apply an Image Enhancing strategy to your chosen category.
9. What is a stratogram?
10. Product supply strategies are validated with which three measures? Define them.

# *4.6- Category Tactics*

This step identifies and validates the specific actions that will be taken to implement the category strategies developed previously. In developing the category tactics, retailers and suppliers identify their options for tactics, complete the necessary analysis to determine the likely impact of a tactical change, and make a final decision on the tactics that will best implement the category strategies, thereby achieving the performance targets of the Category Business Plan.

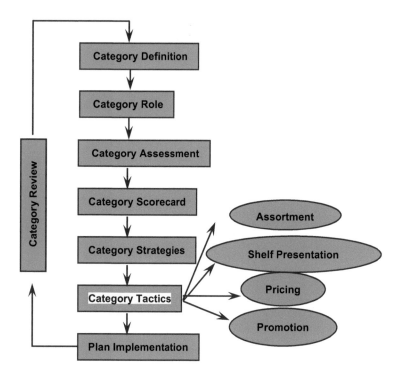

In the Category Management process, category tactics are developed in the following areas:

- ✓ Assortment
- ✓ Pricing
- ✓ Promotion
- ✓ Shelf presentation

Tactics in these areas implement the assigned role of the category and must also link to category strategies. These tactics are to be developed between the retailer and the supplier and should encompass goals from both parties.

**Steps in Tactics Development**

To ensure that tactics are linked to category roles, performance targets and strategies, tactical development should follow these steps:

✓ Determine the tactical choices available.

✓ Select tactical options that will deliver the category strategies.

✓ Validate the impact of each tactic on key category performance targets.

✓ Complete a "tactogram", which summarizes how each tactic will help execute the selected category strategies and the impact of each tactic on category performance.

✓ Review the likely impacts in comparison to preliminary performance targets set for the Category Business Plan and adjust targets or tactics as appropriate.

The next section will describe how this process is completed in the key tactical areas along with some examples that illustrate the outcome of tactics development.

**Assortment Tactics**

The development of an efficient product assortment, one that balances the assortment needs of consumers with the business objectives of the retailer and suppliers, is one of the most important issues in Category Management. Given this importance, some retailers begin their Category Management journey by undertaking an efficient assortment analysis of their categories. While this is only one component of a total Category Management process, it can yield excellent benefits as a first step.

The assortment tactic area establishes the product variety offered to consumers as well as the criteria for carrying and deleting the category's SKUs. Assortment can be an important source of retailer differentiation. To achieve this, assortment decisions must be related to the role and strategies of the category. As a result, an assortment tactic that is correct for one retailer for a particular category may not be correct for another retailer managing the same category. The optimal assortment balances the needs of consumers with the need to avoid unnecessary duplication and the associated costs.

*Assortment Choices*

The tactical choices available in the area of assortment are decrease, increase, swap, uniform vs. cluster, private label, and maintain.

*Decision Criteria*

The appropriate assortment tactics should only be decided after considering the following factors:

✓ Variety Needs of Target Consumer

  o What does the Consumer Decision Tree indicate?

  o What are the minimum coverage levels for variety to meet consumer needs?

- ✓ Current Variety Image
  - How does the current variety compare to competition?
  - Who is perceived to be the current category variety leader? Why?
- ✓ Marketing Strategy
  - What level of variety is consistent with the retailer's overall marketing strategy?
- ✓ Category Role and Strategies
  - What level of variety is consistent with the category role and strategies?
- ✓ Cost/Benefit of Different Variety Levels
  - What are the opportunities?
  - How "long" is the tail? (e.g., last 2% of turnover comes from last 20% of SKUs)
  - What is the minimum performance acceptable to carry an item?
  - What is the gain required to offset the cost on inventory, space, and administration?
  - What is variety and what is duplication?
- ✓ Product Acceptance and Deletion Criteria
  - What criteria should be used for accepting and rejecting products given the category role and strategies?
- ✓ Supplier Capabilities
  - Can category suppliers support tactical decisions?

Since category tactics execute the category strategies, there need to be logical linkages between strategies and tactics. The diagrams below are examples of the preceding questions.

## The Assortment Challenge – Variety vs. Duplication

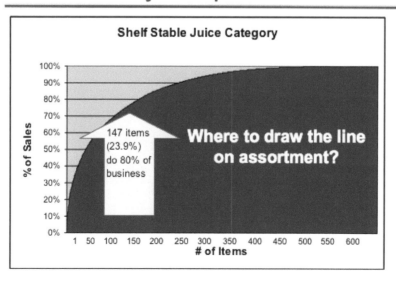

# Assortment Tactics

**Key Decision Criteria and Tools**

- **CDT Switching and Walking Levels**
  - Set Core assortment at Walking Levels
  - Minimize duplication at Switching Levels

- **Market Coverage Levels**
  - Set Coverage Levels based on --
    - Category Strategies
    - Category Role
    - Company Marketing Strategy for Product Assortment/ Variety

# Key Assortment Tool
# Walking and Switching Levels –

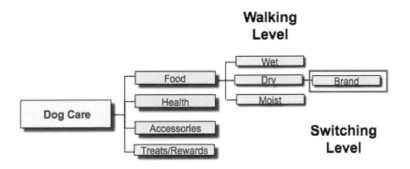

# Key Assortment Tool
# Market Coverage Level

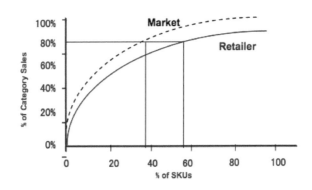

## Tactic Impact Validation

The likely impact of each tactical action must be determined prior to making a final decision on which tactics will best implement the category strategy and contribute most to category performance targets.

### Assortment Guidelines by Category Strategies - example

| Transaction Building | Profit Generating |
|---|---|
| • Emphasize larger sizes of products, premium / trade-up products, products suitable for multiple unit purchase incentives (e.g. 2 for 1), and expandable consumption products | • Focus Private Brand assortment on generating disproportionate percentage of total category profit.<br><br>• Expand assortment in higher "Profit Productivity" segments; reduce in lower "Profit Productivity" segments of category.<br><br>• Increase assortment in higher market growth, higher profitability segments of category. |

## Pricing Tactics

Tactics in this area determine the prices the retailer offers to consumers for the products carried in the category. As with all decisions in all tactical areas, these decisions must be based on the category's role, target performance measures, and category strategies as well as on an understanding of consumer and competitive behavior.

### Pricing Choices

The key tactical choices that exist in pricing are described in this section.

### Decision Criteria

Pricing decisions reflect numerous considerations made by the retailer in its own business judgment including, among others, the following:

o Value Provided to Target Consumer

  o How important is pricing in the value offered to consumers in this category?

  o How price sensitive are target consumers?

  o Which products are the most price-sensitive in the category?

o Current Price Image

  o What does the category assessment reveal?

  o How does the pricing compare to competition?

- o Who is perceived to be the category price leader? Why?
- o What are the key price image items of the category?
- o Marketing Strategy
  - o What pricing is consistent with the company's overall pricing and marketing strategy (e.g., high/low, EDLP, etc.)?
- o Category Role and Strategies
  - o What pricing is consistent with the category role and strategies?
- o Cost/Benefit of Various Pricing Options
  - o Will price increase/decrease significantly impact category turnover and profit?
  - o Are private label items priced correctly in relation to supplier-branded products?
  - o How should new items be priced?
  - o What are likely competitor responses to any price changes?

The diagrams below are an example of some general guidelines for linking pricing tactics to various category strategies.

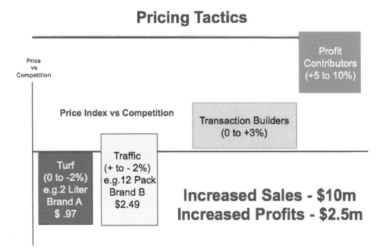

## Pricing Tactics

**Tactic Impact Validation**

As with all tactic decisions, the expected impact of recommended pricing actions must be determined. This is determined by strategy (e.g., "What impact will the proposed pricing changes have on turnover and profit of the items targeted for a traffic building strategy?"). This information provides the pricing "tactogram".

# Pricing Tactics Guidelines by Category Strategies – example

| Image Enhancing | Turf Protecting | Traffic Building |
|---|---|---|
| • Typically these SKUs will be less price sensitive...selling emphasis should be on value of broad and unique SKUs offered.<br>• Pricing levels should encourage consumer to trade-up or add another SKU to their normal purchase in category. | • Clearly define target competitor against which "turf" is to be defended.<br>• Establish competitive Price Index range (e.g. –5% to 1%) for Turf Protecting products vs. target competitor.<br>• Must sustain pricing on Turf Protection products for extended period if necessary | • Set prices for Traffic Building products based on predetermined competitive Price Index range (e.g.. +- 2%) based on competitive pricing history and overall company pricing strategy.<br>• Identify most price sensitive products in category as most likely Traffic Builders.<br>• Identify Traffic Builders in different branches of Consumer Decision Tree (CDT). |

## Promotion Tactics

Tactics in this area determine the retailer promotions to be offered to the consumer in the category. The promotion tactics define the criteria for using various vehicles (advertised features, displays, sampling, contests, etc.) to promote the components of the category (e.g., segments, brands, SKUs, etc.) to execute the category strategies. Specific promotional tactics are defined, and the final output of this step is a detailed calendar of promotional events linked to the achievement of the category strategies. Promotional tactics play an especially important role in the Category Business Plan because they are the main source of creative selling ideas.

*Promotion Choices*

Compared to the other tactical areas, there are more tactical choices in promotion. The diagram below lists some of the most common promotional tactical choices.

*Decision Criteria*

As with other tactical decisions, promotion decisions must be linked to other decisions made by the retailer in the Category Management process.  The factors include:

o Marketing Strategy
  o What promotions are consistent with the company's overall marketing strategy?
  o How will the target consumer respond to various promotions?
  o What is the promotion activity of competitors in this category?
  o How will competitors respond to various promotions?
  o What impact does promotion have on the image of the item, category, and retailer?

- Category Role and Strategies
  - Which promotions best deliver the assigned role and execute the category strategies?
  - What criteria are most important for choosing the right promotions?
- Cost/Benefit of Various Promotions
  - How well do promotions work in the category? Do they increase turnover? Market share? Profit for the category? How much do they cannibalize existing results?
  - Does the promotion attract new consumers, and do they buy other products as well as the promoted item?
  - Which promotions build consumer loyalty?
  - Which promotions create unfavorable purchasing behavior and erode brand and store equity?
  - What do various promotional options cost? What return on investment does a promotion generate?

The diagrams below provide a set of decision guidelines that can help ensure that promotional tactics are effectively linked to some of the key category strategies.

# Promotion Tactics
# Pet Care Consumer Decision Tree

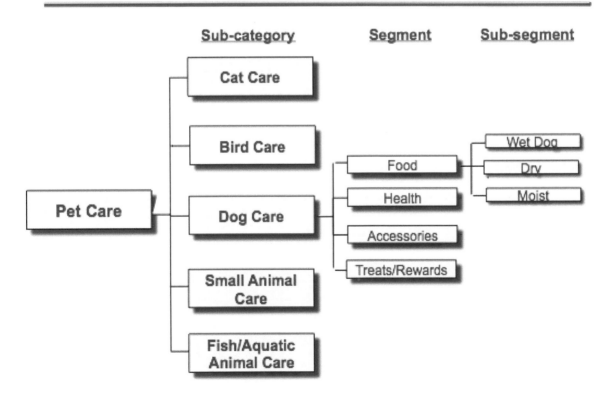

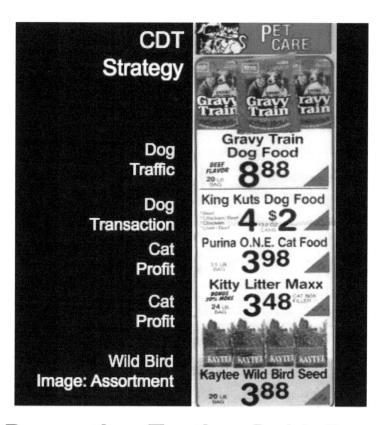

| CDT Strategy | |
|---|---|
| Dog Traffic | Gravy Train Dog Food — BEEF FLAVOR 20 LB BAG — **8**88 |
| Dog Transaction | King Kuts Dog Food — **4** $**2** |
| Cat Profit | Purina O.N.E. Cat Food — 3.5 LB BAG — **3**98 |
| Cat Profit | Kitty Litter Maxx — BONUS 20% MORE — 24 LB BAG — **3**48 |
| Wild Bird Image: Assortment | Kaytee Wild Bird Seed — 20 LB BAG — **3**88 |

# Promotion Tactics Guidelines by Category Strategies – example

| Transaction Building | Profit Generating |
|---|---|
| • Cross-promote Transaction Building products with Traffic Building products to create impulse sales. | • Promote Profit Generators to increase category and promotion mix profit margin. |
| • Promote Transaction Builders as part of a "total solution" where appropriate (e.g. – fabric care, pet care, etc.) to encourage regimen purchases. | • Emphasize larger sizes (e.g. – bonus packs) in selecting Profit Generating products for promotion. |
| • Offer discounts on larger size products to encourage trade-up to larger sizes. | • Promote non-price attributes (e.g. – quality, value etc.) for Profit Generators (vs. promotion only price) to create value image for higher profit margin products. |
| • Use multiple unit pricing (e.g. 2 for 1) to encourage higher transaction. | • Use private label products to promote price-value in category at higher than category average gross margin. |

# Promotion Plan: Laundry Care

| | | Wk 1 | Wk 2 | Wk 3 | Wk 4 | Wk 5 | Wk 6 | Wk 7 | Wk 8 | Wk 9 | Wk 10 | Wk 11 | Wk 12 | Wk 13 | Wk 14 | Wk 15 | Wk 16 | Wk 17 | Wk 18 | Wk 19 | Wk 20 | Wk 21 | Wk 22 | Wk 23 | Wk 24 | Wk 25 | Wk 26 | Wk 27 |
|---|---|---|---|---|---|---|---|---|---|---|---|---|---|---|---|---|---|---|---|---|---|---|---|---|---|---|---|---|
| Fab rainforest detergent lg | Excitement Creating | X | | | | | | | | X | | | | | | | X | | | | | | | | X | | | |
| Tide Kick Stand Appliance | Excitement Creating | | X | | | | | | | | | X | | | | | | X | | | | | | | X | | | X |
| Snuggle Pillow Mist | Excitement Creating | | | | X | | | | | | | X | | | | | | | | | | X | | | | | X | |
| Downey Enhancer | Excitement Creating | | | | | | | X | | X | | | | | | | | | | | | | | | | X | | |
| Savemore detergent - gallon | Profit Generating | X | | | | | | | X | | | | | X | | | | | | | | | X | | | | | |
| Savemore bleach - gallon | Profit Generating | | | | | | | | | X | | | | | | | X | | | | | | | X | | | | |
| Febreze 1000 ML liquid | Profit Generating | | | X | | | | | | | X | | | | | | | | | | | | | | X | | | |
| Dryel refill | Profit Generating | | | | | X | | | | | | | | X | | | | X | | | | | | | | X | | |
| Woolite gentle care | Profit Generating | | | | X | | | | | | | | X | | | | | | X | | | | | | | | X | |
| Scotch Gard 14z | Profit Generating | | | | | | X | | | | | | | X | | | | | | | X | | | | | | | X |
| White King water softener | Profit Generating | | | | | | | X | | | | | | | X | | | | | X | | | | | | | | |
| Purex liquid - 200 fl | Transaction Building | | X | | | | | | | | X | | | | | | | | | X | | | | | | X | | |
| Downey 120 fl | Transaction Building | X | | | | | | | | | X | | | | | | X | | | | | | X | | | | | |
| Sun Classic Detergent 5# | Transaction Building | | X | | | | | | | X | | | | | | | | X | | | | | | | | X | | |
| Tide powder regular | Traffic Generator | X | | | X | | | X | | | X | | | X | | | X | | | X | | | X | | | X | | |
| Clorox gallon | Traffic Generator | | X | | | | X | | X | | | X | | | X | | X | | | X | | X | | X | | | | X |
| Summit laundry tea | Image - assortment | X | | | | | | | X | | | | | | | | X | | | | | | | | X | | | |
| Summit laundry tea w/bleach | Image - assortment | | | X | | | | | | | | | X | | | | | | | | X | | | | | | | |
| Planet Ultra | Image - assortment | | X | | | | | | | | X | | | | | | | | X | | | | | | | | | X |
| Lysol Fabric Refresh | Image - assortment | | | | | | X | | | | | | | X | | | | | | | | | X | | | | | |

## Category Promotion Plan is balanced across the CDT and Category Strategies

*Tactic Impact Validation*

The choice of promotion tactics must be validated to determine whether the actions will be able to generate sufficient sales and profit improvement to warrant their implementation.

The final analysis of this step in the Category Business Plan is a promotion tactogram which summarizes the impact of recommended promotion actions by category strategy, and an annual promotion calendar for implementing the recommended promotions.

### Shelf Presentation Tactics

Tactics in this area determine how the category will be presented to consumers at the point of sale. Some of the key decisions made in this step are the criteria used for managing shelf space (in the category, sub-categories, segments and SKUs), category location in store and in aisle, category layout, on-shelf service levels (e.g., minimum days of supply, case pack out, etc.), and specific sub-category/ segment and SKU space allocation. While computerized space management systems play an important support role in helping make these decisions, the decisions must also reflect important strategic issues, such as the best location for the category in the store and the best overall flow of products on the shelf. Tactical decisions are extremely important because consumers primarily see the result of Category Management at the shelf level.

*Shelf Presentation Choices*

Key tactical choices in this area are shown in the next diagram.

*Decision Criteria*

Shelf presentation decisions must also reflect numerous considerations made during the Category Management process. These criteria include:

o Target Consumer

   o Is the shelf presentation logical and "shoppable" based on the needs and/or wants of the target consumers and how they make purchase decisions in the category (the Consumer Decision Tree)?

o Competitive Positioning

   o Does the shelf presentation help highlight key points of competitive differentiation sought by the retailer?

o Marketing Strategy

   o Is the desired variety image communicated and reinforced by the shelf presentation?

o Category Role and Strategies

   o What shelf presentation is consistent with the category role and strategies?

o Cost/ Benefit of Various Shelf Presentation Options

   o How are operational issues considered (e.g. cost of restocking)?

   o What impact will a particular location within the store have on category sales and profit?

   o What impact will a particular category layout have on category sales and profit?

   o Does the shelf presentation help the retailer implement its customer service strategy at store level?

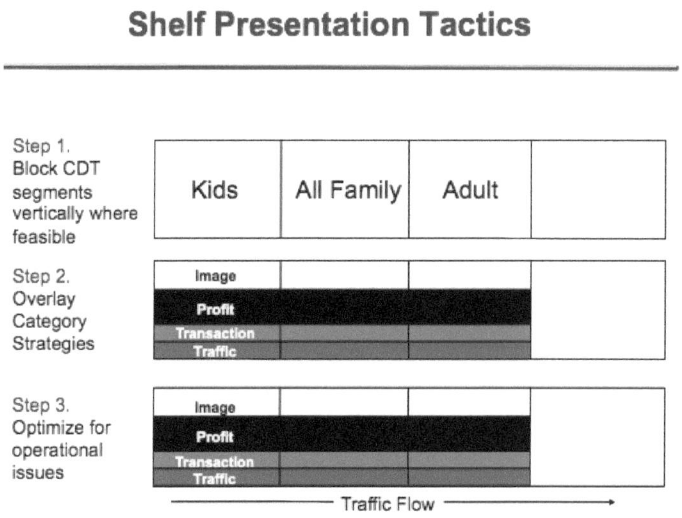

## Shelf Presentation Tactics

The following diagram provides some general guidelines for selecting shelf presentation tactics that support the various category strategies.

## Shelf Presentation Guidelines by Category Strategies - example

| Variety Image Enhancing | Turf Protecting | Traffic Building |
|---|---|---|
| • Group Variety Enhancing products together for maximum impact.<br>• Place at beginning of traffic flow to attract consumer into aisle / category. | • Under-emphasize Turf Protectors in shelf layout – don't give Turf Protectors prime shelf space.<br>• Position Turf Protecting products at end of traffic flow and near Traffic Builders to reinforce broader price value offering available vs. only Turf Protectors.<br>• Position Turf Protectors adjacent to substitute products that are more profitable to encourage switching. | • Position Traffic Builders to maximize potential sales of complementary products in the category.<br>• In smaller sections, locate Traffic Builders at end of traffic flow; for larger size sections place Traffic Builders in more than one location...either at beginning of traffic flow (or in middle of section) as well as at end of traffic flow.<br>• Don't give Traffic Builders prime shelf space (e.g. – on eye level shelf). They should be convenient for shopper but not most visible in section. |

The output of this step is a shelf presentation for the category that presents the category to the consumer in a manner that has "consumer logic," that is, it reflects in some manner the structure of the Consumer Decision Tree and reflects the blend of strategies that the retailer wants to implement in the category. The next two diagrams show an example of how a retailer changed the shelf presentation for the Oral Care Category to better consider these factors. The results from this change have been a significant improvement in turnover, gross profit, and return on space asset investment in this category.

## Oral Care Category
## Shelf Presentation – Before

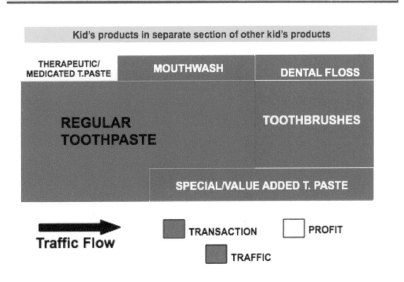

87

# Oral Care Category
## Shelf Presentation – After

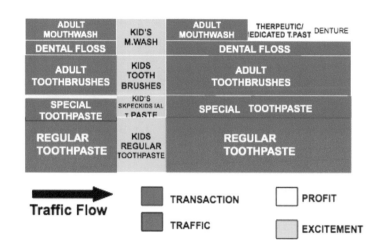

## Overall Tactogram

The final step is the development of an overall summary "tactogram." This shows the total impact of the recommended actions in all four tactical areas. The total impact is then compared to the preliminary target category performance measures established earlier to check if these targets can be achieved. If not, either the targets must be adjusted, or the recommended tactics revised.

# Chapter 4.6 Discussion Questions

1. What does the Strategy Tactic step identify and validate?

2. Define and apply an Assortment tactic to your chosen category.

3. Define and apply a Pricing tactic to your chosen category.

4. Define and apply a Promotion tactic to your chosen category.

5. Define and apply a Shelf Presentation tactic to your chosen category.

6. What are the five steps in the development of Category Tactics?  Briefly define.

7. What is a tactogram?

8. What is the role of the supplier in the Category Tactics, when finished?

# 4.7- Category Plan Implementation

This step in the Category Business Planning process develops a specific implementation schedule and assigns responsibilities for completing all tactical actions shown on the category "tactogram." The potential benefits of Category Management lie in the implementation of Category Business Plans. These plans are of little value if they are not implemented or are implemented poorly.

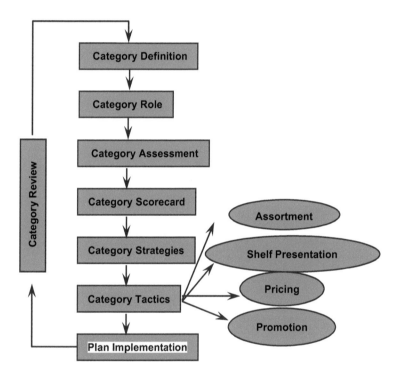

The key components of plan implementation are:

o  Approval Process

o  Assigning Responsibilities

o  Scheduling

*1. Plan Approval Process*

The retailer's and supplier's management must establish the criteria and  process  for approving Category Business Plans. The approval process ensures the commitment to implement the plan and that all trading partners can provide the necessary resources to execute it. The criteria for approval of a Category Business Plan should include:

Strategic Fit- Management should be certain that the Category Business Plan is consistent with the company's overall strategy.

<u>Target Performance Impact</u>- An important aspect of the approval process is to confirm the projected impact of the plan on the category performance targets.

<u>Resource Allocation</u>- The approval process should "sign-off" on any additional resources requested by the retailer and the supplier, especially if the plan requests additional resources beyond what has already been allocated (e.g., a new type of cooler, more shelf space, more promotion activity, etc.).

<u>Impact on Other Areas</u>- If the Category Business Plan impacts other functional areas of a retailer's or supplier's business, the approval process must recognize and manage this issue. For example, will the promotional tactics within the plan have any implications for the supplier's marketing function? Will the retailer's store engineering department be impacted by plans to relocate the category within the store? Answers to these types of questions should have been provided in the development of the Category Business Plan, but it is important that management agree to manage these issues as part of the plan approval process.

## 2. Assignment of Responsibilities

This step involves assigning each tactical action required in the plan to individuals for execution. Retailers typically assign tasks to the category manager, senior management and functions throughout their system (e.g., store operation, logistics, information systems and finance). Suppliers may assign tasks to the account executive, senior management, product supply, information systems, customer service and, frequently, marketing or product development. For example, to implement the assortment tactics, it may be necessary to authorize several new products, discontinue stocking some items, revise the planogram and reset store shelves. The implementation plan will assign each of these tasks to individuals in the supplier's and retailer's organization.

## 3. Implementation Scheduling

This step involves the development of timelines and milestones for the tasks, which have been assigned. An essential tool for quality implementation is a detailed implementation calendar. The calendar includes dates for completion of all tactical actions, as well as dates for reviewing plan progress.

### Implementation
### Success Requirements

- Top management commitment to implementation
- Detailed Implementation Plan
- Involvement of Store Operations
- Category Plans must be "store relevant"
- Review and redesign current implementation processes
- Assign specific responsibility and performance measures at HQ and store levels

# Category Management
# Implementation Phases

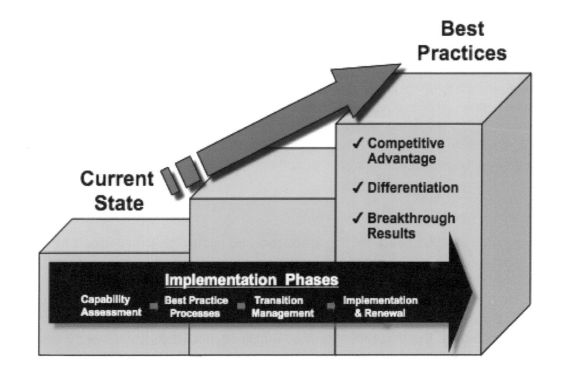

# Chapter 4.7 Discussion Questions

1. What two things are produced by the Category Plan Implementation step?

2. What are the three key components of the plan implementation?

3. The Category Business Plan needs to be approved.  What are the criteria for approval?

4. Assign responsibilities to two of the tactics developed in your chosen category.

5. What are the four Category Plan Implementation phases?

# 4.8- Category Review

The final step in the Category Management business process is to conduct an ongoing review and measurement of the progress of the plan towards the category role and target performance measures, and to modify the plan as appropriate. Category Business Plans are typically annual plans. Their results should he extensively reviewed annually, and less extensive reviews should be conducted at least on a quarterly basis.

## Measuring/Monitoring Category Business Plan Performance

Some of the key questions when measuring the category's performance are:

- How often should the Category Business Plan be evaluated? This will depend upon the category and its role. Destination categories tend to be evaluated more frequently.

- What role does the retailer play in measuring the category's progress? The supplier? This will depend upon the information capabilities of each party.

- What format should this measurement reporting follow? A common review format for all plans should be developed to eliminate the confusion and complexity created by having different formats and measures. This format should contain, at a minimum, a comparison of actual vs. target performance levels, an explanation of any variances and actions to be taken to modify the plan's implementation because of these variances.

## Modifying the Category Business Plan

Category Business Plans are developed and approved based upon assumptions about the expected business environment. If these conditions change, the underlying assumptions of the plan may not hold, and the plan will need to be modified. The key to ensuring timely follow-up is the effective assignment of retailer and supplier monitoring responsibilities, and for the timely identification and communication of relevant changes in the business conditions facing the category.

A disciplined, standardized process for making changes to an existing Category Business Plan should be developed between trading partners. Effective measurement and monitoring procedures can help prevent over-reaction or under-reaction to variances in plan results or changes in business conditions. Modifying a Category Business Plan, however, must be a carefully managed process and approval to make modifications must be a clearly defined responsibility.

# Chapter 4.8 Discussion Questions

1. What are the key questions when measuring a category's performance?

2. Why review results?

3. If your results of your chosen category were negative, what would you do now?

4. Who should initiate the review process?

# *4.9- Conclusion Business Process*

The core work of Category Management is the process of Category Business Planning. The development, implementation and monitoring of the results of these plans is the clearest sign that a company is managing its business through a Category Management approach. Without such a systematic, disciplined, cooperative approach, many efforts become merely a list of projects.

Category Management is an on-going management process that has no real end point. It is a process of continuous improvement in managing consumer-defined business units in a more strategic manner. The process of Category Business Planning is new work for most retailers and suppliers. It requires a significant commitment by management and a substantial investment in people and systems development. The results it produces, however, when implemented well, can be spectacular. It is, at its core, a smarter way to run today's retailer and supplier businesses.

# 5- The Enabling Components

Best Practices Category Management consists of six interrelated components. Two of these components are considered essential and are referred to as the "core components". They are Strategy and Business Process and were described in detail in chapters 3 and 4. The remaining four components of Category Management are referred to as the "enabling components", due to their role in supporting strategy and business process components.

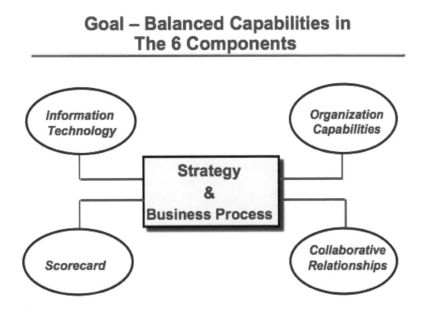

The enabling components are:

*1. Performance Measurement-* The measurement tools used to monitor progress, improve category planning and decision making and serve as a basis of reward and recognition.

*2. Organizational Capabilities-* The development of the organization's Category Management competence through the appropriate organizational structure, roles/ responsibilities, skill/ knowledge development and reward systems.

*3. Information Technology-* The data and systems which support the fact-based decisions of Category Management and improve business process productivity.

*4. Cooperative Trading Partner Relationships-* The synergy created when trading partners cooperate to maximize their unique resources and perspectives for a common objective, delivering superior consumer value more profitably.

Each of these enabling components is described in detail in the following sections. The enabling components are described as they appear in a Best Practices Category Management company environment. We invite you to benchmark the level of development of these components in your own company to the ones described in this chapter. From that comparison, you will understand where your company is strongest, where your company needs to change, and which enabling components need the most attention. How to manage and organize the implementation of this change is explained in chapter 6.

# Chapter 5 Discussion Questions

1. Name and briefly define the four enabling components of the Category Business Plan.

2. How do enabling components differ from the core components?

# 5.1- Performance Measurement

Performance Measurement may be the most important Enabling Component of Category Management. The retailer or manufacturer may have the appropriate organizational capability, sophisticated information systems and the best trading relationships. Unless the progress of the category can be measured, and the people impacting the category performance know what they are working towards and being rewarded for, any progress will be limited. Category Management requires a sophisticated and broad performance measurement system because it impacts all aspects and each function of the company.

> The Enabling Component, "Performance Measurement", is the set of methods and tools used to monitor the progress of the Category Management process as well as the individual Category Business Plans against target objectives and overall company goals, to improve business planning and decision making and to serve as a basis for reward and recognition systems for the Category Management organization.

## Overview

Category Management represents a complete business process for both the retailer and supplier partners. The relationships and communication necessary for effective Category Management require change both internally and externally. These changes include modifications to measurement systems and thus a redesign of the overall Performance Measurement system. Information technology is rapidly advancing in its ability to provide more effective data in readily accessible data warehouses with powerful analytical tools. This is making the reporting of robust Performance Measures available to both business partners at a more reasonable cost.

Three types of Performance Measurement need to be included in the category Management process:

*1. Company Level Performance Measurements-* These measures are specified as part of the Corporate Mission, Goals and Strategies, which the business partners will use to measure the success of Category Management initiatives in their respective businesses. Chapter 3: Core Component- Strategy describes the requirements for corporate Performance Measurements to support Best Practices Category Management.

*2. Category Performance Measurements-* Proper measuring of performance requires a balanced set of key performance indicators for the retailer, supplier and the joint team with a focus on the consumer.

   o *Retailer Category Measures-* For each category Performance Measurements are directly related to individual Category Business Plans and relate to retailers' internal as well as external measures. While they should be developed in concert with the supplier partner, ultimately the target measures tie to the retailer's overall company targets.

o   *Supplier Category/ Brand Measures*- Each supplier practicing Best Practices Category Management will have its own set of Performance Measures for brands and categories in which they compete. While these measures relate to their business across all customers, they should be aligned with the performance targets of the supplier's customers.

o   *Joint Retailer/ Supplier Category Measures*- The retailer/ supplier teams will have Performance Measurements that include important measures of each business partner as well as those related to the success of the team and the relationship itself. Category Management is founded on achieving the triple win: consumer, supplier and retailer. Jointly agreed team Performance Measurements allow for greater buy-in with business partners and importantly, will focus on problems earlier to make faster plan adjustments.

3. *Capabilities Measures*- While related to Performance Measurements, tracking the capabilities of different business partners is also beneficial in selecting capable partners and tracking the evolution of capabilities over time. Scorecards can be valuable for aiding selection of qualified partners if completed objectively. They are not, however, a substitute for corporate and category performance measures to guide Category Management and Category Business Plans.

**Creating the Performance Measurement System**

The steps for creating the required corporate and category performance measurement system are:

1.   Establish Performance Measurement Design Principles

2.   Select the Appropriate Performance Measurements

3.   Design Information Technology Systems to Provide Measurements

4.   Align Reward and Recognition Methods with Performance Measurements

*1. Establish Performance Measurement Design Principles*

Link to Corporate Mission and Strategies- As part of the development of the overall Corporate Mission, Goals and Strategies, quantitative goals should be developed to measure the performance of the total company. Some Performance Measurements will apply only at the total company level, e.g. return on equity, economic value added, share price, etc. However, all measurements will guide the selection of Category Performance Measurements as well as have an impact on category role selection.

For Category Performance Measurements, the category role establishes how the category is to fit into the overall company strategy and how it will help the retailer differentiate itself in the marketplace. The Category Performance Measurements, therefore, must be designed so that in managing the categories, the organization can focus on the key measures that will best achieve the overall company strategies and goals.

Balanced Set of Measurements- Traditional measurement systems tend to be overly reliant on short term, internal financial measures such as turnover, profit, return on assets, etc. Also, most financial measures are historical and only results oriented. A more complete Performance Measurement system must be able to look forward as well as to the past and should reveal how results are achieved. The following are the basic principles for designing balanced performance measurement systems:

- *Internal and External Measures*- The easiest measures to obtain are generally those generated inside the company from existing systems. With the focus of Category Management on bringing value to the consumer, external measures focused on the consumer and the marketplace also become important.

- *Results and Process Measures*- Traditional measurement systems focus predominantly on results achieved. These are reflected in the classic financial and operational measures: turnover, profit, return on assets, expenses as % of sales, etc. While these measures report results, they are limited in explaining how the results were achieved. Process measures add a broader foundation. Examples of process measures are speed of new item introduction, price levels versus target competitors, promotional levels versus target competition, warehouse service levels, average category team longevity, percent of stores implementing Category Business Plans, etc.

- *Appropriate Time Frame*- Most measures tend to be short-term focused. Some of the most important measures will only change over longer periods of time, such as household penetration, competitive position in the market, etc.

- *Total System Coverage*- Performance Measurements need to cover the total system within and between the retailer and supplier. Category Management of strategic business units implies that the success of Category Business Plans relies on all functions in the company to deliver results. Each business unit inside the organization will be impacted by Category Management in some way. The appropriate measures need to be in place to be able to improve all parts of the system that impact the performance of the category. Unless the functional "what counts" factors are modified to reflect the needs of Category Management, a given department will not be making the necessary contribution to Category Management success. For example, supplier finance and marketing will be involved in supplier category teams and have new kinds of contact with retailers. Unless the finance and marketing hierarchies include these assignments on the career path, position qualified people and most importantly, include team Performance Measurements in evaluations, the required changes to sufficiently support Category Management will not occur.

- *Category Measurement Consistency*- A consistent set of measures should be used across categories. This will allow the company to roll up the different Category Performance Measurements into department and overall corporate Performance Measurements. Caution should be exercised not to create too many measurements, however. Practitioners have found that 9 to 12 measures allow focus on important areas for performance and improvement. More than 12 tends to dilute the efforts of the Category Management.

- o *Timely, Accurate and Understandable Measures*- A good performance measurement system provides accurate information at the right time and in an actionable format. While information technology advances are making more effective data available, some measures may need to be approximated, for example, shelf set compliance percent may need to be based on a sample of stores rather than total coverage. Managers need to be clear on the source and accuracy of any measurement being used. Accuracy becomes even more important if reward and recognition systems are to be based on specific measures. Specific areas that have potential accuracy problems for reward and recognition are measures involving gross margin, inventory and store transactions. Consistency of definition, capturing all data in the system and covering all, or a statistically valid number of stores, are the challenges as the measures focus changes from a single department to a single category level.

## 2. Select the Appropriate Performance Measurements

Using the design guidelines for balanced Performance Measurement, Company and Category Performance Measurements should be viewed in four broad areas:

- o *Consumer Measures*- Category Management's foundation is providing increased value to the consumer. Understanding where the category stands with the consumer is critical. Possible measures include consumer satisfaction levels, customer loyalty and/or retention, % target consumer purchasing category, household penetration, etc.

- o *Market Measures*- Retailers choose Category Management as a corporate strategy for competitive advantage. Success must be measured in the context of the market and must not be based solely on internal targets and comparisons. Care must be given to what constitutes the "market." Many traditional grocery categories are being challenged by mass merchandisers, hard discounters, drug stores, and other specialty retail formats. Thus, focusing only on the grocery channel can mislead the company. Potential measures include market share in units, opportunity gaps, index of retailer to market growth in category, category development index, etc.

- o *Product Supply/Efficiency Measures*- This area has the biggest opportunity to focus on process measures. These measures help the organization improve the basic customer processes needed to deliver better business results. Examples of efficiency measures are: time of new item introduction, price accuracy, % acceptance of items presented, new item success rate, % of stores implementing Category Business Plans.

- o *Financial Measures*- Internal financial measures will generally be the easiest to identify turnover in units or equivalent units, gross or net profit in units or %, inventory turns or days sales in inventory, gross or net margin return on inventory, turnover or profit per linear/square/cubic foot.

*3. Design Information Technology Systems to Provide Measurements*

The largest challenge to implementing new Performance Measurements is capturing the information on new measures, especially process measures. The issues involve both capturing data as well as reporting the Performance Measures. Most retail information systems have focused on data by department and store, rather than by category. Also, most retailers do not have profit measurement systems to retrieve category information below gross margin or supplier profitability. Thus, more data needs to be captured and aggregated.

For suppliers, information tends to have been aggregated by geography or by brand rather than by customer or category. Identifying information by customer, especially customer profitability is a new opportunity in part dependent upon activity-based costing (ABC) systems.

For both retailers and suppliers, more data creates more complex reporting. Solutions to the need for more and better measures will impact all functional areas and involve the development of new data warehouse, analytical and reporting technology that parallels the information needs for the assessment portion of the Category Business Planning process.

*4. Align Reward and Recognition Methods with Performance Measurements*

The power of Performance Measurements is unleashed when individual reward and recognition systems are based on the new measures. The closer the reward and recognition system is tied to the category measures, the more likely the desired results of Category Business Plans will be realized. Three aspects are particularly important:

- *Overlapping Performance Measurements*- Success of Category Management depends on the Category Management team developing high quality Category Business Plans, plus the operations area executing these plans at store level. Having managers in different departments jointly responsible for some of the same measures will tend to focus people on the same objectives. To do this, it is also important to align category measures with the functional measures that are currently used to reward managers.

- *Intangible Rewards and Recognition*- Salary, bonus and promotion are not the only reward and recognition tools to be used to further category performance. Senior management behavior and focus on a day-to-day basis can have a heavy impact on the behavior of the organization. For example, management can agree to category Performance Measurements that focus on turnover and gross profit, and then review on a weekly basis the promotion budget. Similarly, in operations, agreed targets for shelving, assortment and out of stock levels can get lost if the store manager's supervisor focuses on labor hours. For operations, what the district manager or regional manager asks about on store visits is the clearest indication of what is, in fact, important.

- *Broad Based Rewards and Recognition*- The Category Performance Measures should not be the only basis for salary, bonus and promotion. Successful companies include other aspects of individual performance such as negotiating skills, coaching skills, creative skills, etc.

## Summary

Performance Measurement is a key enabler of Category Management. Following the design principles will allow the business partners to place company strategies and consumers at the center of attention and drive Category Management decisions towards these strategies supported by the reward and recognition system. Overall, experience to date confirms the ability of focused Performance Measurement supported by appropriate changes in the reward and recognition system to produce superior results from Category Management. Leading retailers and suppliers are making aggressive use of any ABC-based measures available to have better profit numbers to support assortment and pricing decisions. A retailer that has substantially higher than industry average profitability does not use turnover as a corporate performance measurement. Instead, market share is the critical measure.

Creating a successful Performance Measurement for Category Management depends on understanding the appropriate design principles, selecting the best set of Performance Measures for the company and the categories, investing in information system support and modifying the reward and recognition systems.

# Chapter 5.1 Discussion Questions

1. Why would Performance Measurement be the most important enabling component?

2. What three types of Performance Measures need to be included in the Category Management process? Describe them.

3. What are the steps for creating the required corporate and category performance measurement system?

4. List and describe the four consistent Company measures.

5. List and describe the six consistent Department measures.

6. List and describe the seven consistent Category measures.

7. Apply Performance Measures to your chosen category.

# 5.2- Organizational Capabilities

Effective Category Management rests ultimately on the skills, talents and commitment of people within retailer and supplier organizations to perform at the levels required for this work. The appropriate business processes and information technologies can be put into place, but unless the people component of Category Management has the necessary capabilities, Category Management will not succeed.

---

The Enabling Component "Organizational Capabilities" refers to the development of the retailers' and suppliers' competence to perform Best Practices Category Management through the appropriate organizational structure, job roles/ responsibilities, skill/ knowledge development, job performance measurement and reward systems.

---

This chapter focuses on the enabling component of Organizational Capabilities. It defines the principle for an effective Category Management organizational design and discusses the requirements in the major component areas of organizational design: organizational structure, job roles and responsibilities, skills requirements, job performance measurement and rewards and recognition approaches. The most common issues that arise in implementing organizational capabilities are also identified and addressed.

## Overview

One of the fundamental premises of this text is that Category Management involves a retailer and its suppliers managing the category business process together to meet complex consumer demands for superior value. The joint management of co-developed Category Business Plans is usually new work for both trading partners. It calls for organizational skills and interfaces that differ from the conventional "buying and selling" approach of the past. Category Management, therefore, has proven to be a difficult undertaking to launch from conventional organizational platforms. In fact, there are few examples of sustainable success that have not involved substantial change to previous organizational structures, support systems and work processes that link the retailer to its suppliers.

On the supplier side, experience also shows that when the contact with a retailer is solely via the suppliers' sales organization (whether direct or brokered), difficulty implementing Category Management programs and practices is encountered.

Overcoming this difficulty typically requires changes in how the interface is managed as well as changes in the support provided to the retailer via the account manager. Often necessary are reorganizations of the suppliers' promotion, pricing and merchandising planning groups, as well as those groups engaged in acquisition of new data and the support of the hardware/ software systems used to manage the data. Additionally, suppliers often find that the work of Category Management lends itself to the deployment of personnel skilled in information systems and analytic methods with their retailers. Likewise, retailers have found it necessary to revamp their conventional buying/ merchandising departments and reorganize around category-based business processes.

As these changes occur in both retailer and supplier organizations, the implementation of Category Management brings about a shift in roles and responsibilities between and across both organizations. For example, a supplier's role in order management and replenishment often migrates into areas historically thought of as retailer work, while joint Category Business Planning can often move a retailer into areas historically reserved for its supplier organizations, such as consumer research and joint new product development.

Changes in roles and responsibilities between trading partners together with an increase in the complexity of work to be done, often leads to the creation of multi-functional teams to manage the interaction previously reserved for buyers and sellers. As multi-functional, team-based interaction becomes established, there is a clear need for complementary shifts in organizational structures, job descriptions, skill requirements performance measurement, and methods of reward and recognition.

Organizational Capabilities, therefore, become an essential enabling component of Category Management. Simply stated, the implementation of Category Management is made possible by the existence of organizations capable of forming this innovative new business process. Implementing an effective Category Management capability in a retailer or supplier organization is broad in scope and impact.

In the sections that follow, the five organizational areas will be discussed in more detail. Before doing that, however, the basic principles that should guide Category Management organizational designs should be understood.


**Principles for Effective Category Management Organizational Design**

Effective Category Management organizational designs are based on the following essential principles:

- o Category Management organizational designs should be based upon a clear understanding of the work involved in Category Management. As described in previous chapters of this report, this work is defined by the two core components of Best Practices Category Management: Strategy and the Category Business Planning Process. Organizational designs must facilitate the completion of this core work in the most productive manner.

- o The organizational design should empower Category Managers with the responsibility and accountability for the management of their assigned categories.

- o The Category Management organization needs to be staffed with skilled individuals who are trained to perform their responsibilities.

- o Responsibility for managing a group of categories should reflect, as much as possible, similar consumer needs and synergies among the categories, thus maximizing the level of consumer, competitive, and supplier expertise among category managers of their business.

- o A Category Management team organization should be structured and staffed based upon the actual workloads involved in managing categories grouped by consumer synergies.

   o  Effective Category Management support services should be in place, allowing Category Managers to focus their efforts on developing and executing Category Business Plans and relieving them of the mundane tasks that inhibit this goal. Support should also be aligned by category to deepen the expertise in the requirements of managing consumer-based categories.

These principles should guide the design and implementation of these five organizational components: organization structure, job roles and responsibilities, skills requirements, job performance measures, and rewards/ recognition. Each component will now be described in more detail from both retailer and supplier perspective.

**Retailer Category Management Organization**

There are four steps in reaching the most appropriate design decision:

1. Determining category alignments
2. Assessing category management workloads
3. Choosing the most appropriate organizational design
4. Transitioning the current organization to the selected design

*Determining Category Alignments*

The starting point for design of the retailer Category Management organization is to decide on category alignments, that is, how categories will be assigned to Category Managers. Traditionally, categories have been assigned based upon criteria such as aisle adjacencies, common suppliers or common category purchasing characteristics (e.g. giving all commodity-market driven categories such as coffee, sugar, etc. or giving all direct-store-delivery (DSD) categories to one buyer or merchandiser). As a consumer-driven process, Category Management is based upon the premise that categories with similar consumer synergies should be managed together creating the basis for greater knowledge and expertise of consumers amongst Category Managers. This approach is implemented by grouping items into logical "category groups" based upon consumer synergies. The table below provides an example of how retailers have defined some of these "category groups" in their grocery departments.

   Similar consumer-based groupings are defined for non-food areas. These can include category groups for baby and health categories, personal care and cosmetics, leisure and entertainment, seasonal general merchandise, etc. The organizational design concept is to assign, to the extent possible, categories in the same category group to the same Category Manager. This approach significantly increases the level of category expertise of the Category Manager, which is the ultimate competitive advantage gained from Category Management.

| Category Group | Categories |
|---|---|
| Beverages | Soft drinks, coffee, tea, milk, water, juices- refrigerated and non-refrigerated |
| Main Meal | Frozen entrees, canned seafood, canned vegetables, pasta and rice, gravy mixers |
| Breakfast, Baking, Meal Enhancers | Cereal (cold and hot), pancake mixes and syrup, flour, sugar, cooking oils, salad dressing, condiments, spices |
| Indulgent Foods | Confection, salty snacks, nuts, cookies, crackers |

*Assessing Category Management Workloads*

The next step in the organizational design is to assess the level of work involved in managing each category group to determine the number of people required to manage each category grouping, and the amount and type of support needed. Workloads should be assessed using criteria that truly determine the quantity and intensity of effort needed. The diagram below provides examples of some commonly used criteria to assess relative workload levels for category groupings.

Each category group should be assessed using these types of criteria to determine relative workloads. Workload levels will then guide how the line and support Category Management organizations should be structured for maximum performance.

*Choosing the Most Appropriate Organizational Design*

Some companies organized along traditional functional lines have difficulty focusing on consumer value because no one "owns" the entire process. For example, within many supplier organizations, key processes such as product development or order management, cut across so many department boundaries that the only manager to whom all these activities are reported may be the managing director. For many retailers, a similar situation arises with processes that work across functions such as warehousing, transportation, procurement, merchandising and store operations. A well-designed Category Management organization focuses on the key processes of delivering consumer value and designs organizational structures to execute these processes efficiently.

For a retailer, this design usually means the organizational structure needs to facilitate integrated buying and merchandising activities and the development of cooperative relationships with suppliers to create strategic advantage. This advantage can be built through superior and more timely knowledge of consumers and of category dynamics, supplier marketing plans and product supply capabilities. For a supplier, Category Management often leads to the emergence of customer-based multi-functional teams that focus on delivering consumer value through strategic alignment with retailer trading partners.

In a Category Management context, the potential disadvantages of the traditional functionally based retailer and supplier organizations are as follows:

o   No one on either the retailer or supplier side has total ownership for the process that achieves business objectives at the category level.

o   There is no clear-cut overall responsibility of accountability for category performance. Someone may have responsibility for making the sale, someone else may be responsible for placing and tracking the order, another person might develop the promotional plan, and another may be accountable for the planogram. In such an environment, it is unlikely that there will be any cohesion between product and category strategies.

o   The inefficiency of multiple retailer/supplier points of contact results in slow response to consumer-based opportunities, and in unproductive work processes.

o   Traditional structures frequently lack clear consumer focus and stress measures that reflect the contribution of individuals and/or functions. For retailers, the traditional structure generally fails to capitalize on the consumer knowledge and category expertise that exist within supplier organizations.

o   The emphasis on traditional organizational structures tends to be excessively on reactive, tactical level issues, and focused on the short-term, at the expense of longer-term business plans and goals.

In a retailer Category Management-based structure, the Category Business Planning process, which guides the development, execution and measurement of Category Business Plans, provides the logical mechanism for coordinating both demand-side and supply-side activities that deliver consumer value and achieve Category Business Plan objectives. This is due to the business objectives of the plan consisting of a combination of turnover, profitability, market share, and logistical efficiency goals defined at the category level. A fundamental assumption of the Category Management organizational design is that, unless the full range of marketing, procurement and logistics objectives can be applied at the category level, no clear-cut responsibility for achieving these goals will exist. Supply-side activities support the ultimate objective of serving the consumer to maximize turnover while incurring the lowest possible system costs, thus achieving optimal return on assets.

*Transitioning the Current Organization to the Selected Design*

<u>Line Category Management Structure Options</u>- A basic principle of Best Practices Category Management organizational design is to place clear-cut responsibility and accountability for the performance of categories in the hands of the Category Manager. Retailers have usually considered two organizational design options to accomplish this: Integrated Category Management team, and separated, but coordinated, procurement/ logistics and Category Management functions.

In an Integrated Category Management Team, each Category Management team manages a group of consumer-related categories (as described earlier) and has total responsibility for managing all aspects of these categories including procurement/buying, assortment, pricing, promotion, shelf presentation and product supply activities. The Category Management team is supported by Category Management support functions, including store execution and logistics. The typical structure of the team is a Category Manager, an assistant Category Manager/ Category Merchandiser, a replenishment buyer and a category clerk. The actual composition of the team will be determined by the results of the workload assessment for the assigned category groups as described earlier.

The advantage of this structure is that the Category Manager has, within his or her team, the capabilities to directly manage all aspects of the category grouping assigned. However, given the fact that the products of a single supplier may now be managed in several Category Management teams, there is a requirement to coordinate multi-category supplier logistics to ensure that maximum product supply efficiencies occur. This requires assignment of responsibility for the coordinating tasks. This process is significantly aided by computerized efficient replenishment systems. The decision, at this point, is whether to integrate the replenishment process or maintain a separate buying team.

In an organization where the replenishment function is separated from the line Category Management function, the key requirement for this design is to ensure that responsibility and accountability for the management of a category are not fragmented. Effective design requires management supervision to ensure that the necessary coordination between buying and selling activities occurs. One method of facilitating this is to align the replenishment and Category Management responsibilities; that is, within the replenishment organization, categories are assigned in the same manner as in the Category Management organization. For example, a beverage category group replenishment manager works in coordination with the beverages Category Manager. In an organization where the replenishment function is integrated, the results have generally proven to produce more efficient organizational processes, and the function has emerged as the more commonly implemented design.

Category Management Support Organization- For the line Category Management organization to accomplish its principal objective, it requires the assistance of various support functions within the retailer's organization. A specific Category Management support services group is generally established to ensure that this support is provided across the Category Management organization in a productive manner. The most common support tasks provided are category analysis, pricing and planogram support, store level coordination for Category Business Plan implementation and coordination of product supply activities involved in the development and execution of Category Business Plans. The Category Management support organization ensures that the resources required by the line organization to develop and implement its plans are deployed efficiently across the entire line organization. The function of the support group is to provide additional resources to the line organization as required to ensure Category Business Plans are developed, implemented and monitored and in a highly productive manner.

## Supplier Category Management Organization

For supplier organizations, multi-functional designs have emerged as the most effective designs for performing Category Management work. Headed by a team leader, supplier customer teams contain functional expertise such as finance, information technology, marketing, analytical support and customer service. These functional experts can draw upon, as needed, additional support from the home office. The distinguishing characteristic of this multi- functional team is that it is outwardly focused on customers and consumers.

Supplier organizations are undergoing significant changes to implement these designs effectively. Traditional functional-based designs (marketing, trade marketing, sales/account management, etc.) are changing to process-designed organizations. These formats emphasize the multi-functional capabilities needed for the process of developing, implementing and monitoring Category Business Plans with trading partners. This transition is not an easy one for supplier organizations to make. Reasons for this difficulty include: the pervasive impact of such a change (it affects all functions of a supplier's organization), the fact that the supplier is redesigning to meet a major new organizational design and work process being initiated by their retailer trading partners, and the need for a supplier to maintain a hybrid design to meet the needs of accounts that deploy Category Management as well as those that do not. It is essential that suppliers develop a clear-cut strategy and plan for this transition. A phased approach has generally been most successful.

A final point on organizational structure warrants emphasis here. Category Management can have impact beyond the Category Manager and his or her supplier partner. The entire organization needs to be equipped, aligned and prepared for the impact of this practice. This impact is best communicated in terms of the relevance of Category Management to achieving overall corporate objectives. It helps to make clear that previously self-contained functional units within the organization will be called upon to support the core Category Management business process. In fact, the activities performed within functional units are often vital to the process of providing value to customers and consumers.

A broad-based understanding of Category Management throughout both retailer and supplier organization is necessary. Given the multi-functional nature of the Category Management approach, educating only the retailer Category Manager and the supplier account/sales manager will significantly reduce the magnitude of the total benefits possible from Category Management.

**Job Roles and Responsibilities**

Specific Category Management roles and responsibilities are determined by trading partners. For the purposes of clarity however, the following distinctions are generally made concerning the roles of the retailer and its suppliers in Category Management:

o The retailer is typically the "Category Manager", as the retail store is where categories are managed. It is at the retailer's site that all the components of Category Business Planning and implementation come together.

o Suppliers are typically category consultants/ partners to the retailer. They provide important input and experience but are not the final decision makers on how the particular category will be managed, or how it will fit into the portfolio of category roles being deployed by the retailer.

The role of the Category Manager within a retailer organization, or that of category consultant/ partner within a supplier organization, encompasses and expands considerably upon the responsibilities of the traditional buyer/ merchandiser and account manager role.

The Category Manager's (and category partner's) key role is the ownership of the Category Management business process for the categories being managed. This implies not only having responsibility across categories, but also ensuring the appropriate linkages exist between category and corporate/ departmental strategies. It also involves significant responsibility for the coordination of business process activities that flow across traditional functional boundaries within the retailer and its supplier organizations.

The major responsibilities of the Category Manager within a retailer organization are generally:

o To develop Category Business Plans for assigned categories

o Integrate these plans into the broader business goals and strategies of the retailer

o Achieve category business objectives for assigned categories through the implementation of tactical decisions for these plans at store level

These responsibilities involve taking ownership in the development of the following:

o Marketing (consumer-oriented) strategies and tactics for the areas of product assortment (variety, selection, quality) pricing, promotion and shelf-space management.

o Product supply (systems- and cost-oriented) strategies and tactics for achieving the demand-side strategies with optimum cost efficiency in the procurement, physical flow, storage and payment of products within the category. As such, the supply-side focus can include the evaluation and coordination of activities such as continuous replenishment, cross- docking, direct store delivery and electronic data interchange.

o Relationship strategies that recognize the interdependence of a retailer and its suppliers in delivering superior consumer value are the work and responsibility of both trading partners.

The supplier category partner (often supported by a multi-functional team) is charged with meeting company, category and brand/ SKU strategies and objectives, through the co-development of Category Business Plans with a retailer's Category Manager. Objectives for the supplier partner include the traditional focus on turnover and costs, as well as broader considerations such as product line and account level profitability, market share within the retailer, product flow and service elements, return on inventory (ROI) and return on assets (ROA). This implies a strategic alignment between a supplier and its retailer trading partner in each of the key areas outlined above, marketing, product supply, and relationship strategies. It also implies a more strategic role for the supplier and the empowerment of multi- functional teams within the supplier organization.

## Category Management Skills

The nature of the Category Management process changes the role and responsibility of the Category Manager and supplier category partners significantly. Serious consideration must be given to the skill requirements essential for effective Category Management. The most important of these skills are:

- o **Strategy development skills**- Ability to take a strategic perspective when planning actions and making decisions. This ability is evident from Category Business Plans that are consistent with, and reinforce, the overall strategic direction of the company. The plans should also reflect a clear understanding of the target consumer and how to meet consumer demands, considering strengths and weaknesses vs. competition at the category level.

- o **Consumer/retail marketing skills**- Ability to understand and apply the principles of marketing to Category Business Plans that can meet consumer needs. This skill requires a clear understanding of consumer and competitive trends in the category. It also calls for keen insight into the segmentation of target markets and how to reach these targets through marketing strategies in areas of product assortment, pricing, promotion and shelf-presentation.

- o **Financial management skills**- Ability to understand basic financial statements and key financial measures. The concept of asset management, what assets are, and how their productivity is measured, e.g., GMROI, ROA, ROI, etc. needs to be understood by the Category Management partners. The supply-side component of Category Management necessitates a working knowledge of supply chain costs and is increasingly encompassing activity-based costing (ABC).

- o **Merchandising/selling skills**- Appreciation for the importance of the "top line" i.e., selling to the consumer and the ability to relate the procurement function to selling activities. This includes the understanding of what actions enhance, or detract from, consumer appeal in-store. This skill also involves being able to generate store-level excitement creatively to increase category turnover. It also includes the ability to understand and measure the impact of variations in the merchandising mix.

- o **Information management and analysis skills**- Involves both the data gathering and data analysis components of Category Business Planning. It requires the ability to identify quickly and accurately opportunities or problems from data through a process of disciplined analysis. It includes a working knowledge of where to find the information needed, within the company or from outside sources and of the technology available to access and analyze data.

- o **Product supply (logistics) skills**- Ability of the Category Manager and his/her category partners to assess the impact of logistics (product flow) on key competitive factors: the price and costs of delivered product and the quality of product and service. This knowledge will facilitate the integration of supply- side activities into the total Category Business Plan.

- o **Relationship management**- Skills required for managing cooperative external retailer/ supplier relationships and internal cross-functional relationships in such a way that business dealings are perceived by all parties to be based on the common goal of providing improved consumer value. This contrasts with traditional adversarial relationships between buyer and seller, which are a major impediment to Category Management.

The development of effective skills for Category Management requires retailers and suppliers to take the certain specific actions. First, the current skill levels of individuals in the Category Management organization should be formally assessed through skill testing techniques. Experience indicates that typically, less than 50 percent of current job holders will be able to perform the new work of Category Management successfully. Second, because of these skill assessments, a training program designed to address skill gaps should be developed. Programs should establish minimum entry skills for positions in the Category Management organization and define a curriculum of training covering a 1–2-year period to raise the skill levels of individuals to those needed for effective Category Management. Objective skill assessments supported by a relevant and realistic training program are the key ingredients in developing an industry-leading program.

A final point on skills requirements is that it is important that a balance of the necessary skills exists within the Category Management organization. For example, in an integrated retailer Category Management team, it is essential that all the skills required exist somewhere in the team. The Category Manager, for example, might have the most developed marketing and relationship management skills, the Category Merchandiser, the most developed analytical skills, and so on. A team structure allows a balanced set of skills needed for Category Management to be put into place.

## Job Performance Measurement and Reward/ Recognition

As responsibilities expand within the Category Management environment to reflect the respective trading partners' roles as process owners, corresponding changes in performance measurement and reward/ recognition systems are needed. The business objectives specified in the performance measures for a category become the basis for performance measurement for both the retailer and its suppliers. These measures capture key performance areas such as turnover, profitability, system logistics costs, and return on assets. Beyond this quantitative perspective, the performance of the category Manager will also often be evaluated in terms of his or her performance in coordinating activities across functional boundaries within the organization, as well as in the management of the external relationships with suppliers.

In terms of rewards and recognition, in Category Management the focus shifts from activities to results. The compensation plan for Category Managers and their counterparts on the supplier side is often based upon the attainment of the performance goals agreed to by both parties in the Category Business Plan. The Category Manager's (and category partner's) bonuses should be based upon a combination of total company or division performance, and upon the achievement of specific objectives set for Category Business Plans.

## Best Practices for Success

Organizational capabilities, in many ways, are the "make or break" component for Best Practices Category Management. If the right business processes, information systems and cooperative trading partner relationships are supported by the human resource capabilities and processes as described in this chapter, the significant business benefits of Category Management will be achieved. Like all management methods, Category Management is ultimately a people business. A comprehensive, integrated plan for developing these people capabilities is the best guarantee that this area will lead to the achievements of Best Practices Category Management. A comprehensive human resource development plan will help address most of the more common goals and aspirations found in Category Management. These Best Practices include:

- o  Set an objective assessment of existing skills for Category Management
- o  Embrace the need for a defined training curriculum to address individual and group skills
- o  Clearly define job performance measures that are linked to specific job responsibilities
- o  Clearly define the career path throughout the Category Management organization
- o  Ensure Category Management organizational designs are based upon consumer related category groups, which will support the objective of developing maximum levels of category expertise within the Category Management organization
- o  Category Management teams should be structured or staffed based upon a realistic analysis of the workloads involved

A comprehensive and realistic plan to address human resource success is a key ingredient for effective implementation of Best Practices Category Management.

# Chapter 5.2 Discussion Questions

1.  The enabling component Organizational Capabilities refers to what?

2.  Name and describe the five components of Organizational Capabilities.

3.  A retailer organization takes four steps in reaching the most appropriate organizational design. Name and describe them.

4.  What is the role of the Category Manager inside an organization?

5.  Name and briefly describe the seven important Category Manager skills.

# 5.3- Information Technology

Implementing Category Management requires a significant investment in Information Technology in both the retailer and supplier organizations. The business process is complex, data sources are diverse, and considerable analytical effort is needed for writing Category Business Plans and monitoring implementation performance. This chapter focuses on the enabling component of Information Technology. It defines the requirements for effective Category Management systems and discusses the implementation methodology. The most common issues that arise in implementing information technology systems are also identified and addressed.

> The Enabling Component "Information Technology" refers to the development of the computing and communications infrastructure, data architecture and applications software that enable the analysis and decisions required by the Category Management business process.

## Overview

Information Technology Systems are critical for successful implementation of Category Management. To be effective, Category Management systems should span the entire business process, provide readily available and accurate measures and facilitate cooperative trading partner relationships.

The challenge for Category Management Systems lies in the breadth and depth of data to be analyzed and in the variety of analysis required. When implemented correctly, such systems can significantly enhance an organization's capability to practice Category Management successfully.

Since Category Management is generally practiced between retailer-supplier partners, the target architecture for such systems should mirror the complementary needs of the partners.

For the suppliers, Category Management systems architecture consists of three building blocks:

1. Application software to develop Category Business Plans.

2. Multi-Dimensional Data Servers (also called On-Line Analytical Processing Servers) with syndicated market measurement data (market and key account turnover, share and causal data, consumer household panel data), and the retailer's cost and inventory data at a summary level.

3. Data Warehouse to bring together the internal data (customer orders, shipments, invoices, promotions, inventories, etc.) with syndicated key account data (including the retailer's PO.S. data, whenever such data are directly available) at a detail level. The supplier should be able to roll-up all key account plans, monitor performance versus plans and analyze customer profitability.

For the retailers, Category Management systems architecture consists of three building blocks:

1. Application software to develop Category Business Plans. Such software should have analytical capabilities to define categories flexibly, recommend category roles, assess category performance, select category strategies and tactics and monitor Category Business Plan performance.

2. Multi-Dimensional Data Servers (also called On-Line Analytical Processing Servers) with all the internal and external data needed to write category plans at a summary level. Such servers are often provided by syndicated data suppliers who purchase data from retailers.

3. Data Warehouse with detailed aggregated item and store level data for executing and monitoring Category Business Plans and for integration with product supply and marketing applications.

Category Management systems providing these capabilities should be implemented in three phases:

o Phase 1: Client software that automates analytical templates for writing Category Business Plans using a one-plan-at-a-time approach. Such templates can be supported by client-based spreadsheet and/or database applications. While this can help in getting started, it is not workable on a long-term basis due to its intensive manual requirements.

o Phase 2: Multi-dimensional server-based Category Management systems: often such systems can be implemented using the products of syndicated data suppliers (e.g. Nielsen and IRI). However, such systems are inherently limited due to the summarized information provided, typically market/ account and weekly level, and inflexibility in accommodating category definitions by consumer segmentation.

o Phase 3: Integrated Category Management systems that bring together all the detailed and summary data required, and that are designed to reflect the business process accurately. Data from three sources are needed:

    o Point of Sale (POS) price, share and turnover data for both the market and retailer.

    o Consumer household panel data to analyze category consumption and purchase behavior.

    o Retailer cost and inventory turns data.

    o This data should be the lowest level of aggregation; typically, daily, by item, by store. Such systems should allow monitoring of Category Business Plan execution within the retailers' organizations and link tactical applications for Assortment, Pricing, Promotion, Shelf Presentation and Logistics with Category Business Planning software.

While a balanced set of capabilities across each of the six interrelated components is required for successful implementation of Category Management, managing the Information Technology component can be more complex than the other components for several reasons:

- Information Systems need to follow the business process, which itself evolves as Category Management is implemented.

- The data for Category Management comes from several different and disparate sources. The extraction, transformation, aggregation and loading of the required data from internal systems and syndicated sources is a complex process. Integrated Category Management systems require implementing a decision support systems infrastructure and are built upon a data warehouse. The data warehousing technologies are relatively less mature as compared to transaction processing technologies

- Lack of standardized data definitions, item coding schemes and chart of accounts between retailers, suppliers and the syndicated data providers, Considerable effort is thus needed for conversion tables, customized data models and data synchronization processes.

- Information systems generally take longer to implement than the other components.

## Design of Category Management Systems

Category Management is an information-driven process for analysis, planning and execution of Category Business Plans. Therefore, Information Technology must provide the information infrastructure that maps this business process and integrated On-Line Decision Support (OLDS) systems that extract, transform and aggregate the data from internal operational systems and combine it with syndicated data into an easily accessible single source needed by decision makers throughout the Category Management process.

The information infrastructure for Category Management can be viewed conceptually as consisting of three components:

- Computing and communications infrastructure
- Data architecture
- Decision support applications

*Computing and Communications Infrastructure*

This area refers to the computer hardware and software needed to run the computer system (operating system, associated utilities, Database Management Systems, communications software, etc.), the Wide Area Network (WAN) and the Local Area Network (LAN) to support the business process. The computer hardware can be either mainframe, mid-range or microcomputers, linked together with WANs/ LANs to enable communications throughout the network. Retailers require a central server to pull the POS data from the stores or the warehouse withdrawal data from the distribution centers. Manufacturers require database servers or data warehouses that integrate internal and syndicated data.

*Data Architecture*

This area refers to the data architecture for Category Management decision support systems. Weekly and preferably daily, item level price and turnover data by individual stores, along with the acquisition cost data for calculating profit margins, are basic for this purpose. Increasingly, customer transaction data is also being incorporated in the retailer's data warehousing architecture for market basket analysis, closure rates, cross-selling pattern analysis, and for linking Category Management with micro-marketing and customer loyalty programs. Warehouse withdrawal data can be a substitute for POS scanner data, or for adjusting scanner data for missing product or "shrink." However, internal data alone is not sufficient because the category's performance must be compared to the market to assess the opportunity gap. Additionally, consumer demographics, market segmentation, consumer preferences, competitive pricing, market trends, store shelf management, promotion and vendor cost information are needed to manage categories as Strategic Business Units (SBUs).

The different levels of data provide support to different objectives as well as providing different views of the data for the users, e.g.:

- o Operational sources
  - o Up-to-date information on business events across the organization from batch or On-Line Transaction Processing (OLTP) Systems
  - o Up to date information on external market and environmental factors
- o Data Warehouse
  - o A common source for all data decision support
  - o The means by which disparate data sources are consolidated and synchronized
- o On-Line Analytical Processing (OLAP)
  - o Fast analysis of selected data, "Slice and Dice" capability, for comparisons and trending
  - o Advanced analytical capability.

Each part of the data architecture is needed, as each is doing a different job.

Therefore, an effective data architecture requires integration of internal POS and cost data, with the market POS and consumer household panel data from syndicated information providers such as IRI, Nielsen, etc. In some advanced retail applications, micro-marketing (geo-demographic) data is being used to define the target consumer by trading areas or store clusters, and Category Business Plans are deployed down to the store cluster level. Some suppliers are also starting to target category tactics for assortment, pricing, promotion and shelf space management at specific consumer lifestyle/ life stage groups.

Bringing together all the required data is a major challenge. Much of the data needed to support Category Management comes from operational legacy systems. Most of the legacy systems are Transaction Processing Systems (TPS), designed to run day-to-day operations rather than to provide information and analysis for decision support. It can also be very complicated to take information from one legacy application and combine it with information from another. Additionally, the internal data needs to be integrated with syndicated data or supplier-provided consumer data. Successful implementation of Decision Support Systems (DSS) requires a robust data management process that can support routine on-going operation of such systems. Therefore, implementing a data architecture based upon the requirements for Category Management is a prerequisite for success.

*Decision Support Applications*

Category Management software applications are now beginning to emerge because, until recently, there was no standard "best practice" process for Category Management. Plus, there are inherent technical difficulties of building an information infrastructure capable of integrating and processing data from multiple sources in a cost effective and timely manner. Several organizations have implemented their own Category Management Systems using generic third-party tools. Category Management application software should have the following functionality:

- o Category definitions based upon consumer decision trees
- o Cross-category analysis to assist in the assignment of the category's role versus other categories in the store
- o Opportunity gap analysis to evaluate category performance versus potential based on turnover, share contribution, profitability and return on assets (ROA) measures, depending on the performance measures used by the company
- o Sub-category, or item level, trend analysis to develop segment or key item strategies, i.e. which sub-categories, segments or items could be traffic builders, transaction builders, turf protectors, profit generators, cash generators, excitement creators, image enhancers, etc.
- o Analysis of market share, growth rates, competitive pricing, product assortment and promotion comparisons
- o Category tactics development for assortment, pricing, promotion, shelf presentation and product supply
- o Space and assortment analysis to evaluate product variety versus duplication, new product introductions and to maximize return on inventory
- o Monitoring category performances versus Category Business Plan goals on an on-going basis, including identification of over/ under performing categories, sub-categories, etc., (by store cluster, stores, etc.)

To perform Category Management, there is a need for the sharing of information between the retailer and supplier through industry standards and commonly accepted business processes. Sharing of this data is best achieved through standardization of data, application software, compatible hardware and network interfaces.


**Implementation Process**

A three-phase approach is recommended for developing integrated Category Management systems:

- o Phase I: Start with client-based software consisting of linked spreadsheet templates to support a "one Category Business Plan at a time" approach.
- o Phase 2: Implement an online Analytical Processing server-based system with a summary level multi-dimensional database consisting of both internal and external syndicated data. Often such systems are facilitated by syndicated data suppliers that

purchase data from retailers. In addition, organizations have used standard Relational Database Management Systems and query tools to build Category Management Systems either in whole, or in part.

- o Phase 3: Implement an integrated Category Management system based upon a companywide decision support infrastructure and data warehouse. This system stores data at the lowest level of detail, which can then be rolled up for multi-dimensional analysis.

The work in these phases is guided by an implementation team, which should consist of both users and information systems professionals. The project must be sponsored by top management, with an executive steering team accountable for successful implementation.

During the **first phase**, which usually lasts about six months, the implementation team should:

- o Capture the Category Business Planning process using a series of linked analytical templates.
- o Identify what data is available and assess the quality of the data.
- o Learn the steps and analytics involved in developing a Category Business Plan.
- o Develop a "blueprint" for implementing an integrated system in a phased approach.

At the end of this phase, the implementation team should have a good idea of the current state, the future state as defined in the blueprint and the transition plan, with feasibility grade cost/ benefit estimates.

The **second phase** should consist of the developing and testing of a pilot system. This usually involves testing a system from one of the syndicated data suppliers (such as IRI or Nielsen) or building an OLAP server-based system. At this stage, the pilot system does not have to be supported by a data warehouse that integrates internal and external data. Some organizations begin with a small Data Warehouse that can act as the platform for the pilot and be used to prototype the data quality reviews, measures and analytics. This work can then be the foundation for Phase 3. The application software may not map entirely to the business process or have the full functionality desired. However, the pilot should have the typical 80/20 solution for a representative subset of users, which can be modified as the basis for the eventual production system to be deployed throughout the organization. Experience suggests that the second phase lasts from 6 to 12 months and automates the Category Business Planning process substantially.

Moreover, being able to develop a Category Business Plan does not necessarily mean successful execution. The plan needs to be linked to store operations and its progress monitored against plan goals. Performance by business units (divisions, store clusters, stores, etc.) needs to be monitored. Under-performers need to be identified, causal factors isolated, and corrective action taken. Ideally, turnover trends need to be monitored daily for "events" such as promotions, pinpointing stock outs and managing the supply chain, etc.

Therefore, fully operational Category Management requires implementing a data, warehouse-based solution with daily item level and transaction level data. This is usually done in the third phase, which consists of a large central server connected to distributed servers via local area networks.

While there are different architectural models (centralized mainframe base, two tier, or three tier client servers, etc.), the critical success factors are:

- o The ease with which the users can learn and use the application.
- o The availability of all the data needed and the accuracy of the available data.
- o The use of a common and consistent process for the development and monitoring of Category Business Plans.

The **third phase** normally lasts from 12 to 18 months, depending upon the existing legacy systems, scope and the resources assigned to the data warehousing project. Therefore, it is not uncommon for the total Category Management systems implementation to take two to three years.

If appropriate for the organization, some of the later tasks, particularly the preparations for a comprehensive Data Warehouse, can begin early on and can be run in parallel to other work. For example, the organization may have a commitment to establishing a Data Warehouse to provide decision support applications other than Category Management, which will in turn make use of the Data Warehouse. In this case, work done to establish the data needed for the Data Warehouse and to ensure its quality can be done early in the process.

Implementing integrated Category Management Systems in a phased approach requires careful balancing of implementation costs, switching costs and the opportunity cost of not gaining the business benefits because of IT Systems limitations.

**Data Requirements**

An overview of the data needed for Category Management is as follows:

*Point Of Sale (POS) data*

POS information is gathered through scanning of the item at the store level. The information can be used at the store level for groups of stores or for a total retailer view. Major uses of this information include helping to determine efficient store product assortments, consumer demand planning, shelf management, out-of-stock identification and prevention, promotion planning and acquiring of pricing information. A key benefit of POS data is that the retailer and its suppliers are using actual sales information to make business decisions.

The POS data is available to the retailers from both their internal systems and from syndicated data suppliers that purchase these data from the retailers for resale. Increasingly, named account, i.e. retailer specific data, is being made available for Category Management.

The syndicated data suppliers add value to the data purchased from the retailers in two ways: by cleansing the data and by adding causal data (distribution, features, displays, out-of-stocks, pricing) collected through retail audits. POS data is normally available daily and weekly. Daily information is typically more actionable in its use to adjust promotional inventories, eliminate out-of-stocks, follow price and feature prices by store and identify merchandising performance. Daily information is also needed for use with direct store delivery (DSD) business.

Weekly data can also provide many benefits. Some major uses of this information are in shelf management, items to be stocked, promotional evaluation and pricing analysis.

The limitation of POS information is often the reliability of the data, since scanning errors at the store level can affect accuracy. Other issues include the massive amount of data available, and the resources required in terms of technology and people to support the use of the data. Increasingly, retailers are implementing data warehouses to process daily POS data.

*Warehouse data*

Warehouse inventory and withdrawal information by SKU is needed for monitoring distribution of SKUs, warehouse stocking/ reorder levels and forecasting of inventory requirements based upon historical demand patterns. In addition, warehouse information is used to determine item selection and to make merchandising decisions.

Warehouse withdrawal information is captured by the UPC code and can be summarized at various levels based upon needs, i.e., weekly, monthly and so forth. In addition to warehouse data, direct store delivery (DSD) information is also required to identify all sales within the category, properly.

While it is not uncommon to chart Category Management using warehouse-level data, the key limitation of warehouse data is that it is anticipated demand vs. actual consumer purchases. Warehouse data, along with actual point-of-sale scanner data, give the Category Manager a more complete picture of product movement from the warehouse to the store to the consumer.

*Market-level data*

Market-level data is important to Category Management because it gives the retailer and its suppliers a broader picture of what is happening in the marketplace. Examples of market-level data include comparative pricing, assortment, promotional data and share of market information. Normally, a supplier is also able to provide market-level shipment data for its products by various groupings, e.g., consumer segments.

Another source of market-level data is the syndicated data suppliers. These organizations provide timely access to data on a broad scale at all hierarchical levels, i.e. category, sub-category and SKU levels. They have the capability of looking at data in distinct templates such as product and market trends, comparisons and analyses.

*Consumer preference data*

Most suppliers invest in market research to identify consumer preferences, which is a key source of category definition and consumer segmentation (consumer decision tree) data. This information is gathered by suppliers through vehicles such as focus groups, consumer testing, controlled store tests and test markets.

*Consumer household panel data*

Syndicated data suppliers monitor consumer-purchasing behavior through on-going household panels. This data can be used to project marketplace purchasing behavior as long as it is statistically representative of the trading area. This information can also be provided by suppliers who are the primary customers of household panel data. This information is useful in the Category Management process for determining category roles, strategies and tactics.

*Geo-demographic data*

Geo-demographic information is valuable because it assists a category manager in determining individual store cluster (or store) consumer preferences, buying habits and behaviors. Information available can include age, income, population density, ethnic groupings, consumer lifestyles and media viewing/ reading patterns. This information can be used to optimize Category Business Plans for different trading areas or stores and for developing category tactics by target consumer groups.

*Competitive pricing data*

Determining everyday price points that affect category profits is an ongoing process for a retailer. Information that can help a retailer make these decisions can be obtained in one of two ways. First, a retailer collects the information itself by using its own people to observe retail prices at competitive outlets and to monitor weekly feature prices and weekly advertising. Second, from outside sources, syndicated data suppliers conduct retail audits to collect causal data for resale.

*Shelf space data*

Increasing the sales and profits of a category, improving inventory turns and lowering inventory carrying costs through improved utilization of shelf space are key goals of most Category Business Plans. Software packages that assist the Category Manager in space allocation are widely available. Shelf management software generates planograms using POS scanning data, gross margins, product attributes, shelf space and layout for each store. In addition, other information should be considered for optimizing space allocation: customer service, stockouts, labor and handling costs, minimum shelf space requirements, sales, profits and return on inventory investment.

*Promotional data*

To support merchandising decisions, promotional data shared by the retailer and its suppliers is helpful. The following information is needed for tactical promotional decisions:
- What was planned versus what occurred?
- Seasonality figured into baseline sales
- Cost of promotion and financial results- retailer and supplier

o Impact of promotions on category sales, share, growth and profit

o Consumer response analysis and incremental sales analysis

Successful promotion tactics require that the supplier and retailer plan promotional strategies as part of building the Category Business Plan. The supplier/ retailer partners should coordinate a promotional calendar that includes promotion scheduling, price points, volume expectations, spending requirements and so forth.

## Key Issues

The key information technology issues that need to be addressed for successful Category Management implementation are:

✓ Company strategies and business processes must drive IT systems design. Too often, companies allow themselves to be constrained by existing tools. The way to manage technology is to take a phased approach to systems implementation: prototype, pilot, and only then implement a production system. However, there should be an overall strategic systems vision that must be driven by the company strategy and business process.

✓ The need to integrate Category Management systems development with the overall Category Management development program. The development of Category Management systems should be coordinated with the other components of the program. Too often, a gap develops between what the organization can, or wants, to do versus the systems capability. This can become a serious limitation and can prevent organizations from maximizing the business benefits from Category Management.

✓ Assessing objectively current IT strengths/weaknesses. The IT assessment should be done in the very first phase of the Category Management program. A "blueprint" of the future state should be developed and compared to the current state. Is all the data needed available? What applications and databases will be required? How long will it take to implement? All these questions need to be answered early in the implementation plan for Category Management.

✓ Cost versus Benefits of Category Management IT investments. The IT investment required for Category Management can be substantial, depending upon the project scope. Every organization cannot justify integrated applications, with fully implemented data warehouses. Therefore, careful cost/ benefit analysis is essential before proceeding too far into full-scale execution.

✓ Realistic Implementation Plan. Information systems development is not an exact science, it is analogous to new product development. The scope generally changes from start to finish. Legacy systems vary from company to company, maintaining large decision support databases is a challenge (especially when data comes from different sources) and programmer productivity is highly variable. The net result is that unless the scope, schedule and resources are managed carefully, the risk of coming in behind schedule and over budget is substantial.

**Lessons Learned**

Experience to date in implementing Category Management systems across a range of retail formats and suppliers, reveals several key lessons:

- ✓ It takes time to implement integrated high quality Category Management systems. Data quality and integration is always an issue. Therefore, managing project risks through a phased approach and focusing on data issues is a must.

- ✓ The business process development must drive the technology implementation. Almost invariably, it minimizes rework. It is unrealistic for the users to define what they need when they do not fully understand the Category Business Planning process, data sources, data accuracy, data interpretation, and are not comfortable with the use of technology. All these issues can be managed by letting the business process development lead. The challenge is to ensure that IT systems implementation does not significantly lag business process development.

- ✓ The sharing of data between trading partners, and within internal functions, is essential for Category Management. The Category Management application should interface between suppliers and retailers using common data definitions, linked networks, "groupware", or internet delivery.

- ✓ Preference should be for "off the shelf" solutions with 80% of the functionality, that can be customized to a particular organization's needs. A totally customized solution should be implemented only when it is the only way to meet the functional or data requirements, or if the application offers the possibility of competitive advantage.

- ✓ Top management commitment and support is essential. While this is generally true for all major information systems projects, it is even more important for decision support systems where "quantifiable payout" calculations are imprecise.

- ✓ Finally, while there is a general model for Category Management information systems design and implementation, the specific details vary from location to location depending upon technical and organizational factors. Therefore, project planning and management skills are even more critical to Category Management systems applications, than for most information system projects.

# Chapter 5.3 Discussion Questions

1. The enabling component Information Technology refers to what?

2. To be effective, Category Management systems should provide what three traits?

3. What three building blocks are involved in the retailer architecture of the IT system?

4. The IT infrastructure can be viewed conceptually as consisting of what three components?

5. Name and briefly describe the three-phase approach to developing an integrated Category Management system.

6. There are nine key data requirements for an IT system. List them, and then define four of them.

# 5.4- Cooperative Trading Partner Relationships

Category Management changes the relationship between retailers and suppliers dramatically. Traditionally, the relationship between suppliers and retailers is limited to adversarial contacts between the buyer on the retail side and the account manager on the supplier side. Category Management broadens the relationship between retailers and suppliers and introduces direct communication between functional counterparts.

> The enabling component, "Cooperative Trading Partner Relationships", refers to the synergy created when trading partners collaborate to maximize their unique resources and perspectives for a common objective, enhanced business results by delivering superior consumer value.

Cross-functional multi-functional teams are given authority and accountability to improve the supply and demand side processes and thus better meet the needs of the consumer for value, variety, and service. The new relationships can create opportunities for unique and lasting competitive advantages based upon a combination of total system cost efficiencies and superior consumer demand management.

Of all the levels of cooperation between retailers and suppliers, Category Management requires the highest degree of partnership and commitment. Where electronic data interchange (EDI) is principally a cooperation of a technical kind, Efficient Assortment, Efficient Promotion and Efficient Product Introduction of an organizational kind and Efficient Replenishment both of an organizational and a technical kind, Category Management is an approach that integrates all four concepts and, thus, requires a more strategic relationship. Therefore, Category Management requires strategic choices and long-term commitment from both trading partners.

Top management plays a critical role in smoothing the path for mutually beneficial relationships between retailers and suppliers. The need for meaningful, top-down executive commitment is critical in achieving successful deployment of Category Management. The challenge is the ability to create more open and trusting relationships, which harness the unique perspectives and skills of the retailer and its suppliers to create business "wins" for both organizations and better value for their consumers.

Category Management has a dramatic impact on the relationship between the cooperating trading partners. This relationship undergoes a fundamental change in nearly all its aspects. The need to define the way a company cooperates with its partners is always evident in Category Management. This chapter describes the principles that should be at the core of Category Management relationships. It also describes the different levels of cooperation that can work for Category Management and how the benefits expected depend upon the level of cooperation between the retailer and the supplier.

## Principles of Cooperative Relationships

There are some principles that allow cooperative trading partner relationships to grow in an atmosphere of mutual trust and respect between a retailer and its suppliers. This chapter explains what these principles are and why they are important.

### *The consumer is the common focus*

By using consumer value as the common measure of success, a retailer and its suppliers develop common ground for co-creating Category Business Plans. Too often, retailers and suppliers start up Category Management projects with intentions other than improving consumer value. Suppliers sometimes try to push their own products while eliminating products of their competitors through Category Management, totally disregarding the consumer perspective. Similarly, retailers sometimes use Category Management purely to obtain better purchase conditions. These retailers and suppliers have experienced major problems in building long-term cooperative relationships in which Category Management can really produce benefits.

### *Mutually agreed objectives, strategies, tactics and performance measures*

Trading partners can increase the likelihood of successful Category Management practices by co-developing Category Business Plans that serve as the blueprint for leveraging their complementary capabilities. These plans become a key enabler of cooperative relationships, as they transform "my plans" and "their plans" into "our plans".

Without mutual agreement on each decision along the Category Management business process, the strategies and tactics are unlikely be implemented effectively. Some retailers go through the Category Management business process with their supplier without mutual agreement or commitment to decisions made along the process. Afterwards, the Category Business Plan is not implemented, and the retailer uses the consumer information obtained in the process to develop its private label market share in the category to the detriment of the supplier. Perhaps this kind of behavior can bring the retailer some short-term benefits, but it will certainly not result in sustainable competitive advantages that real Category Management can bring.

### *Rewards support cooperative business goals*

Both the retailer's and supplier's recognition and reward systems should be based upon the accomplishment of agreed business plan objectives. History and common sense teach that people will do what they are paid to do, as opposed to what they are told to do, or even what is necessarily the right thing to do. Rewards, therefore, should be congruent with desired results so that the vote of the purse is the right vote.

Ideally, the reward systems of the Category Management team members are linked to their job performance measures, which are linked to business objectives set for categories they manage. Experience has shown that only few retailers and suppliers have a well-designed reward system that considers total system improvements. As some retailers have just changed the title of their former buyers into Category Managers, it is not difficult to imagine that the applied reward systems still contain mainly "buyer objectives". These objectives are in most cases not in line with the objectives raised by the category performance measures. This will then result in poor implementation of the Category Business Plan.

*Relationships and trust are earned, not given*

Recognizing that cooperation is a successful way to maximize total system efficiency and deliver value to the consumer, trading partners need to demonstrate their willingness to change and adapt to Category Management business practices over significant periods of time. A company that cannot resist short-term expediency will find itself less than successful in Category Management.

Trust and partnerships are not obtained overnight. Only professional behavior and objective decision making, along with consumer focus along the business process, will lead to growing trust between trading partners.

*Information sharing is essential*

Retailers and suppliers possess different and important information relative to:

- ✓ Consumer needs
- ✓ Consumer purchase behavior
- ✓ The competitive environment
- ✓ Creative and marketing approaches and programs
- ✓ Systems costs and methodology for improving efficiency

Where appropriate, and observing safeguards to protect confidentiality, this information should be shared between trading partners in an environment of trust and openness for the full benefits of Category Management to be achieved.

The keys to successful sharing of information are first, for partners to be very clear on what information needs to be shared and what results will occur as a product of this sharing and, second, to establish procedures to rigorously protect the confidentiality of each partner's shared data. Many companies address this need by signing mutual confidentiality agreements to protect data confidentiality.

*Neither trading partner has all the expertise for Category Management to succeed*

Category Management is comprised of two separate but complementary sources of expertise, the retailer and the supplier. Neither is sufficient by itself to deploy Category Management successfully. Category Management combines retailer knowledge about the consumer as a buyer with supplier knowledge about the consumer as a user. Bringing this kind of information together is at the heart of Category Management.

*Retailer, supplier, and consumer win (the "triple win")*

The outcome of win-win-win results is critical for the establishment of cooperative relationships. Both trading partners need to understand how they and the consumer benefit from a particular course of action. It is recognized that a retailer and its suppliers may achieve wins in different areas and measure success differently. Both parties, however, must recognize measurable gains to sustain the relationship.

*Multifunctional access and communication*

Category Management is enhanced by the linkage of multiple functions within, and between, trading partners. For cooperative trading partner relationships to flourish, the access between these functional counterparts must be understood and must be open and easy to use in terms of policy, practices and communications.

*Openness to change traditional attitudes and relationships*

Trading partners should enter into Category Management recognizing that change is very likely, and that change is often a key ingredient of business success. Stated simply, a company should recognize at the beginning that the execution of Category Management usually leads to substantial change. Attempting to do new work with old solutions, old tools and old thinking may be unproductive

It should be clear that the attitude and expertise required for productive Category Management is very different from the attitude and expertise one might expect from former buyers and salespeople. Changing the organization and attitudes towards managing categories as strategic business units from a total process view is the main challenge for retailers and suppliers in the implementation of Category Management.

*Leadership, leadership, leadership*

To succeed, at all the above, requires leadership, at a variety of levels. Top management needs to lead the changes within their organization and to assign accountability for that change. Functional management should lead in opening the trading partners to the synergies that exist between aligned systems, different data and perspectives and different skill sets. Both the retailer and its suppliers should empower their respective leaders to make decisions and be the interface between the two organizations

## Category Management Cooperation Models and their Benefits

The methodology of Category Management can be applied with different levels of supplier-retailer cooperation. The more intense the cooperation, however, the more both trading partners will benefit from it. This section's goal is to explain what the different levels of cooperation can be and what these cooperation levels will produce in terms of benefits.

*Best Practices Cooperative Category Management Model*

In this model the retailer chooses a knowledgeable and capable supplier that best fits into its corporate strategy. The chosen supplier is involved in the whole decision process along all steps of the Category Business Planning model.

The decision process is no longer owned by the retailer alone but is shared in a partnership characterized by trust and common objectives. The supplier and retailer work closely together and go through the steps in a constructive dialogue. This cooperative relationship is the necessary basis for the full realization of the synergy between retailer and supplier know-how. It is this synergy that will produce the most successful ideas to enhance consumer value.

Selecting the right partner for this kind of relationship is of vital importance. Capability, commitment, attitude, consumer and market knowledge and trust are the main criteria of the selection of the right partners, size and market share are less important criteria.

If needed and appropriate, both trading partners may still wish to complete their category know-how with the insights of another capable supplier. This action is most frequently done when there is a part of the category that is not covered by the supplier, and where a non-competing supplier can add value to the business process. It should be clear that the Best Practices cooperative relationship model will produce the largest benefits for both trading partners.

## Conclusion

Of all the enabling components of Category Management, the cooperative relationships component is the least technical and the most readily actionable. It may, however, be the hardest to achieve because it requires an open, cooperative atmosphere between suppliers and retailers. It is, however, the essential glue that binds all the other components together and allows them to work.

All retailers and suppliers will agree that Category Management requires a certain minimum level of supplier-retailer interaction. The models for Category Management described above show how retailers can work together with suppliers to maximize results for all parties (triple win!). The experience of most Category Management practitioners suggests that those who cooperate the closest will provide superior value to the consumer and will be more successful. Achieving these benefits begins with leadership decisions in cooperative relationships.

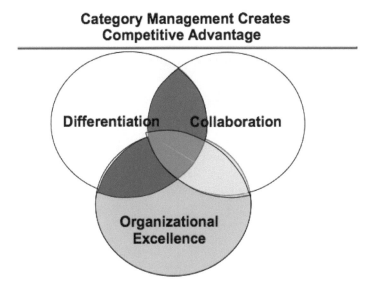

**Category Management Creates Competitive Advantage**

Differentiation    Collaboration

Organizational Excellence

# Chapter 5.4 Discussion Questions

1. The enabling component Cooperative Trading Partner Relationships refers to what?

2. Name three areas of the Category Business Plan that can be enhanced by retailer and supplier collaboration. Why are these areas better when collaboration is involved?

3. There are ten Principles of Cooperative Relationships. Name and define them.

# 6- Successful Implementation

In the preceding chapters, the scope, work processes and support requirements for achieving Best Practices Category Management have been defined. As with any management approach, however, merely understanding Category Management will not yield significant benefits. Benefits only occur with the successful implementation of this approach in the strategic and tactical operations of retailers and suppliers. This chapter will focus on the requirements, the issues and the most common obstacles that a retailer and a supplier will need to understand and address to implement Category Management successfully. This chapter describes recommended steps for getting started and then rolling out Category Management within retailer and supplier organizations.

The information contained in this chapter is provided to assist companies in the development and implementation of an effective plan to achieve the substantial benefits made possible by Category Management. The experience and learning of the companies from their work assisting retailers and suppliers around the world is the basis of the recommendations provided.

A word of caution is appropriate at the outset. Since each company's starting capabilities in the six component areas of Category Management will vary, the actual implementation needs and priorities will also vary. For example, if a company already has a well-defined and documented set of business strategies capable of supporting Category Management, less investment of time and effort will be needed in this component area. More implementation effort should then be focused on the other components, where capability deficiencies may be greater.

This chapter follows the following outline:
⇒ Critical success factors
⇒ Common implementation issues in each of the six component areas of Category Management
⇒ Recommended phases of implementation programs for a retailer and a supplier

## Critical Success Factors
For both retailers and suppliers, experience indicates that there are several essential conditions that must be in place at company level for Category Management to work effectively. The eight most important factors are:

### Top Management Commitment and Leadership
Category Management has pervasive impacts on the organization. It impacts strategy as well as tactical aspects of decision-making. It impacts virtually every functional area. It cannot be implemented quickly. It represents not only a tremendous opportunity, but also a significant change in management processes. It is not merely a project or set of projects. Leadership from the top is essential in this environment. Category Management cannot be driven from lower management levels. Top management needs to take the time to understand the Category

Management approach so that delegation of the actual day-to-day implementation work is based upon the appropriate level of top management knowledge and commitment. Retailers and suppliers that have benefitted most from Category Management have this commitment and leadership as a highly visible, common characteristic.

*Realistic Expectations*

The transition to Category Management takes time. It must be seen as a two-to-three-year implementation process. Benefits in the form of better business results, however, can be achieved as early as six months into the process. Efforts to compress the implementation process into shorter time frames have not proven to be successful. The key requirement is to develop a comprehensive implementation plan, covering all component areas of Category Management and based upon an objective, realistic assessment of starting capabilities in each component area, as it relates to the current total supplier as well as the client structure.

This implementation plan should encompass a phased development of capabilities in each of these component areas. A common mistake is to attempt to develop one or two component area capabilities (e.g., focusing on information systems development or organization redesign ahead of beginning work in the Category Business Planning area). Capabilities should be planned and developed in a more balanced manner, usually in a phased category-by-category and then supplier-by-supplier approach from retailers; as well as a category-by-category and then retailer-by retailer approach from manufacturers.

*Defined Business Objectives*

Management should set specific business objectives to be accomplished following the introduction of Category Management. These should include goals for increased turnover, gross profit inventory reduction and improvement of other business areas. These goals will drive, in a more consistent manner, the priority of implementation work and the allocation of assets. They will also cause appropriate performance measurements to be put into place to see that these goals are being achieved. With specific goals, progress and payoffs from Category Management will be easier to identify and quantify.

*Defined Business Risks*

Since Category Management introduces new business processes into retailer and supplier organizations, there will be certain risks involved in making such a change. These risks should be clearly identified at the start, so they can be addressed during the implementation work. For example, a risk to a supplier could be the potential deletion of slower-selling SKUs. The development of a consumer decision tree for the category will help provide early warning of this or could provide the basis for a more consumer-driven reason for why some SKU deletions could actually negatively impact category performance. A retailer, for example, might see as a risk, the potential loss of private label sales in some categories. The process of objective assessment and delineation of the appropriate strategies for private labels in each category provides the basis for both defining and addressing this potential risk.

*Willingness to Change Company Cultures and Organization*

Category Management will challenge several current business practices of the retailer and the supplier. These practices are likely to have shaped the corporate culture. The cross-functional and cross-departmental nature of the Category Management process requires new perspectives on responsibility and accountability. Team-based internal processes and cooperative external trading partner relationships are, in most cases, dramatically different operating approaches. Even in basic areas of Category Management, such as how categories are defined and how they are presented to consumers on the shelf, new thinking is often required. The scope and impact of the cultural adaptations involved must be recognized and managed if Category Management is to be successful.

*Willingness to Invest Resources*

As has been described in earlier chapters of this report, investments in people and systems will be necessary. These investments need to be quantified, incorporated into the overall implementation plan, and made based on this plan. "Start-stop-start" investment support approaches will be highly disruptive to the achievement of Category Management goals. It is better to lengthen the implementation schedule than to deploy an inconsistent resource investment plan. Also, while some implementation costs are shared by retailers and suppliers, e.g., developing and implementing Category Business Plans, internal costs e.g., systems and training, should be borne by the respective parties. Requesting supplier funding for retailer system development, for example, is likely to diminish commitment levels on both sides.

*Recognizing the Learning Curve*

The learning curve for Category Management cannot be significantly reduced by waiting to learn from the experiences of others. The changes involved and transitions required will take most companies similar time frames to implement. A "wait and see" approach can result in a serious competitive disadvantage. It is important to begin the process as early as possible and then adjust the time frames as conditions and resources permit. Experience to date has shown that retailers and suppliers that begin implementation earlier are more likely to gain a higher share of the benefits. Followers may have fewer options, for example, in such areas as defining their destination categories if a competitor has already completed their work in this area.

*Seeing Category Management as a Creative Process*

If Category Management is positioned only as a more disciplined, formalized, planning-based business approach, much of its potential benefits will not be achieved. While these processes and disciplines do provide the basis for business benefits, they should be seen only as the means to an end and not the end itself. The basis of Category Management is customer value enhancement and competitive differentiation through better management and presentation of categories in the store. This process requires creative thought processes. The result of Best Practices Category Management is not the use of category planning methods. It is improving business results for retailers and suppliers by presenting categories and products to target consumers in more need-relevant, exciting ways that create competitive advantage and happier, more satisfied consumers. The creative opportunities of Best Practices Category Management should be at the heart of how it is implemented. The results of more exciting product presentations, cross-category marketing programs and even new store layouts are already being achieved by some retailers and suppliers.

**Implementation issues**

Successful implementation of Best Practices Category Management involves a balanced development plan covering all component areas of Category Management. Each of these areas, experience indicates, will have its own unique implementation requirements and challenges. The most important implementation issues that typically need to be addressed in each area are described in this section.

*Core Component: Strategy*

The essential requirement is for a written, coherent, communicated set of strategies, covering both demand and product-supply sides. Also required is a trading partner relationship strategy to be in place to guide category level plans and decisions. The most common issues and obstacles in this area are:

⇒ Strategies must be defined in sufficient detail to guide category strategies and tactics consistently. Many companies have overall mission and corporate strategies, but do not translate these strategies into operational terms. For retailers, corporate strategies must link to department level (grocery, meat, etc.) strategies; for suppliers, brand and category strategies must be written and linked.

⇒ Category roles (destination, etc.) must be balanced. Roles provide the links between category strategies and higher-level strategies. The most important decision a retailer makes is the assignment of roles across categories. This should be driven top-down rather than bottom-up to ensure that category level decisions are consistent with broader company goals and strategies.

⇒ Corporate-level goals and strategies should not be sacrificed to short-term pressures, such as period-ending sales quotas or income needs. While corporate-level goals and strategies should not be sacrificed to short-term these short-term needs will always be a fact of business life. They must be balanced with the longer-term benefits of strategic category development. Setting clear policies for how these two goals can be met (e.g., which categories to focus on for each objective) is the correct starting point to address this issue.

⇒ An unwillingness to share strategies significantly undermines the Category Management process. Productive Category Management requires that a retailer and a supplier be willing to share at least a minimum amount of information on their strategies and goals to guide the effective development of Category Business Plans. Clear guidelines for sharing this information are essential for making the process controlled and consistent.

*Core Component: Business Process*

The development and execution of Category Business Plans is at the core of Category Management. Without this on-going process in place, Category Management reverts to project work in areas such as organization redesign or information technology. As such, its requirements should define the organization designs and information systems needed for Category Management. The key issues that need to be addressed for implementation are:

$\Rightarrow$ A common Category Business Planning process should be used across all categories (fresh as well as center store) and, to the extent possible for suppliers, across their retail customers. Varying formats for writing Category Business Plans significantly reduces both the efficiency of the process as well as the quality of the plans produced. The ability to roll up different Category Business Plans into higher level budgets and plans, and to develop cross-business plans (e.g., a plan that integrates a perishable category with a non-perishable category, such as a total Juices plan) are lost when inconsistent planning formats are created.

$\Rightarrow$ Category Business Plan development without effective implementation is poor Category Management practice. Effective implementation requires that operational conditions and expertise be incorporated into plan development, that field managers (Store Managers and field Sales Managers) be trained in the Category Management process, and that the responsibilities and performance measures of key field level managers be modified to reflect the importance of executing the company's Category Business Plans at the store level.

$\Rightarrow$ Clearly defined policies should be in place to govern information sharing and confidentiality between retailer and supplier partners. The process must be carried out efficiently and consistently if the Category Business Planning is to work.

$\Rightarrow$ Defined criteria for the selection of suitable category partners (retailers and suppliers) should be established. Unless minimum capabilities are understood and proven to be in place, Category Business Planning is likely to be a frustrating, unproductive and unenlightening process. Matching unqualified partners has proven to be an almost certain cause of disappointing end results

$\Rightarrow$ Multi-functional input is essential for high quality Category Business Planning. Expertise from the areas of consumer marketing, product supply, data analysis and store level execution must be incorporated into a category plan. This process cannot be carried out effectively by only the Category Manager and the supplier Account Manager.

$\Rightarrow$ Policies are needed to guide Category Business Plan decision-making. These could include, for example, policies relating to how private label should be managed, or any conditions relating to acceptable or unacceptable shelf presentation layouts for categories. These policies, which should be based on broader company strategies, will prevent unnecessary rework to plans that propose actions not consistent with policies.

$\Rightarrow$ The Category Business Planning process should be flexible enough to handle different store formats, competitive conditions and consumer target market definitions. In many cases, adjustments at the Category Tactic step in the Category Business Plan will accommodate these variations; in other cases, different category strategies or even different category roles might need to be assigned to the same category to handle operating differences. The Category Business Planning process is designed to address differences but must be used with flexibility.

*Enabling Component: Organizational Capabilities*
Category Management cannot succeed without trained, motivated individuals within the Category Management organization. The key issues that must be addressed in this area are:

⇒ Category Management involves new work, which requires new skills. When retailers and suppliers begin Category Management, the quantity and quality of the necessary skills rarely exist at the levels needed. Management must assess skill levels objectively, identify deficiencies, design an on-going skills development program and manage the reality that not all current jobholders will be suited to the new responsibilities involved. Failure to address these issues is one of the most common causes of unsuccessful Category Management programs. A well-designed and implemented people-development plan is an integral component of effective Category Management implementation.

⇒ As a multi-functional process, Category Management must transcend traditional boundaries. The transition from functional to process-based working methods is never an easy process and it requires senior management leadership and support.

⇒ Category Management cannot merely be an exercise in title changes. It must define new job responsibilities and empower category-level managers to action these responsibilities. Finally, performance measurements and reward systems must be congruent with job responsibilities and authority levels.

⇒ Field and store level organizational issues must also be addressed. Job descriptions and accountabilities, performance measures and reward systems of individuals charged with executing Category Business Plans at the store level (the consumer interface) are also essential to effective Category Management. These issues are often neglected, the result being that Category Management becomes a "headquarter" approach. In more decentralized decision-making environments, such as in hypermarket formats, store level organizational issues are even more essential to the success of Category Management.

*Enabling Component: Cooperative Trading Partner Relationships*

The most significant change being brought about by the practice of Category Management is evolution in the methods and attitudes of retailers and suppliers. Unproductive, more traditional, adversarial relationships give way to relationships based on the common goal of enhancing consumer value through better-managed categories. The notion that "a poorly managed category hurts all involved (the consumer, the retailer and the suppliers serving the category) is proving a reality. The task of changing these relationships is not an easy one. Leadership and risk-taking are needed to break the traditional boundaries. While Category Management does not take away the need for tough negotiations in the daily practice of business, it does focus these negotiations on more productive win-win-win (the "triple win"- consumers, the retailer, and the supplier) outcomes.

To implement this difficult transition successfully in relationships, several important issues must be addressed.

⇒ Written relationship strategy statements should be developed by retailers and suppliers to guide the new, more cooperative work processes. Without strategic statements, commitments and actions lack consistency. The statements should clearly define what each party brings to the process and what each party can expect from the other.

⇒ The need to share information, some of which can be considered highly proprietary and the basis for negotiating power and leverage, is at the core of these new relationships. For this reason, the nature of relationships will vary depending upon the value of information provided. Relationships based on the availability of, and willingness to share, information and expertise will operate on a higher plane than those involving minimal availability and sharing of information. The latter situation will remain in the domain of more traditional relationships. Written, clearly defined policies regarding information sharing (defining what information will and will not be shared, who has the responsibilities in this area, etc.) are essential to direct this new activity.

⇒ Criteria, on both sides, for the selection of Category Business Planning partners, should be clearly established and communicated. These criteria set the standards for identifying target capability levels to achieve Best Practices Category Management.

⇒ The number of supplier category partners that a retailer chooses to work with is also a common issue. The decision revolves around capabilities and process productivity. The most common, although not the only approach, is that the retailer selects the most Category Management-capable category supplier as the primary partner. If other suppliers have relevant expertise also, the retailer should attempt to obtain information from them, too.

⇒ The "acid test" of Category Management is the willingness to make fact-based decisions based upon overall category improvement, rather than on single SKU or brand impact. This requires a major philosophical change for many suppliers and retailers that have traditionally been focused primarily on SKU/ brand management. The fact-based premise for Category Management provides the rationale for making decisions that benefit the total category. Nevertheless, this perspective is novel, and its implementation requires strong leadership commitment and support.

*Enabling Component: Information Technology*

Information technology provides both the "fuel" and the "engine" for productive Category Management work. It provides the data, the analytical tools and the ability to measure the results of the Category Management process. While Category Business Planning can begin as a more manual process, it cannot begin to achieve its full potential without appropriate information systems. There are several important implementation issues that arise in this area:

⇒ The work of Category Management should drive the design of the Category Management Information Technology support system. Too often, retailers and suppliers make expensive investment decisions without adequate knowledge of the work involved in Category Management. Process must lead design, not the other way around. Time spent learning the Category Management process will assist in specifying the required capabilities of systems and in making better system decisions.

⇒ A phased Information Technology design and development plan is essential. This allows Category Management benefits to be obtained at earlier phases, even though full system implementation may not occur for quite some time.

⇒ A technology skills development program for users of these systems is essential. One of the most observed skill deficiencies for Category Management is computer-based analysis and presentation. These capabilities must be developed in parallel with Category Management information technology systems.

⇒ Clearly defined data responsibilities for the retailer and the supplier partners in the Category Business Planning process will leverage the investments made independently by each party. These responsibilities should be related to data responsibilities for template completion as well as for monitoring the performance of Category Business Plans.

*Enabling Component: Performance Measurement*

The statement that "If it cannot be measured, it cannot be managed" is highly relevant to the design and implementation of the Category Management process. The Performance Measurement component provides this capability. Experience suggests that several implementation issues need to be addressed in this area:

⇒ Performance measures need to be balanced. Improvements in category performance should be measurable across a range of consumer, market, internal financial and asset productivity measures, encompassing both demand and product-supply activities. An unbalanced set of measures can lead to incorrect decisions. For example, turnover increases could be misleading without measures of changes in market share, consumer penetration, or asset productivity.

⇒ Performance measurement methods are most effective when linked to individual and earn rewards and recognition. This linkage is what produces the behavior that leads to continuous improvement in category results. Too often, changes in expected performance are not supported by changes in reward methods. When pre-existing reward and recognition methods do not change, the necessary continuous improvement behavior that is central to Category Management is not fostered.

⇒ There must be some overlap in performance measures to produce consistent, coordinated actions. There are often no common performance measures for a Category Manager and a Store Manager, or a Category Manager and his or her supplier Account Manager. In these situations, it is difficult to produce coordinated, mutually incentivized behavior among managers. There should be at least one common performance measure for all parties involved in the development and implementation of Category Business Plans.

**Implementation Program**

To achieve the "best practices" level of Category Management requires a carefully planned, comprehensive implementation program that covers the development of the necessary capabilities in all component areas. The keys to a successful implementation program for both the retailer and the supplier are:

⇒ An objective benchmarking and understanding of the current capabilities in each area
⇒ A clear understanding of the "desired state" of capabilities to be achieved in each area
⇒ A phased program of development to achieve the desired capabilities

This section of the report will describe a recommended phased implementation program that has guided several retailers and suppliers as they transition their organizations from current practices to Best Practices Category Management. While, in general, the same phases apply to both retailers and suppliers, the specific actions that need to be taken do vary. As such, the recommended implementation program for retailers and suppliers will be described separately.

*Retailer Implementation*

The most effective approach for the retailer is to follow a phased implementation approach. It is important to remember that Category Management is an on-going process of improvement. While the journey has a definite starting point, it does not have an ending point. Best Practices Category Management is an evolving, continuous improvement process whereby the retailer develops and implements its strategic management processes to achieve consumer satisfaction and competitive differentiation. At the Best Practices level, Category Management becomes an integral management method used on a day-to-day basis.

A five-phase approach is recommended for retailer implementation. The phases are:
1. Category Management Capabilities Assessment
2. Category Management Infrastructure Development Plan
3. Initial Category Business Plans
4. Category Management Process Refinement/ Transition/ Roll-Out
5. Expanded/ Next Level Category Management Implementation

Phase 1: Capabilities Assessment

This initial phase of implementation involves completion of the following three tasks:
⇒ A comprehensive and objective assessment of the retailer's current capability levels in the six areas of Best Practices Category Management:
   o Strategy - the current level of development of company and department level missions/goals/strategies to guide Category Business Planning processes effectively.
   o Business Process - the current practices used to manage categories strategically and tactically and the ability of current business practices to support and be upgraded to deliver Best Practices Category Business Plans.
   o Performance Measurement - the current methods used to monitor and evaluate the performance of categories and of buyers/merchandisers/Category Managers, as well as the ability to develop and implement performance measurements suitable for Best Practices Category Management, are assessed.
   o Organizational Capabilities - the capabilities of the current organization to perform Best Practices Category Management work. This assessment should also include the current capabilities in support areas, such as planogramming, pricing, inventory management, field merchandising, etc., as well as capabilities of store management to implement Category Business Plans.
   o Information Technology - the capabilities of the current IT systems to support Best Practices Category Management, including an assessment of current Category Management tools, internal and external data sources used, and any decision support architecture. Current supply-side IT capabilities that relate more

directly to Category Management processes (EDI, CRP, etc.) should also be assessed.

- o Cooperative Trading Partner Relationships/Supplier Relationships - in this phase, the overall status of current relationships with suppliers is assessed whilst any philosophical or other obstacles (to more cooperative relationships) are identified. The most qualified Category Management suppliers also begin to be identified in this phase.

⇒ A detailed 1-2 year development and implementation plan that specifies the tasks necessary to achieve the Best Practices Category Management level, the recommended sequence of implementation actions, and a specific timetable for completing these tasks.

⇒ Estimates of the likely costs and benefits to the retailer arising from the implementation of the recommended Category Management program.

The ability to migrate to the Best Practices level of Category Management in an efficient manner can only begin with objective knowledge of the starting point. This initial assessment of capabilities must be done objectively. If an effective assessment of capabilities is not carried out, or is carried out inadequately, the journey into Category Management will not be a smooth one. Time spent completing high quality work in this initial phase will be more than offset by benefits achieved in subsequent phases.

## Phase 2: Infrastructure Design and Development Plan

Based upon the findings of Phase 1, the design and development of a few infrastructure components, essential for achieving the desired Category Management capabilities, begins. The typical areas of work during this phase are:

⇒ Strategy Development - The development or refinement of company and department level mission/goal/strategy statements to a level that is adequate to guide Category Business Planning work in a consistent manner.

⇒ Category Business Planning Process - The selection of templates to guide the development of Category Business Plans, the development of criteria to select categories and suppliers for Category Business Planning and the actual selection of categories and qualified supplier partners for completion of the retailer's initial Category Business Plans.

⇒ Category Role Development - The identification of potential "Destination" categories for the retailer and, based upon cross-category analyses and visits to the retailer's and its key competitors' stores, the preliminary assignment of category roles to all categories.

⇒ Organizational Design - The design of suitable consumer-based category alignments and completion of an analysis of workloads involved in managing categories aligned in this manner, the design of a recommended Category Management organization design, covering line, support and field execution organization components, suitable for use by the retailer. Skills assessments of current and/or potential Category Manager candidates are also typically completed during this phase, as is the design of a skills development training curriculum for the Category Management organization.

⇒ IT System Design - During this phase, work should also begin on the design of a suitable IT platform (databases, analytic and decision-making tools, hardware requirements) to support Best Practices Category Management.

## Phase 3: Initial Category Business Plans

With the infrastructure development plan described in Phase 2 completed and, in some areas being implemented, the first Category Business Plans need to be developed. Tasks typically completed in this phase are:

⇒ Selection of Categories and Suppliers for Initial Plans - Preliminary selections made in Phase 2 are finalized. Categories from different departments (grocery, HBC, general merchandise, and perishables) should be chosen for initial plans. This begins to demonstrate the applicability of the Category Management process across the retailer's entire business, given that priorities and improvement potentials are assessed correctly.

⇒ Plan Development Framing Sessions - The development of all phases of initial Category Business Plans are completed during a series of meetings between the Category Manager/ supplier teams. These sessions achieve two purposes: training on the Category Business Planning process and completion of the Category Plans. The process typically takes 10-12 weeks to complete.

## Phase 4: Process Refinement/Transition Plan

Based upon the learning from prior phases, the retailer's Category Management approach will be further enhanced and modified as deemed necessary to achieve the Best Practices capability level. The most common tasks completed in this phase are:

⇒ A review of the Category Business Plan development methodology (templates, team composition, role of suppliers, etc.) used in the initial plans and agreement on any modifications.

⇒ The further enhancement of processes for implementing Category Business Plans at store level. This often includes the training of store-level managers on the basics of the Category Management approach and on their responsibilities in the Category Business Planning process.

⇒ The development of an overall transition and roll-out plan to implement all capabilities developed or in development over the next 1-2 years. These capabilities include organizational redesign, IT systems development and further enhancements of the Category Business Planning process.

⇒ Once these tasks are completed, an additional round of Category Business Plans are developed. This sets into motion a process in which the goal for each Category Manager is to complete 3 to 4 Category Business Plans per year for the next 1-2 years.

## Phase 5: Next Level Category Management

The work required to complete the major tasks in Phases 1 to 4 typically takes a retailer 18-24 months. Experience indicates that any shorter timeframe is likely to cause dislocations that impede effective progress towards the goal of Best Practices levels for Category Management. Phases 1 to 4 establish Category Management as a fundamental business process for the retailer. Once the basic disciplines and business management processes are in place, the next level, or "next generation," of Category Management capabilities can begin to be developed. Some of the work currently being undertaken by the most advanced Category Management retailers includes the following:

⇒ Cross-departmental Category Business Planning e.g., a plan for a "Meal Center", which uses the Category Business Planning process to combine categories from various departments (grocery, bakery, meat, etc.) into a single Category Business Plan.

⇒ Enhancement Category Business Planning to enable plans to be developed and executed on a micro-merchandising basis, down to store cluster, or even specific store level.

⇒ New generation store designs based on blending category roles with destination categories to provide the hubs of new store design formats.

The extent of the impact of Category Management on a retailer's organization and business practices, in addition to the need to maintain current business performance, requires a carefully thought-out and planned approach for implementation. The phased approach described above has provided a realistic roadmap for several retailers that are successfully implementing the Category Management approach and that are committed to achieving "Best Practices" capability levels.


**Supplier Implementation**

A similar phased implementation approach should be followed by suppliers to achieve Best Practices Category Management effectively. A brief description of each phase follows:


Phase 1: Capabilities Assessment

The goal for this phase is the same as for the retailer, to objectively assess current capabilities in the component areas of Best Practices Category Management. Based upon this assessment, a detailed implementation plan and timetable is then developed, as is an initial estimate of likely costs and benefits from implementing the program. The areas that need to be addressed in the assessment are essentially the same as in Phase 1: Retailer Capabilities Assessment, described in the previous section, with modifications in several areas. Some of these include:

⇒ Strategy - the need to assess the current linkages (if any) between overall company, category, and brand level strategies. (It is uncommon for suppliers to have written, linked category strategies prior to Category Management).

⇒ Organization - the current capabilities to perform multi-functional teamwork, which is typically a more difficult challenge for suppliers than for retailers.

⇒ Retailer/Supplier Relationship - since Category Management is a retailer- initiated change, it is typical to find more resistance to changing traditional relationships on the supplier side than on the retailer side. The extent of, and reasons for, the attitudes that prevail need to be clearly identified in this phase.


Phase 2: Infrastructure Development Plan

Based upon the capabilities that are found to exist or not exist in Phase 1, the key areas of internal, "back end" capabilities development work are now addressed. The most common areas of work are:

⇒ Development or refinement of company and brand level mission, goals, and strategy statements to be able to support Category Management work with trade customers. The development of written category strategies that link to brand strategies is important work that should be undertaken in this phase.

⇒ Development of policies and processes to guide each step of the Category Business Planning process. These include how the category should be defined and the consumer decision tree to be recommended to retailer customers; recommended roles for the category based on differences in a retailer's target consumer, competitive situation, and overall corporate goals and strategies; and recommended strategies for category segments to support different category roles.

⇒ Policies on data sharing and confidentiality, criteria for selection of customers as Category Business Planning partners and the response to the situation where the supplier's competitor is chosen as the lead category partner.

⇒ Development of a Category Management Capabilities Presentation to position the supplier's capabilities to retail customers in a consistent manner.

⇒ Appointment of a multi-functional Category Management leadership learn that will spearhead the execution of high-quality Category Management work throughout the organization.

⇒ Skills assessments of current and potential customer account managers to identify current organizational and individual skills deficiencies for Category Management work.

⇒ Redesign of current organizational structure, Job definitions, performance measures and reward methods to support headquarters and field level Category Management work.

⇒ Design of Information Technology systems to support Best Practices Category Management at headquarters and field as well as at customer interface levels.

## Phase 3: Category Management Pilot

With infrastructure development plans completed, and in some cases with implementation underway, initial deployment plans with selected key retailers should begin. A successful implementation process depends heavily upon an accurate assessment of category improvement potentials and retailer prioritization. The tasks to be completed in this phase are:

⇒ Selection of suitable pilot trade customers based on a combination of both business as well as learning opportunities.

⇒ Approvals from trade customers based on the reaction to the supplier's presentation and levels of retailer commitment to the Category Management process.

⇒ Completion of all steps of the Category Business Plan, through a series of joint retailer-supplier team training and plan development sessions, presentation of the completed plan to both managements and approval of management to proceed to plan implementation.

⇒ Implementation of the pilot plans in retailer's stores and monitoring of business results against established performance measures.

## Phase 4: Process Refinement/Transition and Roll-Out

Based upon the learning from the Phase 3 pilot work, the following tasks are usually completed in this phase:

⇒ Review of Category Business Planning methodology, company policies and processes to identify suitable modifications and enhancements.

⇒ Training of an expanded base of company personnel who will be involved in the roll-out of Category Management work with customers. This should involve individuals from all major functions (sales/ account management, marketing, marketing/ consumer research, information technology/ data analysis, logistics/ product supply/ customer service and financial systems).

⇒ Development of a detailed transition plan to guide the changes the organization will need to make to implement Best Practices Category Management work with minimal disruption to current business.

⇒ Selection of category and trade customers for completion of additional Category Business Plans and the development of a timetable to deploy the necessary resources to execute plans.

### Phase 5: Expanded/ Next Level Category Management

Once the basic capabilities, processes, and disciplines described in Phases 1 to 4 are in place, a supplier can begin to develop capabilities that are designed to further enhance its leadership position in joint retailer/supplier Category Management initiatives. Some suppliers are beginning to work with their customers in areas such as the following:

⇒ Developing and implementing micro-merchandising-based Category Business Plans at store cluster, or individual store level.

⇒ Integrating activity-based costing measures into category plan performance measurement systems.

⇒ Applying Category Management principles to the development of "new generation" destinations with retailers, such as meal solution centers, baby centers, pet centers, etc.

⇒ Integrating frequent/ loyal shopper data into Category Business Planning databases.

Like the retailer, the supplier should transition to Best Practices Category Management capabilities through a well thought-out, phase-by-phase plan. The implementation of these capabilities has pervasive impacts on the supplier's organization. It challenges and calls for changes in several traditional supplier business practices, and its impact is felt across all functions of the supplier's operation. The phased approach described above, based upon experience, should provide the general roadmap for how to achieve Best Practices Category Management. The road is neither easy nor short (Phases 1 to 4 will typically take 18- 24 months or more to complete) but, if driven effectively, can lead to significantly improved business results and competitive advantages that are difficult to imitate.

# Chapter 6 Discussion Questions

1. Name and describe the eight critical success factors to implementing a Category Business Plan.

2. Of the two core components, name two issues that must be avoided to successfully implement a Category Business Plan.

3. Of the four enabling components, name two issues that must be avoided to successfully implement a Category Business Plan.

4. Name and describe the five phases of the Retailer Implementation Program.

5. Name and describe the five phases of the Supplier Implementation Program.

6. What have you learned from the Category Management Process?

# *Category Management Conclusion*

The Category Management model provides a standard definition and framework around which this important management approach can be discussed, evaluated and successfully implemented. Most importantly, it is hoped the knowledge of this approach will stimulate retailers and suppliers to challenge their current practices, beliefs and assumptions as they search for effective solutions to the realities posed by emerging industry trends.

In concluding the report, several points should be highlighted:

⇒ Category Management is an integral part and therefore a major component of the food industry. While the primary focus of Category Management is on demand-side practices, its strategies, disciplines and business processes enable demand and supply-side management to be integrated at the category business unit level.

⇒ Category Management also provides the necessary organizational designs, cooperative trading relationships and strategic linkages to facilitate an integrated management approach. As has always been the case, winning requires a combination of superior consumer-based, demand-side management practices and cost-efficient business processes. Category Management can deliver this combination.

⇒ Category Management is an evolving, "back to basics" approach to management. It focuses management attention and processes upon what is ultimately the most important ingredient for success: understanding and meeting consumer needs in a competitively superior manner. It is a consumer driven approach from start to finish, but none of its tenets are revolutionary. It draws from the proven disciplines of strategic marketing, asset management and cooperative relationship management and applies these to the category level of business. Its growing acceptance has much to do with its "back to basics" approach.

⇒ It challenges all business practices that do not add perceived value to consumers. Today, many such practices are present in our industry. These range from the simple naming of categories to the artificial departmental boundaries that fragment categories, to the use of tactics that confuse rather than enlighten and excite consumers, to unproductive retailer-supplier practices. Such practices do not add value to the final arbiter of our success- the consumer. Category Management challenges all such practices.

⇒ Category Management is not a project or a program. It is a continuous process that manages categories in a disciplined, strategic manner. It should not be confused with category improvement projects that, while often producing positive results, do not lead to the profound, on-going changes and benefits that are associated with Category Management. It is the cross- departmental and cross-functional process by which retailers and suppliers "go to market".

⇒ For Category Management to succeed, it must be guided by a carefully designed implementation plan supported by top management commitment. This takes time, resources and patience, but the returns that Category Management can produce far outweigh the costs.

⇒ Most important of all is the impact of Category Management on the capabilities of people. Business success in the 21st century will ultimately depend upon the people who manage our organizations. The ability of Category Management to enhance their management skills will prove to be its greatest contribution. It will allow retailers and suppliers to attract, grow and retain individuals with the skills the industry needs for future prosperity.

⇒ Category Management is merely one step in the evolutionary journey of our industry. Its principles and disciplines are already providing the stepping stones for new opportunities in areas such as different store layouts, new insights into how consumers make their shopping decisions and integrated, single system retailer-supplier marketing planning and execution. Category Management provides the platform of disciplines, processes, skills and creative retailer-supplier cooperation from which these next generation competitive advantages are emerging.

Finally, experience has conclusively shown that those retailers and suppliers that lead the way in Category Management will achieve a greater share of its benefits. The "sitting on the sidelines" approach has proven to be a major competitive risk with Category Management. We hope this text will encourage retailers and suppliers to evaluate their potential within their organizations and provide a roadmap for achieving significant benefits for those that choose to adopt it.

# Trends, Tips, and Tactics for Today's Grocery Industry

**Including Revenue Growth Management, Retail Media Networks, and GenAI**

# *Oh boy!*

Sometimes in this food and consumer packaged goods industry, you step back and just say, "**oh boy**"! Sometimes, that's a good thing, as in, "oh boy, this pizza program rocks!". Sometimes, it's not a good thing, as in, "oh boy, these customers really are hurting for cash!". But, either way, this industry has a cornucopia of "oh boy", served with a side of "wow", all smothered in a gravy of "let's go!". It's a wild industry, essential to the public, integrated into the fabric of our lives, with some impressive innovation and evolution!

In our annual look at the trends impacting us, how categories and segments have changed, and best practice tips, you'll hopefully find this book one that should be read throughout the year and passed on to your merchants and store operators.

*We've got a lot going on!! So, let's go!!*

# *Start with the Customer*

Of course you start with the customer, and, by extension, the consumer. It's why we exist, right? Two willing parties, exchanging something of value, both are better off after the exchange. The definition of marketing, and what we do every day.

It's *assumed* the customer cannot make their own Oreos, Cheez Its, or Gatorlyte. We need Mondelez, Kellanova, and PepsiCo for that. It's *assumed* the consumer packaged goods (CPG) company is pricing their product at a price that will cover all fixed and variable costs, and return an acceptable margin rate. It's *assumed* the reseller (whether it's an online retailer, brick and mortar retailer, direct to consumer, or an omni mix of all the above) has appropriately marked up this product, to cover all fixed and variable costs, and return an acceptable margin rate. It's also *assumed* that the customer has entered this transaction willingly and is exchanging something of value (money), to acquire this product. Then, after all that, it's *assumed* both parties are better off after this exchange.

That's a lot of assuming! What happens when the customer is stressed by years of inflation, but has no offset of a salary increase? What happens when the CPG is hit with inflationary input cost increases, and has little relief in being able to increase their costs to resellers? And, likewise, when retailers are hit with higher costs (including rampant theft), how do they recoup at least some of these cost increases? Add to that a political environment where every headline turns profit into "corporate greed". *Oh boy, have we got a situation!*

# How is the Customer?

Rough. Feeling rough. That's all you can say. Customer sentiment is clearly showing the impact of 20% food inflation from the last three years. It's everywhere, too, in all sectors. The interest rate spikes have not only sent home buying to an absolute screeching halt, but it's also much more expensive to remodel stores, open new stores, invest in infrastructure, etc. If you wanted a recipe for stagflation, just look at this country.

*Stagflation: Once believed to be impossible by economists, a combination of stagnation and inflation, normally caused by slow growth, high inflation, and high unemployment.*

You cannot keep printing money as a country, raise taxes, raise interest rates, mandate increased minimum wages, impose regulations on pretty much everything, oppose all mergers and acquisitions, without the resulting rampant inflation and customer depression.

The customer is stretched and struggling. Even if you "have money", you're seeing it, too. **You trade down, you cook more at home, you avoid eating out, you put off that new car, you put off upgrading your home, you put everything off.** That's stagflation. We're not depressed, we're just existing.

This is not meant to be a downer of a book, but we also cannot ignore reality. In case you were looking for a cherry on top, companies feel the same way. Wages cannot even come close to helping assuage inflation for your associates, you cannot buy new plants and equipment, you're not sure if you should invest in people, and cutting costs is imperative. If you can't get it from increased retails, you need to cut overall costs, or drastically improve effectiveness of your resources! We'll talk about all of this! First, let's look at some overall top trends, before we talk about how our organizations can ensure *we are there for the customer every step of the way.*

# *Top Trends*

This period of stagflation, inflation, cutting back, re-defining value, is having a palpable impact on the food industry. Additionally, though, technology, ease of shopping, health and wellness, weight loss, and the usual suspects for trends, are also steering consumers, shopping patterns, new items, and value areas like store brands. Besides our annual sriracha shortage, let's talk about a few of the overall trends, the ones that permeate all categories in the store.

**Overall costs!** We've reached $8 Big Macs, $18 bags of Halloween candy, a $5 regular bag of chips, and prices for things we never thought we'd see at these levels! It's an overall feeling that *everything has gone too high*. The dream of owning a home, or even being able to afford rent, is slipping away for most young people. As the reality continues to settle, the feeling that "it's going to get better" is fleeting.

*We can still do something.* All hope isn't lost, it just needs to be cultivated. My top solution? Be special. There you go, right? Nice and easy? Just be special. You can stop reading now. Everything's going to be okay. Be special.

## What makes you special?

You *can be* special. These are your differentiators. The things you defend, the things you cannot give up to competition at any cost, the things that make people drive past other stores to come to you, the things that make customers lock into your online ecosystem and never want to leave. The best way to understand what makes you special, so you can defend your position, is by asking your customers. Ask your customers, especially your loyal ones.

You have the data, you know who is loyal, ask them why they are loyal, why they continue to choose you over the rest. Break out your questions into the 4P's. Remember, the 4P's are always there to help you. Price, Product, Place, Promotion, they are how a business connects with customers, and a great way for you to understand what makes you special. Understand what you offer that makes you special in your **customers' eyes**, then defend it to the death. That's all you've got, you know.

**Ozempic, Wegovy and other GLP-1's.** If there is one thing you can count on, it's that anything helping you lose weight without exercising and starving yourself is going to catch on. It's human nature. Diet is just "die" with a "t". Everyone would like to "lose a few pounds", but food and drinks are just so darn good! Glucagon-like Peptide-1 (GLP-1's) agonists can help regulate blood sugar and lead to weight loss and are a hit!

According to users, *it is highly uncomfortable if you try to exceed the amount of food you can eat*, while on this medication. As you can imagine, the focus on protein in your diet increases exponentially when you drastically limit your intake. Yes, there are a ton of side effects that are all over social media, like "Ozempic eyes", which reflect the massive amount of muscle you also lose on these drugs; plus, nausea, vomiting, etc. But it's a tradeoff.

As someone who loves what food brings to life in celebrations, gatherings, and overall life enjoyment, the side effect that bugs me the most is GLP-1's take the enjoyment out of food. I don't like the idea of making food intake something transactional. Losing weight is worth the side effects for **a lot** of people, though.

The numbers are astounding! Within the next few years, it is expected that 20M people will be on a GLP-1, roughly 15% of the population. What's even more incredible is what the drug does to consumption. 92% report eating less, 61% report eating fewer meals (or skipping one per day), 51% report eating fewer snacks, and 33% report totally quitting sugary sodas. In beverages, 24% report drinking less coffee, and 11% report drinking less alcohol.

Nestle was first to market with a GLP-1-specific food line announced, Vital Pursuit, to acknowledge the protein-focus within fewer overall calories. As with 100-calorie packs, Atkins, keto, paleo, and every other trend of its kind, we can expect other CPG's to follow suit. Just be careful, many Ozempic users do not even finish out their first cycle, so I would choose a name for your product that implies it's part of the diet but can also survive any public backlash against these drugs.

I'm going to add **protein focus** to this section, namely since touting protein in foods is not a new trend, but it does keep growing. Understanding what protein *is*, and why it should be pursued, has not grown as quickly as the number of products focused on it. Macronutrient, micronutrients, protein with added sugars, etc., all need to be part of the discussion.

There will always be trends, and they will continuously involve customers and their relationships with food, which also means their relationships with you.

**Are we in a caffeine bubble?** Caffeine is everywhere. Not only in the usual beverages, but caffeine has been infused into gummy bears, drinkable shots, powders, pills, gum, taffy, and even shampoo (yes). And now Starbuck's is having a sales issue, McDonald's is selling less coffee, coffee houses are closing, are we falling out of love with coffee? Are we so inundated with caffeine, we need to pop the bubble a little bit? This one isn't clear. Not sure we can blame an issue with sales at Starbuck's on over-caffeination, rather than $8 drinks, but something to watch. At some point, enough is enough, and customers move on to some other way of infusing energy into their lives.

**Are we becoming carnivores again?** More specifically, are we becoming grass-fed carnivores? More studies continue to show eating meat is not so bad for you. Let's focus on red meat, since that is the one meat source that has been vilified for years. In fact, pork made a point of making sure it's *not* lumped in with red meat, hanging out with its buddies, chicken and fish. Red meat was the one always picked on, unfortunately, mainly due to the feed used for raising cattle (plus, that ozone impact). In a unique twist of irony, *it was the onset of plant-based foods that highlighted the need for three main vitamins and minerals: iron, zinc, and Vitamin B-12.*

Yes, iron, zinc, and B-12 can be found in other foods or supplements, but red meat is a complete protein with the full amino acid chain. As with any new trend, or renewed trend, extremists are everywhere! Eating only steak for every meal, skipping all vegetables, etc. The internet is great at encouraging extreme behavior. Ignore that. But, as a retailer or CPG, understanding how red meat is making its way back into favor, particularly grass fed, is important and we all need to adjust in stores and in product development. And, hey, while we're at it, steak and hamburgers need sauces, buns, cheese, salads, and on and on and on.

**Good and bad oils for cooking.** It's been interesting watching the discussion of the "good" cooking oils and the "bad" cooking oils. Most every customer has known vegetable oil is not good for you. It's just cheap. For the "bad" oils, seed oils have become the new villains. Corn oil, grapeseed, sunflower, canola are all made from the seed of the plant, not the actual plant. The high heat needed to process the seeds is the issue. *Coconut oil?* Well, this one was such a hit a few years ago, and now is being picked on by everyone! Some studies are showing coconut oil to be unhealthy, being high in saturated fats and raising LDL cholesterol (the bad one). Other studies say it's great for you. Follow the science they say....

Now, on the "good" side, extra virgin olive oil is usually the clear winner, but some have been stating it's best added *after* the cooking process. The heat either reduces the benefits or may even produce harmful byproducts. The trend now is to focus on cooking with *ghee*, and *grass-fed butter* (there's that grass-fed, again!). Then, you can add olive oil at the end, for more health benefits and taste. **Ghee is a rocking trend right now!** If you're not expanding your assortment of ghee, you're being left behind.

**WFH Fridays.** In this new world of hybrid scheduling, Fridays are the new Saturdays, in the sense of shopping and catering to personal needs. Lord help the person who schedules a meeting on Friday afternoon! In one study, 28% of all meetings are being scheduled on Tuesdays now, with Friday barely registering 5%.

What does this mean for us? *First*, it's possibly shifting shopping into Thursday nights, or earlier in the day on Fridays. *Second*, the opportunities, especially for those stores with bars or cafés, or gyms next door, is to make Friday into a celebratory and festive kind of day. Schedule demo days, or "taste of" events, or mid-afternoon brunch specials, or Friday brew specials, etc. Make it fun. If you have a sit-down area in your store, enhance the power of your available wi-fi, to encourage Friday workers to work from your store; plus, make it easy to order from your table. The last thing anyone wants to do is get up and lose their coveted seat in your sit-down area.

**What is up with these shock flavors?** Yes, you hear me talking to you, Sour Patch Oreos. We used to think swicy was an odd combination, as a new word was formed to describe sweet and spicy. But now, that would be *kind of tame*. What is it about the consumer psyche that has brought us to Sour Patch Oreos?

*First*, it's an odd world right now, anyway. With so many people worried about inflation, jobs, seemingly endless wars, we need a little fun in our lives. Like the taste or not, a Sour Patch Oreo is fun. Fun sells, fun goes social, we need fun in our lives.

*Second*, it's a social media world. Sometimes, it's cool to pick up something unique and then tell the world you got it. We love likes, we love engagement with others, and the chance that our post can "go viral" is exhilarating. A package of Mustard Skittles is low-risk for the consumer, and high-reward for uniqueness, social media interest, and overall buzz. We all win.

*Third*, LTO's win every single time!! I love Limited Time Offers, for all the reasons we just stated; plus, the fact they could be gone tomorrow. An LTO is a great way to compel a purchase, since we need to "get ours" before the next person does; then, we need to tell everyone about it. LTO's rock!

*Fourth*, if you can dream it, someone will try it. Mustard Skittles, Hidden Valley Ranch ice cream, gravy-flavored Jones Soda, Lay's Flamin' Hot Dill Pickle chips, Peeps Pepsi, and even Kraft Mac and Cheese ice cream, are all dreamed up as unique combinations, usually to be tried once. What's the harm in trying them?

*Fifth*, any combination of sweet, salty, spicy, and sour is being tried right now. Gen Z may not have great prospects for home-buying or being able to afford much in life, with our inflation the way it is, but they do like to have fun and try new things! I would also add global tastes move around the world at light speed. A dish in India cooked with ghee becomes a trend in the United States in very little time. The world is getting smaller.

*Sixth*, face it, you're not going to just buy the unique flavor. There's a risk involved in buying the LTO flavor, so you normally buy that one <u>plus</u> the original flavor. You will not cuddle up to Netflix with a package of Sour Patch Oreos, but a pack of Double Stuf? Now, that's a night to remember!

*Seventh*, humans have the attention span of a squirrel. We are programmed to be entertained in about 8 seconds or less on social media, and that lack of focus transfers over to the rest of our lives. "Regular" is another way of saying "boring". We need newness in our lives, and we love trial. Bring on the shock flavors.

*Eighth*, for the CPG's, shock flavors and co-branding are a great way to remind customers of products they have not purchased in a while. You may not even buy the Sour Patch Oreos, but you've just been reminded of Sour Patch and maybe you haven't thought about that brand in a while. Next time down the candy aisle, it'll connect.

These shock flavors are here to stay. They are fun and catchy, and why not have a little fun?

**Organics continue to roll!** It's not the first year we've said organics are on fire, and it won't be the last. The sweet spot for organics is either price parity with non-organics, or a slight premium in price. Once prices are close, it's natural behavior for consumers to move towards organics. Why not? *There's only upside for consumers.*

Produce is still the leading category in organics, with 20% of the $64B in sales last year, followed by bread/grains, condiments, dry breakfast, and baby food. At the current CAGR, organic sales will top $400B in the next three years.

What's interesting is the <u>$6B in nonfood organic sales</u>. You might be wondering, what's a nonfood organic item? **Cosmetics, personal care items, alcohol, and textiles**. For *cosmetics and personal care* items, the products must be plant-based/non-synthetic to be labeled organic. The FDA regulates personal care products and cosmetics and has determined any items aiming for the organic label need to follow the *USDA procedures* in place for food items.

For alcohol, there are some nuances between wine, malt beverages, and distilled spirits. A *wine* can be certified organic, if no sulfites have been added in the process of making the wine. A wine can also be labeled as "made with organic grapes", though, and still have added sulfites.

For *malt beverages*, which includes most seltzers (also called flavored malt beverages) and all beers, neither organic nor "made with organic ingredients" allow for added sulfites. You can use non-organic hops, and still be labeled "made with organic ingredients", if only 30% of the hops are non-organic.

For *distilled spirits*, certified organic products must be made from all organic ingredients (unless organic yeast is not available). "Made with organic ingredients" spirits are not required to use organic yeast and must be at least 70% made of organic ingredients.

For *textiles*, which includes *apparel, bedding, towels, and curtains*, the product must be made with certified organic fibers, which have followed the USDA guidelines for organics. If any part of the textile is non-organic, you cannot carry the certified organic seal.

If you want to show true price and quality comparisons, the standard rule is to shelve organic items next to non-organic items in center store. For produce, the practices are mixed. Some retailers shelve all organics together, and some integrate them with their non-organic counterparts. *Both methods of merchandising have pros and cons.* Separating organics from non-organics has a pro in the sense you can find all of them in one spot. To the contrary, though, you must have vibrant easy-to-locate signage, or you run the risk the customer will not find the organics. As a rule, if the signage is eye-catching, you can merchandise organics separately or together and be just fine.

One last thing on organics, with the new Strengthening Organic Enforcement (SOE) addendum in effect, attention to detail in organics is paramount, and a complete review of your production process is in order. The new amendment to the USDA organic guidelines has been added to strengthen oversight of production, handling, certification, and selling of organic products, and went into effect March 2024.

**Stores as solutions.** Lots of talk lately around stores as solution centers. Whether it's offering access to dietitians, knowledgeable cheese mongers and butchers, wine stewards, prepared foods, or the like, grocery stores are perfectly positioned to offer ways to make lives easier for customers. The inherent knowledge necessary to determine appropriate assortment, shelving, depth of variety, and trend spotting translates easily into a full solution center for customers increasingly hurried and distracted.

**Phygital is here to stay.** The blurring of lines between the physical stores, and the digital experience (phygital) is continuing. Overall customer contact points, signals, contribute to the brand experience. Yes, "contribute" can mean in a positive or negative manner. The more you can enhance that connection and use components of each to maximize the customer's interpretation of your value, the stronger you'll be.

Think of a store that uses geofencing to buzz the customer as they are about to skip the condiments section and reminds them they have not purchased mayo in a while, or highlights a deal on ketchup this week, that is a helpful phygital experience for the brands, the customers, and the retailer.

**Labor will always be an issue.** Stores have run 60%-80% turnover for as long as I can remember. It's just part of the service industry. Your best bet is to continue to focus on your team. Remember, *pay is somewhere around #7* in the list of "things most important to me where I work". Culture, acceptance, diversity of thought, embracing identities, being part of the solution, feeling like you have a voice. All are important.

Drucker's phrase "culture eats strategy for breakfast" is true. You can tell when a store is "sick" as soon as you walk in the door. Conversely, you can tell when the total store is "bought in". It takes effort to make your store, your department, your category management team, your product development team, your people all believe in "the cause". The higher purpose, or unified purpose, is real.

**Diversity reigns.** In the United States, 21% of those over 75 years old are non-white. 46% of the US 18-21 years old are non-white, including 22% identifying as Hispanic. *It is expected 90% of the US population growth the next five years will be coming from non-white.* Look at your team. Do you reflect the future? Look at the stores. Does the assortment reflect the customer? Those who choose to work with us want to feel like they are part of the team and part of the solution. It's difficult to feel part of the team if the team looks nothing like you. This does not mean pandering, or just checking a box, it means diversity in your team can be a competitive advantage, as that team will then connect with your customers more seamlessly.

**Limited Time Only rocks.** I'll never back off LTO's! LTO's are timeless. The LTO strategy adds *scarcity*. The customer will pay a premium just because they also want to share with their friends, they got something no one else could get. *Scarcity works!* Tell someone there is a "limit of 6", and they'll buy 6. LTO never fails to awaken the competitive spirit in customers.

We're all treasure hunters at heart, and discovering something limited in availability, that's the epitome of finding the treasure chest! Please don't confuse LTO's with a seasonal program. Seasonal programs are expected, and a normal part of working your way through the year (both customers and companies). LTO's are that little bit of extra topping, a neat way to drive incremental sales.

**Tell your story.** *Customers want to know your story.* You are special for some reason. Tell people about it. Why should they care about you, your products, your store? People want to know you are run by real people and you have a story. Integrate that story into everything you do, and all marketing messages. Did you start in a farmer's market, are you third generation, did you raise cattle growing up, they are all part of your story.

**Tired or Inspired.** The customer who says *"I love to cook, give me cooking tips"* yesterday is the same one saying *"simplify my life and stop making me work so hard"* today. The best thing you can do is be prepared for both types of customers- **tired or inspired**. Offer meal kits and ready to eat for the *tired*. Offer ingredients, recipes, healthy ideas for the *inspired*. And be prepared for it to be the same person. It's a good issue to have. You're not one dimensional. If you were, you'd have bigger issues. You could be a mattress store....see our discussion on ReGenAI for more on tired or inspired.

**What's going on with plant-based?** It's been interesting watching the launch of plant-based meat options, and the rush to offer the items in supermarkets, restaurants, and so on. Then, just as quickly, the demand dropped precipitously. There seem to be several reasons, including the realization that plant-based products trying to replace animal proteins are not considerably healthier, and sometimes less healthy, than animal proteins.

Additionally, there's a tremendous uptick in the carnivore diet, which is clearly the opposite of plant-based, as iron, zinc, and B-12 are necessary nutrients readily found in proteins like beef, and flexitarian diets. Plus, you don't necessarily need a burger lookalike or steak lookalike to avoid animal proteins, there are great meat substitutes like tempeh, tofu, and even portobello mushrooms.

Remember, *it still comes down to taste*. Plant-based milk alternatives are doing exceptionally well, so it's not <u>plant-based</u> that's the issue, it's the *taste* of plant-based *meat*. Plus, looking at the plant-based meat ingredients, they fall below the nutritional needs of most humans, and contain significant levels of salt, sugar, and saturated fat.

Assuming you're still wanting to be in the plant-based business, clear signage is always number one when trying to show variety and options to customers. I'd also suggest a plant-based section in the meat case, at least until the various options become mainstream. Clear signage and its own section will help. Staying on top of variety with also help, with bacon alternatives, pork alternatives, chicken, and even fish. As each animal protein has a plant-based option, it makes sense to carry the variety.

I'd also suggest staying on top of research, to understand why many choose plant-based options. *Flexitarian diets are showing a super trend*, so you need to ensure the customers knows you are trying to offer options, not make a statement against animal proteins.

Those who buy plant-based meats tend to be younger, have college degrees, and higher household incomes. Wherever your store locations have those demographics as their predominant customer, plant-based meats should be offered in a wider variety.

**Conscious consumerism is here to stay.** Yes, we are all conscious of environmental and social issues, plus health issues, and it plays into food choices. Understanding how each of the generations views consumption is paramount for food retailers. Older generations focus on *elimination* of ingredients like sugar and salt. Younger generations are focused on being *cause-based* or empathetic to growers, pickers, and workers along the supply chain. But, be careful not to paint a broad brush and assume these concerns are worth paying a premium. Yes, we care. No, we don't care so much we want to pay a 40% premium for the cause. Remember, our guests are loyal to themselves and their families first.

**Third Party Shoppers need to get out of the way.** At some point, the number of "shoppers" in the aisles shopping for other shoppers becomes quite annoying to those shoppers shopping for *themselves. The ones who got in their vehicles and made the trip to walk into your store.* Plus, the nature of these services makes the fulfillers pushy and aggressive. And this goes for both third-party, like Shipt and Instacart, and our own personal shopper fulfillers. When speed is an incentive, it causes friction between those shoppers and the ones in the store shopping for themselves and making decisions at the shelf.

**Add microbiome to the probiotics and prebiotics discussion.** It's not new to talk about probiotics, but the discussion has expanded to prebiotics, and the movement has expanded to the entire store. Add to that the deeper discussion on your microbiome, and its link to overall health, and this trend is solid.  Where we might have previously stopped at yogurt and cottage cheese, you can now add sauerkraut, kimchi, tempeh, kefir, kombucha, and miso to the list. Watch for this trend to continue growing, as the healthy bacteria in your gut and your microbiome continue to be at the forefront of health discussions.

**Protein is a constant buzzword.**  Protein grams on packages is the norm now and is driven by customer-demand.  We need to work on helping the customer understand what it means to have protein in something.  Many are pointing to macronutrient percentage as a better way to understand the balance between protein content and the content of other ingredients- good or bad.  Macronutrient percentage measuring is coming to the forefront as a solid way to communicate balance.

**Frozen foods are rocking!**  We've been saying this for a few years now, and there is no abatement in sight.  Frozen foods are so helpful to customers.  Frozen foods offer an option for certain items in households that would otherwise spoil too quickly or couldn't travel to that area in a "fresh" state.  Keep on top of frozen sales, as they are with us for a while.  Everything in the store is offered in a frozen state, so maintaining the trends from the center store is imperative in frozen assortment.

Some de-SKU'ing in the "diet" section could help alleviate some of the space pressure. *There are soooooooo many diet brands, and they each have appetizers, main meals, desserts, etc.* You can probably choose one or two, and de-sku the rest.  Hot right now?  Frozen fruits, frozen vegetables, frozen Asian foods, and all these new versions of peanut butter and jelly, ham and cheese, grilled cheese, chicken sliders, etc.  Probably the one needing some attention would be frozen hamburgers.  They seem to be mostly uncooked in the frozen aisle and could use an expanded cooked variety.

**Local and Regional are still hot.**  Everything from local foods to regional tastes, the desire to "support local", as well as the assumption that local means healthier (maybe not a fact-based assumption, but an assumption either way), is still trending.  Look for the expansion outside produce to *meats, sauces, condiments, and bakeries* to continue.  And if you don't already have a *local honey* program, it's time to pick up the pace on that one!

**Private brands continue to steamroll!**  This trend of private brand strength is becoming stronger each year.  Originally built for loyalty, margin rate, and an everyday value option for customers, private brands are so much more today!  A good strong opening price point (OPP) label for an inexpensive option in most categories, a national brand equivalent (NBE) label for a less expensive version of the national brand leaders, then a premium label for upper-tier, value-added, special ingredients….they're all important.  Treat your private label like a complete brand, with research and development, beautiful and impactful labels, quality assurance, new launches, etc. Private label is a winner year after year.

Each year, we have these over-arching themes of health and wellness, technology, customer connectivity, and the impacts of the economy and the government.  Each year, the industry rises to the challenge and offers the best experience possible, no matter the challenges. We're going to walk the store, *but let's talk about a few major structural changes first.*

# Hello, RGM

Let's talk a bit about Revenue Growth Management (RGM). In some iteration, the need to effectively maximize your resources has always been prevalent in this industry. *Margin rates are so tight, it's the nature of the game.* Then, we went through a few years of supply chain issues, bath tissue being hoarded, a multitude of distractions, you know the story. One main key result of the supply chain issues was the removal of promotions. Why promote, when there's *nothing to promote*? Why promote, when your supply chain is so disrupted? Normal replenishment on the shelf, and on shelf availability, was just a dream for a while.

Now that supply has been somewhat normalized, we've been hit with a contracted economy and inflation. Both factors impact us in several ways: we sell more on promotion, shoppers become promiscuous (it's okay, I'm just talking about a lack of loyalty to one format), store brands rise in popularity, and customers "circle the wagons" around their own family and their own interests.

So, the focus has turned back to Revenue Growth Management. And, not surprisingly, there's no firm consensus on the definition of RGM. Let's break it down, so we can understand what we're trying to accomplish with RGM.

**Goal:** To successfully manage net revenue in a manner consistent with company goals for sales and profits, effectively utilizing multiple levers, to ensure market share stability and/or gains.

**Levers:** Here is where multiple sources differ. Some sources point to the 4P's of marketing as your levers. Hard to disagree with that. In most cases, the 4P's will always be your friend. They are your marketing toolbox, and what you "encode" into your offer, to secure a connection with your target market(s). Looking at it that way, price, product, place, and promotion fit perfectly. To make these P's more retail-specific:

- **Price:** How you effectively manage your pricing to maximize profitable sales. It's easy to sell $5 for $3, anyone can give product away. Maximizing pricing involves understanding repurchase cycles, how your product is perceived by customers (decoded), your differentiators, breakeven analysis, and the best balance between spend and incrementality.
- **Product:** In the retail sense, this would be an effective assortment. How many flavors optimize your customer connection, shelf presence, brand value message, etc. I'd also add in here your product forms. Do you need singles, multi-packs, club packs, liquid and dry form, consume with one hand or two, etc.? Everything you need to ensure your product is unassailable by competition.
- **Place:** In retail, this can mean various things for retailers vs. CPG's. What is the maximized distribution of your products in various formats? Obviously, a limited assortment store has a different value proposition vs. a traditional store, and the assortment must match the value offer. Similarly for retailers, do you need a store every five miles, every 20 miles, etc.? Inventory and stores are resources, and they need to be maximized.

- **Promotion:** This P is one of the more misunderstood P's, as many simply interpret promotions as ads. Not necessarily, although ads (and commercials) are the face of your value proposition. In a social media focused world, your value proposition lives in many forms, like how you communicate with customers, how you encourage dialogue, how you convey value in stores, your signals, etc.

The main lever, which does not fit neatly into one of the 4P's is *trade spend optimization*. This aspect of RGM is the most talked about in companies, and rightfully so, as this aspect of the business shows the most potential benefit from the appropriate analytics. Remember the saying, "50% of my spend is wasted, I just don't know which 50%'? Trade spend is in a similar situation. How can you maximize the effectiveness of your trade spend, while also maintaining customer connectivity and shelf/brand presence in stores, plus encouraging trial by new customers?

Like Category Management, all these levers are supported by enablers, such as well-trained people, appropriate metrics and measurement capabilities, the right tools and processes, even top leadership buy-in. At the risk of offending bread, *you're toast without top leadership buy-in.*

We could write an entire book on RGM, but let's talk some tips, to help ensure RGM works:

- **Measure <u>units</u>:** In an inflationary time, units are the key. In the last three years, almost every category has shown unit declines. Some of that unit decline is the result of shifting consumers into multi-packs, of course; but, most is from inflation skewing sales data. Units, or equivalent units, or stat cases, they're all there to help strip out inflation's impact on retail prices. If you only measure dollars, you're solely looking for numbers that make you look good. Your job is to seek the truth in the numbers, not just seek the good.

- **Market share:** Kind of a no brainer, but an inflationary period shows sales increases for everyone. You need to compare yourself vs. the rest of the market, if you want a true picture of results.

- **Measure sales per point of distribution:** If items are only brought in for promotions, they show tremendous lift, of course. On the flipside, sales and lift per point of distribution will give you a truer picture of a SKU's performance against demographics, against distribution, against geographies/regions, against rural/urban, etc. You cannot just measure lift in a vacuum.

- **Maximize SKU's on both sides of the desk:** You cannot measure effectiveness inside a CPG, while also working to make sure *every SKU is carried by every retailer*. You also need to look in the mirror and determine if you are also contributing to inefficiencies. Sure, it all rides on the same truck to the retailer, but every SKU requires a warehouse slot in everyone's distribution center, production stops to change labels, formulation management, item set-up, etc. Efficiencies can be found on both sides of the desk, which can increase everyone's effectiveness.

- **Same-store, as a concept, works.** If you are not working to strip out new products or new stores, you are letting the data skew. Measure "like for like", as in stores open a year ago vs. those same stores now (the name same-store). Adding ten stores over the year, then being amazed at how great your sales are trending, is a false flag.

The RGM framework is valuable in understanding how to maximize resources on both sides of the desk. There are a ton of similarities to Category Management, with an enhanced focus on promotional spend optimization. Whatever you call it, it's healthy for us to be focusing analytics on understanding how to connect more effectively with our customers.

# *Hello, RMN*

Retail Media Networks (RMNs) have dominated the discussion for the last year, or so. As with so many other hot topics, is it clear what we're talking about? If I asked you today to define your RMN, *what would you say*? If I asked you an even deeper question, like what are the goals of your RMN, what would you say? If you can answer succinctly, and define your RMN, then great. *Skip this chapter.* For the rest of us, let's try to break it down a bit, in hopes of ensuring we are all steering in the right direction.

In easy-to-understand terms, RMNs refer to advertising within retailer sites and apps, usually by brands that are directly selling products with retailers. At the same time, other advertisers can utilize this space to connect with customers, even if those products are not directly sold by the retailer. The value from the RMN is the closed loop, and relatively captive audience (no audience is captive, honestly). The hope is we are catching the shoppers close to the decision point of purchase.

A few definitions before we continue, to help understand RMNs:
- **Customer signals:** This term is popping up everywhere and has certainly replaced "touchpoints" in the lexicon of trying to understand the various interactions your brand has with customers along their path to purchase. Similarly, signaling is being used as describing the trigger mechanisms in place to understand when a customer is ready to purchase. The better your network is on picking up signaling, the better conversion rate.
- **Conversion rate:** Not a new term, but the primary measure of effectiveness. Your RMN should be built upon the premise that every customer signal is an opportunity to convert to a purchase, thus converting signals into purchases.
- **Context:** In our recent conference, context was the word of the two days. Every presentation involved setting the paradigm for how marketing interacts with a customer's context. In many ways, context is quite like utility. Utility is the usefulness of your offer. Every customer is approaching your brand from *their own context*. Remember, the customer owns decoding how they connect with your brand, and *their* context plays a key role.
- **Relevancy:** Yes, this could fit inside the context discussion, but this one is highly applicable to RMNs, RGM, and all the ways you are using data to connect with your customers. The moment your algorithm spits out dog food offers, and you've never purchased anything dog-related at the store, credibility is shot. Not only that, but *you've wasted your time and the customer's time*, and not one signal, purchase decision, or conversion will come from sending irrelevant offers to customers.

Like RGM, there could be an entire book on Retail Media Networks, so the aim of this book is how to apply what is going on out there, and to understand some best practices from key retailers and CPG's.

*First,* why do we need RMNs? They accelerate ecommerce growth, they provide robust first party data, the data is inside the closed loop of the RMN, the retailer or CPG controls the message, you have a clear understanding of your audience, you can flex in and out various brands.

*Second,* how does loyalty fit into the RMN discussion? Of course, everything is about customer loyalty, but how about specifically with RMNs? Loyalty is measured by digital engagement (back to those signals again). If you are increasing traffic growth, digitally and physically, some aspect of this engagement is working.

*Third,* the entire industry is about analytics now, and RMNs are in the same boat. Understanding how algorithms are being used to nudge for trial purchases, personalize the customer relationship, compel initial purchases, time re-purchases, include commodities the customer is skipping, encouraging revisits, and even increasing basket sizes, all comes under a robust data analytics team that *must have heavy interface with the merchandising team.*

*Fourth,* artificial intelligence (AI) and generative artificial intelligence (GenAI) do come into play in RMNs. They come into play everywhere, yes, but specifically GenAI is allowing RMNs to tailor content, formulate personalized recipe ideas that lead to conversion, and link clicking to purchasing. The warning from anyone investing in GenAI is it is imperative to cleanse all data before embarking on a GenAI path. GenAI platforms are intelligent, but they use parameters and data provided by humans. Humans play a part in making sure the data is accurate before feeding it into GenAI platforms.

So, back to the beginning of this section, what are the goals of your RMN? Based upon multiple sources, the goals of RMNs should be:

1. Unify 1$^{st}$ party data
2. Plan with insight
3. Turn insights into audiences
4. Activate those audiences
5. Meet their expectations
6. Measure impact and learn

Other areas to explore are the intertwining of shopper marketing and RMNs, how does sampling come to life in RMNs, LTO's, loyalty events, cooking classes, nutrition? And probably the main question, *how does Tik Tok fit into your life* as a brand or retailer?

Remember, always remember, you grow sales by **acquiring new customers, selling more to current customers, and/or increasing purchase and re-purchase frequency**. RMNs can help with all three. With attention spans down, data availability up, and media fragmentation at an all-time high, you need a strategy to bring attention to your brand, store, service, and value.

# GenAI and ReGenAI

In the slew of new acronyms rising to the top, it's hard to find one more ubiquitous than AI. Artificial intelligence (AI), Generative AI (GenAI), and Regenerative AI (ReGenAI), have all been piled on top of Machine Learning (ML) and Deep Learning (DL), to pretty much confuse everyone. Honestly, using Siri is using AI, so we're already surrounded.

If you want to know the layers, here's a simple chart and explanation from Amazon Web Services:

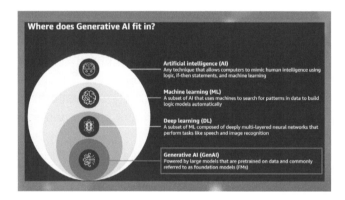

We took the idea of GenAI and ReGenAI and tagged it to the concept of nudging, a much more applied aspect of GenAI, where we are able to use a platform to combine a number of shopping/shopper variables and use them for helping customers meet their goals, manage allergies, figure out "what's for dinner tonight", and a combination of all of the above. We called the framework ***Tired or Inspired: A Conceptual Model for Using Regenerative Artificial Intelligence to Create Context, User, and Time-Aware Individualized Shopping Guidance***, using "tired or inspired" as a situational context for what is going on in the customer's mind as they are shopping in grocery stores or online.

This research conceptualized a consumer-centric, regenerative artificial intelligence ("ReGenAI") model for the Fast-Moving Consumer Goods ("FMCG") retailing channel. The system uses its awareness of context, time, and users to (re)generate customer touchpoints and other marketing communications. Its output provides deep insights into regular and altered FMCG customer journeys, such as shopping behaviors under stressors like lifestyle choices or cataclysmic socio-economic and weather events.

The recursive model advances from current, generative AI systems. It uses "tired or inspired" as a simplified bifurcated grocery shopper taxonomy to operationalize customers' purchasing and consumption behaviors into actionable data for demand planning and retail operations. The research involves GenAI concepts in an applied manner that can advance customer connectivity in the food and CPG industry.

Artificial Intelligence systems collect and analyze significant amounts of complex, multivariate data, predicting outcomes, comparing these to actual results, and learning from this analysis to optimize their models and decision-making functionalities

GenAI is characterized by its ability to recognize its environmental circumstances *and* users' psychological factors and so become "aware" of the context and time it is operating in, making the context integral to data collection, analysis, and developing solution decision-sets and implementing these toward achieving its set goals and objectives. Because of this comparative understanding of current and desired reality, GenAI can then apply its creative abilities to recommend or "nudge" its users to change their attitudes and behavior toward retailers, brands, and, by extension, specific purchase decisions in the context of FMCG or grocery shopping. This constitutes a dramatic leap forward from using demand data in sales and supply planning or non-generative AI, i.e., not including demand management through customer touchpoints. GenAI, therefore, also represents a significant opportunity to improve demand and supply integration in FMCG retailing.

Whether shaping food shopping behavior towards healthier choices, understanding the impact of cataclysmic events on long-term behavior, or matching caloric goals with retailer formats, ReGenAI can significantly assist customers through trait inputs, label comprehension, lifestyle factors, and intent. For retailers, the generated insights and predictions can now become the inputs for sales and demand planning, both in the short term (e.g., in case of immediate weather events) but also in the long term, where insights into diet choices or the benefits of personalization will now drive assortment, pricing, promotion, and the content and format of customer touchpoints will increase the efficiency of retail operations and the effectiveness of marketing efforts, increasing the return on investment (ROI) of ReGenAI's use and in doing so, the customer lifetime values for retailers and brands.

Using ReGenAI, as suggested in our conceptual model, FMCG manufacturers, retailers, shoppers, and consumers will thus benefit as shoppers' wants and needs are satisfied throughout satisfactory omnichannel customer journeys. FMCG brands and retailers benefit from streamlining business processes and generating more efficient business planning, product innovations, channel structures, and marketing communications. Delivering on the up-to-now elusive promise of mass customization (e.g., Goodrich, 2007) will be significantly helped by applying the ReGenAI model.

Here is a representation of the model:

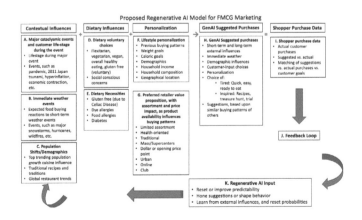

A *very* quick review of the boxes (for the entire article, see the *Journal of International Consumer Marketing* 36(3)):

### Major cataclysmic events (Box A)

One's belief system and its influence on food consumption and purchasing behavior is a long-term trait influencing many consumption decisions, irrespective of life stage. For GenAI, the proposal is that life stages and events will determine shopping probabilities.

### Immediate weather events (Box B)

If one of the model's outputs is a recommended shopping list, weather conditions will be a significant consideration and decision factor.

### Population shifts and demographics (Box C)

In the example of the U.S. population growth concentrating in specific regions of the United States, the ensuing impacts on cuisines, tastes, and recipes will first be at home, then transfer from ethnic to general cuisine restaurants, eventually transitioning from ethnic supermarkets to becoming part of traditional grocery stores' assortment and buying patterns.

### Voluntary Diet Choices (Box D)

As the name indicates, some diet-related consumer traits are not religious or health-related but are followed willingly and voluntarily for consumers' aspirational health, or goals and objectives. Voluntary choices can include flexitarian, vegetarian, vegan, socially conscious, and so forth.

### Necessary Diet Choices (Box E)

Required or necessary diet choices represent mandatory lifestyles, such as diabetes control, celiac disease, food allergies, etc.

### Lifestyle Choices (Box F)

This consumer trait grouping includes the previously modeled and discussed consumers' buying decision-making and behavioral schemas, weight and other health goals, attitude, and intent towards FMCG brands and retailers. Also included are control factors such as household income and composition, geographic location, and other user, context, and time awareness that operate as input variables to the "Tired or Inspired" model.

### Retailer Value Proposition (Box G)

From the perspective of the individual shopper, a retail location (brick-and-mortar or online store) represents a unique combination of utilitarian and hedonic factors that constitute its value proposition.

### GenAI suggested purchases (Box H)

The GenAI model, as presented here, generates original content for customers based on its awareness of user, context, and time variables. To conceptualize the highly dynamic and customer-specific factors determining a shopper's mood and demeanor on each shopping trip, we added "Tired or Inspired" as an independent variable to the model, i.e., as a system input. Being tired or inspired will reasonably result in vastly different customer journeys. For instance, a "Tired" shopper will seek to complete a short trip only, goal-orientated towards choosing quick, easy, and ready-to-eat recipes and meal solutions. On the other hand, "Inspired" shoppers may explore complex recipes, try new foods, and spend more time in the store to complete their "treasure hunt."

### Shopper Purchase Data (Box I)

AI computational models build upon pre-existing parameters and use cases, with multiple users' data composing the input variables for the system's learning functionality. Not all journeys end with customers purchasing the AI-suggested products. Impulse buys, changes of plan, and recovered inspiration are but a few examples of changes in utilitarian or hedonic shopping factors (variables) that obstruct or change shoppers' journeys and, thus, the predictive accuracy of the GenAI system. It is here that the depicted feedback loop compares suggested versus actual purchases. This data will then again become input to the ReGenAI system.

### A feedback loop (Box J)

As part of a fully functioning AI system, machine learning is only possible if it can access deviations, standard optimization, and some form of behavioral data to compare to the outcome predictions it suggested before, based upon the same variables. Augmenting the actual versus predicted data with additional external variables increases the system's understanding of behavioral patterns, allowing it to improve its predictive capabilities and suggest ways to influence human attitudes and behavior.

### Regenerative AI input (Box K)

At this stage of the conceptual model, the outcomes and suggestions from earlier iterations are taken together with the input variables from the current iteration. By comparing the input variables between "then and now," the system will learn to assess changes in these variables' impact. The ReGenAI system could suggest "better than" alternatives, at least nudging consumers to choices that are "as good as they can get, based upon their circumstances."

Whether shaping food shopping behavior towards healthier choices, understanding the impact of cataclysmic events on long-term behavior, or matching caloric goals with retailer formats, ReGenAI can significantly assist customers through trait inputs, label comprehension, lifestyle factors, and intent.

For retailers, the generated insights and predictions can now become the inputs for sales and demand planning, both in the short term (e.g., in case of immediate weather events) but also in the long term, where insights into diet choices or the benefits of personalization will now drive assortment, pricing, promotion, and the content and format of customer touchpoints will increase the efficiency of retail operations and the effectiveness of marketing efforts, increasing the return on investment (ROI) of ReGenAI's use and in doing so, the customer lifetime values for retailers and brands.

Using ReGenAI, as suggested in our conceptual model, FMCG manufacturers, retailers, shoppers, and consumers will thus benefit as shoppers' wants and needs are satisfied throughout satisfactory omnichannel customer journeys. FMCG brands and retailers benefit from streamlining business processes and generating more efficient business planning, product innovations, channel structures, and marketing communications.

# *Let's Walk the Store*

Now that we've discussed some overall trends impacting every category in the store, we're going to take a walk around a store. As a special feature each year, we get to walk the store together. There is *nothing more important* than being able to complete an effective and impactful store walk. We're taught it first thing as we enter this industry, and it never ends. You see so much on a store walk. It's quite literally putting yourself in your customers' shoes. **Let's go for a walk!**

# *Come on in*

Nothing can say "welcome" or "go away" more than the front of your store. And it's <u>everything</u>, the parking lot, the cart corrals, the bottle and can redemption areas (if you have them), the entrance and exit options of the parking lot (can you go left from your parking lot easily?), the propane cylinder refills, are you allowing RV's to make your parking lot a home, it all matters. Either *everything matters*, or *nothing matters*.

The entrance to your store sets the tone. Go to your store at night in the winter, do you feel safe in the parking lot? Is there enough lighting? Most of us get out of our car and look around. It's one of the reasons the fronts of stores look so majestic. You are entering a beautiful bastion of bounty, and the front needs to look like a castle. It's the first impression!

You get out of your car, and what do you see? A beautiful display of flowers, plants, and lawn items. What do you think? *Fresh, summer or spring, lively, beautiful.* That's the tone. You sell *food* and it's *fresh*. Food comes from the earth (mostly), and you can trust this store.

Now, what if you get out of your car and you see a massive truck trailer with pallets and pallets of paper towels and tissue on it, and a big sign for a great price? What's your interpretation of the retailer's message? *Value, price, best deal in town, get it while it's hot!* In both scenarios, your trip through the rest of the store? Same impression. The fresh outside makes the store fresh inside. Value and price outside? Same result.

*Now flip the scenario.* What happens when you drive up to the store and must get out and move a shopping cart to get into a parking place? Add that cart to the hundreds that are out in the parking lot, dodge a flying piece of debris as you get out of your car, and walk quickly past the employee smoking by the propane cylinders (it's happened, don't laugh), to get into the store. Now, what's your impression? Yup, this is an easy one. This store doesn't care about *you*. They think you are fine with an un-safe environment that is wrought with peril. And that's how you're going to feel as you shop in that store. The outside makes a difference. You might want to skip the sushi in this store.

We've parked, are walking in, and the outside has met whatever expectation we have for the store. We slip through the sliding glass doors as they welcome us as only sliding glass doors can welcome us- come on in, stay a while! You walk into what we like to call the **De-compression Zone.** That big bad outside world was nipping at your heels, but here you are. A cool collection of some of the world's best food products grown or made by some of the most skilled artisans in the world. Take a deep breath….de-compress.

What's the first thing you see? What's the first thing you should see? Let me introduce you to one of my favorite phrases- *It depends.* What should you see? It depends. If you're a value format like Walmart, then you should see **value**. If you're a traditional format like Meijer, Kroger or Family Fare, then show off what makes you different. Go for **fresh**. If you're a club store, like Sam's or Costco, you start with **treasure hunt** down the middle, with everything else surrounding the hunt. Your value proposition should be communicated every step along the way. Remember, *what makes you special?*

# Flowers and Plants

Picture walking through a wall of beautiful **flowers** and **plants** as you head into the most *luscious, bountiful produce department ever*! Yeah, that is a beautiful picture. Every store should have floral at the front. It's on no one's list, except for Valentine's Day, and is a perfect upsell for every customer. Fresh sells in floral.

A well-run floral department at the beginning of the store? *Now, that's selling!* Get someone to run your floral departments who is the most passionate and effusive person in the store or in the company. Really, that person will make your floral departments resemble their passion. Floral calls for *flamboyant leadership*. Seriously, find someone a little crazy and energetic. That person.

Some other tips, have the correct mix of **plants, flowers, and bouquets**. Make it known you can make any arrangement or corsage or centerpiece on demand. The only other section of the store that demands this much artistry, personal touch, and love is cake decorating.

A few more hints, always have the $10 to $15 **bouquets in water buckets by the registers**. The registers are perfect for that last impulse buy of flowers. And make sure you have the bouquet dry bags connected to the displays. *They're wet, you know.* Now, how else do you get someone's attention? **Balloons! Balloons!** What is more attention-getting than a bunch of balloons? Have them on the flowers, have them in floral, have them near the special occasion cakes in the bakery. Balloons can still sell, you know. Go to any dollar store and look at the displays of balloons. If you are a traditional store, you've pretty much given this business to dollar stores. If you don't think you have the labor for balloons, dollar stores carry balloons and have **one person working and a store manager that runs five stores at a time**!

A last tip, many customers have turned to growing their own herbs and some vegetables at home. Make sure you have small plants, as well as seeds. You're helping customers, and you really should be the only place customers think of when it comes to food. Play up the savings that can had by growing your own food at home. *On to produce!*

# Fruits and Vegetables

The beautiful collection of fruits and vegetables in your stores should rival any farmers market in the country! In fact, go visit the farmers markets on the weekends, and see what they are doing. There is no reason *any* customer shouldn't feel the same about your produce department as they do about farmers markets. Fresh, local, earthy, and healthy. It's a showcase of beauty.

Ask customers why they choose their favorite store, and **produce** is almost always number one. Even the mass merchants understand how important produce is in keeping a customer coming back. What makes a great produce department? Start with the *first look*. What do you see? Does it scream "fresh picked", "good for you", "straight from the earth", "trust"? If so, then good, *you're in the right place*. A beautiful and fresh produce department should delight your eyes and make you feel like you're at one with the earth. Seriously, that's how important the produce department is to customers.

Even the table or fixtures should scream earthy or fresh or "straight from the field". The fixture should **showcase the product**, and should blend in. To complete the ambience, there should be lighting directly on the beautiful produce, maybe even dimmed on the aisles, to showcase the product even more. Use special floors that are different from the rest of the store. An earthy wooden floor is a perfect complement to a produce department.

Let's talk **navigation**. A customer has an expectation to be able to walk around your department and *take their time* to pick out their produce. They'll also want to know who grew it, is it local, etc.? Make sure you give the customers *spacing*! Customers want to be able to make a thoughtful decision in produce, and that can only be done if they don't feel like they are in everyone's way. Make the aisles wide and clean and let them think! They're thinking through their food needs for the week.

So, what's new in produce? The newest trending area is the **ready to eat** section. Normally reserved for deli, ready to eat is popping up all over the store. Everyone is rushed and not wanting to spend a ton of time on meal prep. The margin you can make in ready to eat salads is off the charts, if you order and rotate it properly. Add to that, ready-cut vegetables and fruits are still trending well. Make it easier to consume produce, and the guests will appreciate the effort.

**Packaged salads**, usually adjacent to ready to eat salads, are not new, but have been holding strong. Make sure this section reflects new combinations of greens and is also rotated properly. These bagged (or plastic container) salads have extremely close dating, and they need to move out of your store as quickly as they came in! Very importantly, maintain variety in this section. Your eyes can easily make anything green look like variety, but 30 rows of spinach, without any options for kale, arugula, romaine, etc., is <u>not</u> what the customer's want.

**Seasonality** is obviously key in the produce department. If that is new news to you, then kindly close this book and use it as a drink coaster, please….it's not going to help. Let's talk about product layout in produce. The seasonal part is the most obvious: apples in the fall, local corn mid-July, etc. Seasonal items need to be front and center. You need to remind customers it's cider time, it's pumpkin time, it's stone fruit time!

Please remember there are *apple customers year-round*. Demand might shift a bit and be a little heavier in the fall, but you still need a base assortment of those items you call seasonal. You just get them from somewhere in the world that is still growing and harvesting the product. I'm convinced that is why we have two hemispheres- *when one takes a break, the other one picks up the slack*.

**Local** is continuing its meteoric trend! Remember, all produce is local to somewhere, so this is a balancing act. You want to play up local, show your local growers, but do not ignore great items solely because they don't fit a rigid definition of local arbitrarily determined by drawing a circle on the map around your store. If you followed that map unwaveringly, you'd have a boring department and risk being constantly out of items customers want. As with everything, don't rank *your* definition of value over the *customer's* definition.

Seasonal items towards the front, then break out into stone fruits (those with pits or seeds), other fruits, cooking vegetables, regular vegetables, greens, then bagged salads, and the green wall! **A green wall!** Now that's a differentiator! Angled almost vertically, the green wall makes or breaks your produce department. It yells freshness, earthy, healthy, wellness, fit, etc. *It's all about the green wall.*

What about stocky items like **potatoes, carrots, stewing vegetables**, etc.? They are bulky and, frankly, not very exciting. You need to ensure you have variety and sizes for all customers. As more customers have started cooking, look for this section to have a nice expansion trend. Vegetables are back!

And the "extra" section with **kombucha, live probiotics, pomegranate juice, immunity shots, and everything superberry?** Yeah, that's a big part of the department. If you're not focusing on these trendy items, you are missing a whole segment of the population that likes to "juice" (as a verb). Everything is now available in liquid form. Make sure you have the full variety. They started in produce, but now superfood beverages are everywhere! There really isn't a healthy food group that isn't also available in liquid form.

**Organic produce.** Organic is the growth trend of the last four years and shows no slowing at all, as we discussed at the beginning of this book. This one area, along with local, is going to carry produce growth for the next five years. Please, please, please do not treat organic items as "we carry them when we have them". Make sure they are part of the set and are a *mandatory part of the minimum assortment*. In the produce department, it's best to have an organic section separate from the rest, simply because it showcases variety better when all grouped together. Plus, you can show a keen focus on maintaining organic assortment when you have a plan for all commodities in the organic section.

Just make sure the customers can find it. Maybe even put it first in the traffic line. Or, if you have a spacious department, go ahead and place organic sections closer to their non-organic friends. Have an organic potato section adjacent to potatoes. Have the carrots and celery near the other carrots and celery. Just call it out big and bold! Customers *are* looking for organic.

A tip for **cut fruit and vegetables, "loose" nuts and seeds**, etc., procure them from a producer who is skilled in manufacturing these items in a hyper hygienic environment! You cannot replicate these clean environments in a store, and someone's going to get sick! Go tour one of these facilities, and you'll see what I mean. I'm talking full body suits and walking through a sanitary mister. *That* clean! Anything someone picks out of the canister and immediately eats needs to be produced in a highly sanitary environment.

Carry sizes that encourage **full consumption** of the products at home. At least 30% of all produce is thrown away at home, and we can help. Shrink some of the pack sizes. No, offering loose individual fruits and vegetables is not the only, or best, solution. Bagged produce is easier to shop, easier to checkout, easier to bring home, and easier to consume.

Lastly in produce, what about pricing? *Price is not a differentiator.* Repeat after me- not a differentiator. If people shop in your stores because of price, it's because that's all you have to offer them. Yes, price operators have something to offer besides price, but not much. The reason they exist is because of price. Unless you work in this price-oriented format, make it about the product- variety, service, cleanliness, customer service. *Make it about the experience.*

One thing on produce pricing, make sure you know the key items people will notice. Number one? Yup, you guessed it- **bananas**. One of the most noticeable prices in the store. Keep regular bananas at a highly competitive price without losing money. How do you make up the margin? *Expand your offering on organic bananas* and make them competitively priced. The only way the math works on competitive banana pricing is if you offer competitive organic pricing and can increase those sales.

And, while we're at it, self-checkout is a major part of the future of shopping. The more you can do in the produce department to *help the customer ring up their produce easier at the front*, the better off you'll be. Plus, the more you can distinguish organic produce from non-organic, the more likely you'll be to have the organic produce rung through as organic by the customer. A major area of shrink is self-checkout organic produce going through as non-organic!

For the rest of produce pricing, just keep it competitive. People eat produce for health, for beauty, for just about everything except price. Everyone knows healthy items are more expensive. Giving it away makes no sense.

# Deli Meats, Cheeses, Salads

In many ways, the **deli** and **foodservice** are related from the customer's perspective, and in many merchandising departments. For this book, though, we're going to keep them separate. Probably the best way to think about it is the difference between ready to eat **hot food** and **cold food**, with cold food being in the deli. The deli is the area selling things to be eaten immediately cold, eventually put together and consumed at home, or a combination of both. The one main ready to eat product in the deli would be the **sandwiches**, and there is a decent argument that even sandwiches should be in the foodservice area. The best way to stay on trend is to think like a customer. Have we said that before? Maybe a few thousand times.

The deli is an area being pressured by the *health and wellness* trend, like every other category and department in the store. The health and wellness trend has forced another look at the amounts of nitrates, sodium, and additives that have been thrown into processed meats- then labeled as healthy. In some cases, eating a deli meat sandwich is just as bad for your body as a Big Mac with fries! Things are changing for the better, and we'll all be healthier for it.

There is a "processed and cured meats rejection" happening in this country. We're seeing products labeled as unprocessed, uncured, etc. The only issue is deli meat is a bit like jerky. It *needs* something to bind it and preserve it.

How do we win in the deli? After everything we've said about processed meats, **deli meats** and **cheeses** are still popular, as are the deli salads. One of the best practices in the deli involves a *three-tier pricing structure* and variety. Everything else revolves around these two principles.

For the three-tier pricing, it is commonly known amongst customers that you can flex quality of ingredients in and out of deli meats. It is also commonly known that the price will fluctuate with the quality levels. Some customers just want a **cheap product** they can feed their family. A rock-solid price on ham, turkey, yellow American cheese, and maybe a roast beef is necessary to satisfy a certain segment of the population. If you do not offer that tier today, *do not be afraid to attack it*. In multiple retailers, it has been proven that an opening price point deli meat offer *does not cannibalize* the better-quality cuts. It just brings people back over to the deli that had been skipping you and going to a price-only operator.

For the other tiers, you need a mainstream quality product in both a private label and one national brand. Then, you need a **premium tier** brand, like Boar's Head. You may choose to also offer a store brand in the higher quality tier, but be careful. That might become a major area of spoilage, if you are trying to sell a store brand next to Boar's Head or Dietz and Watson.

Then, take care of variety, like all the **Italian cuts**, the more obscure cuts, the varieties of cheeses, and anything that helps you shout assortment. These cuts do not need to be low priced, as that is not why people are buying them. Keep them wrapped until a customer wants them and wrap immediately after. They do not have a ton of volume, so watch for shrink. Keep variety, though. Do not control yourself out of business.

In-store made **guacamole and hummus** are showing no signs of slowing down. The multiple ways we can incorporate guacamole and hummus into our diets is astounding, and *mostly healthy.* If you can sub hummus for mayo, that's a healthy alternative. **Red beet hummus** is rocking! Think from a customer viewpoint (there it is again!), we all know beets and avocados are healthy. *Well, how much fun is it to take a beet bunch and slice it and cook it?* It's a mess, you look like you're bleeding, and you have this massive green top that is supposed to be healthy, but tastes like sand and grit. **Solution: red beet hummus.**

Now the guac. Avocados are like these little cantankerous angry things that love to act like they will ripen nicely and evenly. But what happens? Yes, you go to bed and they are green, the next morning they are brown and ready to be thrown away! **Solution: guacamole.** The customers usually invent solutions before the food industry does. That's why we always stress "customer first".

A few other points on the deli. *Face the slicers towards the customers.* It's a simple thing but makes a huge difference in appearance and implied customer service. The associate takes the order, grabs the wrapped meat, and takes it around the table to then face the customer while cutting. Seems small, but it isn't. The rule for anything in a store is to avoid turning your back to the customer.

Last thing on deli (we'll get to cheese and pizza later) is *scheduling.* Watch your labor in the deli during peak shopping periods. Cutting labor in the deli is a self-fulfilling prophecy. You keep cutting, the *sales go down* accordingly. Cut some more, and *sales go down again.* When sales go down, you then cut labor. Stop it! Some customers will wait in line for their chance at the deli slicing associate, but some won't. Those are the silent voters who looked at the line, and decided it wasn't worth their time or effort. In other words, you have no idea how much you can sell because you are eliminating those who *do not want to wait.* They'll go somewhere else.

Are there things you can do to help alleviate the pressure when busy? Of course. **Pre-slice** the higher-volume meats. Pre-slice the ham, turkey, American cheese, roast beef, and maybe even bologna or whatever is on sale that week. I've never seen a customer balk at it. You can also **pre-package** deli salads and have a spot on the floor for anyone who does not want to wait. Excellent solution.

Speaking of deli salads, you just need to focus on **macaroni salad and potato salad.** These two are the big kids on the block. You need variety, but these two salads are more than 50% of your deli salad sales (including red skin potato salad). Now, with macaroni and potato as your base, you can go crazy. Add different sizes, different flavors, mustard-based, mayo-based, onions, no onions, etc.

The deli is a quality and signature area for many retailers and needs to be run by someone with a keen view on how to maximize sales while controlling shrink. *Control, don't eliminate.* Eliminate shrink and you'll eliminate your sales. Have plenty of areas with sandwich breads, toppings, etc. and you can complete a picnic right there in the department.

One other thing to consider is **fresh pasta.** Many retailers have moved all fresh pasta products into the deli. Many other retailers keep those products adjacent to the deli. Whatever you do, shelving these items, along with homemade pizza-making supplies, hummus, cheeses, etc., makes for a robust presentation of these types of items. I say "these types", because they really do not have an inherent home or category. They need refrigeration, are seen as toppings (like hummus and spreads), go well with charcuterie trays (all the rage right now), and present themselves well near the specialty cheese sections.

# Hot Ready to Eat

The reason I separated foodservice from the deli is the incredible growth that is coming from the **foodservice** side of the business. In today's world of grocerants- a hybrid of grocery store and restaurant, the old days of potato logs and fried chicken are over. This part of the business is rocking!

First thing's first, *hire someone with restaurant experience* for this area of your store. You are proactively offering a dining out or dining at-home option to your customers. You are working with, or competing against, restaurants and real chefs. You need restaurant expertise. Now, having said that, make sure it is a restaurateur who either understands grocery stores, or can learn quickly.

*And, where do you go from here?* The sky's the limit. With the right amount of imagination, combined with the appropriate demographic, this area of your store can be the area everyone talks about! First, though, you can stop reading if you just do this: *Copy everything Wegmans is doing and bring in enough volume to support the operation profitably.* Do that, and you're fine. Stop reading.

All kidding aside, Wegmans does an outstanding job in their restaurants, but you may want to make sure you have enough customer traffic to offer what they do. Otherwise, just doing what they do is going to be the death knell to profitability. For everyone else, let's talk about how to put the offer together.

Let's talk about **cold** and **hot** differences first. The ability to offer a large assortment of **cold prepared foods** is desirable. Cold pizzas, cold chicken, cold everything, they are all fine and part of a convenient offer. But do not confuse offering cold food to be heated at home as running a restaurant. It is necessary for your assortment but does not differentiate you. *The hot foods are your differentiator.*

The most visible highest volume item of them all? The **rotisserie chicken**, or the roaster! The largest tonnage item in most prepared foods areas tends to be the rotisserie chicken. It was first on the block, it was highly touted as one of the first meal solutions offered by grocery stores, and it still reigns supreme today. As with everything else in this book, you need to pay attention to health and wellness. These things can be sodium-packed! At some point, work on your offer to the degree where you can reduce the sodium content without impacting taste.

You can address trends by ensuring you carry **organic rotisserie chickens**, and make sure you communicate they are *probiotic free, pesticide free, growth hormone free*, etc. They will cost more, so the customer wants to know why. For the flavors, *regular is the top seller*, then please make sure you have a variety of flavors. Most customers will pick up a regular *and* a flavored bird. That's how customers think- I'll choose a "safe" one and then spread my wings (couldn't help it) and try a new flavor. Make sure you have a steady supply of roasters cooking throughout the day and can meet demand for the afternoon shopper. *Do not cook everything in the morning and let it sit there all day.* Once you have established a solid business of rotisserie chickens, try some rotisserie turkey breasts, etc. They all sell well.

Balance out the roaster area (the chicken coop) with hot turkey breasts, hot pasta meals, hot macaroni and cheese, hot sides, packaged hot items from your service hot bar, etc. Surround the coop with dinner rolls and drinks, and you've got a solution center!

Get into the club stores and see what they are doing for roasters, as well as everything else. Club stores love the rotisserie chicken statement. They tend to have a bigger bird (cooked weight around 36 ounces) and a better price. Compare to the traditional grocery store's 26-28 ounce cooked weight, and you can see the issue.

One of the most difficult aspects of grocery store foodservice is being able to be *trendy*. It takes a long time for new techniques and new preparation methods to make their way into the operation. But, being trendy is how you stay relevant. When sushi was on an uptrend, most stores found someone who knew what they were doing and offered them a space to sell their goods. Similarly, find some chefs or cooks and work with them as a test kitchen for new offers and new items.

Now, what about **pizza**? Great opportunity to have another differentiator in the hot foods area. In many ways, the grocery store can offer a *better selection* of pizza, have more affordable lunch options, and take care of customers *better* than pizzerias that are covering all their overhead expenses with one commodity. The only issue....the pizzerias deliver. If you really want to establish yourself in the pizza business, figure out a way to **deliver the pizza**. And do it like the pizza shops- *piping hot, friendly drivers*, etc.

You know what's hot again? Chicken wings and chicken tenders. They never really went away, but the focus went to the chicken sandwich. Now, customers are coming back to chicken wings and chicken tenders/boneless wings. If you got out of the game, get right back in. Make some meal bundles with pizzas, and get the party re-started!

The rest of the foods to be offered hot? That would be driven primarily by the demographics surrounding the store. **Asian food, Mexican food, soups, a service hot bar**. They all can work, if you know your potential for lunch, your potential for dinner, the customers surrounding your store, etc. A word of caution, if you want to establish yourself as a place for dinner, be open and ready for dinner *during dinner*. That is one of the quickest ways to drive people to "real" restaurants that are open late. Remember, grocery stores are not known as places to visit late for anything fresh. We can change that perception.

Let's talk **sushi** one more time. Although sometimes served hot in restaurants, it's customarily a cold offer in grocery stores, and most customers look in the foodservice area for sushi. Not only is sushi a high dollar sale at the register, but nobody buys just one pack! Treat sushi like a *signature area* of the store! An authentic sushi offer is table stakes these days. Have a regular assortment, have a cooked section and raw, then try new limited time only offers, and also plant based. Sushi can be a super area of the store to show you know food!

The foodservice area of the store has *so much potential* for trend, for awareness, for repeat traffic, for takeout, for drive-through....just keep going. It's a fun part of the store!

# *Breads, Rolls, Cookies*

As we make our way from foodservice, we head into the **bakery** department! And it should be gorgeous! There is no excuse to have an anemic bakery department. Not everything in the department is incredibly healthy for you, but it *sure does taste good*. Plus, bread has this connection to the earth that is unmistakable. The nature of the bakery department is it's almost all impulsive. You will entice impulse sales by having bountiful displays, with tremendous variety.

The best way to ensure the bakery department has an excellent appearance and suitable variety, is to divide into segments consisting of **"carriers"** (yes, bread is a carrier of everything) and **sweets**. Once you look at it that way, you can then go about allocating space in your "carrier" section for artisanal breads traditionally used to "carry" a topping, like baguettes, French bread, and most crusty breads. Great for olive oil, butter, hummus, and those kinds of toppings.

That's not the only use for those breads, just the primary use, you then need a selection of the same types of **breads sliced**- especially sourdough, pumpernickel, and those normally used for sandwiches. Having the bakery so close to the deli makes perfect tie-in opportunities. Rolls and other packaged buns can also be in this section. As a rule, make sure those ugly white pricing labels with all the ingredients listed are facing down. The star of the show is the bread, not the label. But, please make sure the labels are correctly completed, so those who have celiac (or those just avoiding gluten) can find what they want in the bakery.

*A money-making idea?* Take half your batch of **French bread** and add **garlic spread** to it, then place it in those foil packs you can place directly in the oven (make sure it is the one you can place in the oven without a fire). *A germ prevention idea?* In the "old days", artisanal breads were open at the top, so they could cool. As you might imagine, today's packaging will need to be *entirely enclosed* all the way around the product. As much as we love the idea of handing someone a loaf of bread, make sure all cleanliness guidelines are in place.

What about **locally baked bread**? This is somewhere you'll need to decide. Do you fight local bakeries and carry your own, or embrace local and bring everyone up together? I'd vote for teamwork. Local artisan bread will never take all your business, and it shows you are connected to your community. *Carry the local breads, and your customers will appreciate it.*

On to the **sweet stuff**! The bountiful abundance of products doesn't stop with the "carriers". The sweet goods are just as important, if not *more* important. More important as sweet goods are usually *unplanned impulse* purchases. Walking around seeing baked products is like walking around farmers markets. Almost every purchase is incremental and is great for the retailer (and the person consuming it). Sweet goods should scream "buy me!".

Start with those handheld bundles of joy! **Cookies**! Perfect for snacking, after school, anytime. **Chocolate chip** leads the way, as Captain Obvi would state. *If you're out of chocolate chip, you're out of cookies*. Big buckets, large cookies, small cookies, decadent, over the top....you cannot have enough chocolate chip cookies. Their little forgotten siblings oatmeal raisin, sugar, peanut butter, or macadamias are to be carried; but, only if you took care of the OG CC first. The club stores are all over cookies (and cakes and pies and all sweet goods). If you want to be in the cookie business, you need to have an idea of how the club stores view cookies, especially around the holidays.

As for **cakes**, you should have a full lineup of *sheet cakes and special occasion cakes*, along with *cupcakes* of the same flavors, even the smaller "cake pieces" sold as "for one"- not a cupcake and not a cake, a piece of cake. As for flavors, *chocolate and vanilla* base layers, then go crazy from there with types of frosting. Keep in mind, **sheet cakes** are usually for special occasions. The variety **artisan cakes** are the "try me" cakes, like German chocolate, strawberry, devil's food, and my all-time favorite: carrot cake (with cream cheese frosting and little raisins).

Your cake decorator should be as passionate about cakes as your floral person is about the floral department. This is the one part of the store where you can truly tell who has passion and who is just "dialing it in". Passion wins every time!

And, how about **doughnuts and bagels**? Absolutely! Primarily morning-focused, you need a variety of glazed and jelly-filled doughnuts, as well as the "everything" bagel, blueberry, and plain. Have the variety and encourage the customers to buy in bulk. This department can still stand out as a playland for *decadence and taste*!

# *Seafood*

Talk about a department where the tide has been rising the last few years, in alignment with the trend towards health and wellness, the **seafood** department is poised to continue that trend, *if....if*, we can *keep the impact of inflation from polluting the waters.* We may have a new generation of vegetarians on the way, and it would have everything to do with the *price of proteins.* When you start to see **red snapper** and **sockeye salmon** hovering around $15/lb. or more, the more viable alternative is to doctor up some *pasta, and maybe add some canned mackerel.* Pasta has gone up in price, too, but not like all the proteins- fish included.

Inflation is a big story, but let's put it aside for a minute and focus on the department. Let's talk about how the set looks. Any store selling *food* has a need for a *seafood* department. If you are in a lower income area, or are a price-oriented store, then it might be best to go with wrapped fresh or frozen seafood. And, if you're heading in that direction, the types of seafood lean more towards mainstream species than specialized. A Pacific halibut does not belong in these stores. **Flounder, shrimp, haddock, surimi, tilapia, farmed salmon** are the types of fish that are affordable and able to be offered at competitive price points for those who are mostly looking for something relatively healthy to feed their families.

And, speaking of feeding your family affordably, make sure you have multiple forms of seafood to offer as well: the **fully unadulterated** fish, the **uncooked but seasoned** fish, and the **cooked** fish. Not everyone knows what to do with seafood. And, in the cooked section, make sure you have an ample selection of **fried seafood**, mostly haddock and shrimp. Since it is served cold, it's also able to be purchased on SNAP, and you should point this out as a convenience to those customers using SNAP. In a recession, those on SNAP benefits will continue to increase. *Cold fried is a super area to drive incremental volume in seafood!*

In some retailers, they will offer to *fry anything* for anyone. Anything in the case can be chosen and fried right there in the seafood department. It works well and gives the customer the sense of being in a downhome fish fry. Make sure you have some kind of hush puppies or French fries, along with some cole slaw. Served as a dinner and talked up as Fish Frydays (or something corny like that), and you may find yourself selling around 10% of your seafood volume as fried fish! You make more gross profit, offer a unique experience to your guests, and may offer something other competitors do not.

Now, let's talk about the *higher-end stores*, where the demand for seafood is significant. Everyone knows seafood is good for you, but not all can afford it. Those who *can* afford it, *usually buy it.* In these stores, you should be offering a *service seafood case*, where you train your seafood professionals (sure, call them fishmongers) to talk about recipes, how to best prepare, how to best serve, what's new, all the things someone would appreciate as they are planning how to feed their family. *A well-trained fishmonger is essential in higher demographic stores.*

In these stores, quite important, steer away from farm-raised, unless it's something like **trout**- which is usually sustainably farmed. The media on farm-raised has been so bad, there's a good chance the industry will never convince anyone that a farm-raised fish is good for them. *Wild caught* is the preferred fish for anyone who can afford it, and filling your case with farm-raised will mostly raise the suspicion that you have no idea what you are doing.

Remember, customers are trusting *you* to maintain the cold chain, maintain the cleanliness of your cases (*if you can smell the seafood, don't buy any from that store*), source your fish sustainably and socially consciously….it's a big responsibility.

You need to accept that customers are looking for a base variety (primarily **sockeye salmon, haddock, cod, perch, trout**, etc.) and then a mix of in and out items like **halibut, red snapper**, etc. Read up on trends and healthy items and feature those kinds of items. A customer in this type of store is up to date on health trends in every department. Ensure there is a good mix of lake fish and ocean fish and communicate with the customers the importance of cooking certain varieties more than others (lake fish needs to be cooked longer).

And, keep in mind allergies, like shellfish allergies. **Maintaining a barrier between shellfish and fin fish is a must**, as is changing your gloves between orders if a fin fish and shellfish is ordered. This allergy is deadly, so do not take it lightly. In fact, it might be best to have little tin trays for each type of fish. The least amount of liquid mixing between species, the better off the customers (and the stores) will be.

How about **lobsters or octopus**? There are certain species of fish or crustaceans that are showing a tendency to "think" or "react". You must make up your own mind on this one. There's a reason we don't carry dolphin in our stores (or dogs or rabbits, or any other animals sometimes domesticated). Like I said, decide as a company and stick with it. If you happen to be in a predominantly Asian market (where **live fish** is customary), and have no idea how Asians eat seafood, you might want to get up to speed quickly. Either buy the expertise (acquire someone) or hire an expert. You need to understand the Asian customs, preferences, normal selections, and how the Asian customers like to choose their fish (usually live and swimming).

You cannot talk seafood without talking **shrimp**! Shrimp are a go-to item for parties, get-togethers, holidays recipes, etc. Have multiple types of shrimp in the fresh case, as well as the frozen case. *Cooked and uncooked, peeled and unpeeled*, and even the surimi rings posing as shrimp rings.

Another area where you can show a ton of variety, but not have it spoil so quickly, for you or for the customer, is in the **frozen seafood** section. Not frozen fish like fish sticks, frozen seafood like **wild caught red snapper, coho salmon, branzino, sea bass, tuna, swordfish, and halibut**. Use the frozen section to expand variety, while not worrying as much about the fish going bad in two days.

# *Pork, Chicken, and Beef*

The **meat** department is a signature area for any store. You must have a quality offering, large variety, affordable packs, and excitement. It's a lot to ask of a department, but well worth it. Like meat's blue friend the fish, *inflation is having a major impact on the meat department.* Luckily (?), the meat department has been through this before. If handled properly, a meat department can operate quite well in an inflationary time, and be seen as a solution for customers.

We'll lead the meat discussion with the top tip for an inflationary time, or a recession: **train the meat cutters to package the product with the <u>end price point</u> in mind.** It's the most impactful thing you can do to help the customers during these times! In the past, you lowered the price per pound, and then made the packs as large as possible. You needed volume. Today, with the price per pound so much higher, even a discounted product is going to be inordinately expensive when packaged in a larger "family size" or "value pack". Give explicit instructions to ensure there are packages of red meat under $10, between $10-$15, and then $15 and up. If it's a sliced item, make it thin sliced and convey a value message.

Next, make sure you have plenty of **grass fed, organic, No-No-No** red meat (meaning no preservatives, no antibiotics, no anything added). Grass fed may be the brightest future for red meat, as we discussed in the carnivore section. "Regular" red meat, full of preservatives, high yield feed, tight spaces, and unhealthy animals will still sell, but the heyday is over. Most people who avoided meat because it upset their stomachs have figured out *grass fed* alleviates the digestion issues part of the meat experience.

The **plant-based** option came on strong and has now settled. As a food retailer, it's important to offer the options for the customers, and let them make up their own minds. I'd suggest you stay away from the word "alternative" in all categories. If people want to avoid certain meats or cuts or animals, that is solely up to their discretion- it's an *option*. You're a food store, and you offer options. After a euphoric rise in trend, mainly because there were so few plant-based products previously, these products leveled off for a while and now have a steadier runway in front of them. To the degree plant-based might be cheaper to make, I'd expect steadily increasing growth for the foreseeable future.

Pay attention to **grilling steaks** in the summer, **roasts** in the winter. Maybe have a *Summer in January* sale, just to try something new. You'd be surprised how many people will buy a steak just because you made it interesting. *Local ranchers* and focusing on *knowing where the beef comes from*, is trending. Knowing the source of all our foods is something desired by customers, and we're here to help. While doing so, it's also a great practice for merchants of food to understand the entire supply chain.

One more point on red meat *packaging*. There is a groundswell of acceptance of what we call **vac packs** of red meat being available to the customer. The benefits of this pack to the consumer are enormous. This type of packaging offers excellent dating, gives more time to use the product before having to freeze it, is ready when you need it (not having to be thawed), and is all-around one of the most consumer-friendly packs available. Something to consider, when thinking customer-first.

Let's move on to **pork**. Another category that is seeing inflationary pressures. Make sure you have *organics or natural*, have some thick cut and some thin cut, have some large trays and some small trays, and stay in stock. The pork industry tried the "Pork....the other white meat" campaign", and it was able to get pork on the radar for a little while. Now, it's a solid category that should have a wide assortment of various sizes.

One area with a nice trend is the previously mentioned vac packs when applied to pork. In fact, we're seeing quite a few new items in vac pack in pork. Most consumers worry about drying out their pork when cooked. **Seasoned packs of pork** help solve that issue for customers. Seasoned pork tenderloins can be stored for multiple days, are pre-seasoned, can be cut into any size the customer wants, etc.

**Chicken!** What was once described as the healthy alternative to red meat, chicken is now under a major attack for well....the fact we now seem to be growing "super chickens". The feed given to chickens these days is turning them into monsters! Chicken is one of the few categories in the meat department stabilizing in pricing, and maybe even deflating a bit.

It still makes sense to follow inflation tactics in chicken, though. Place smaller portions in packages, show a family of four they can still offer some meat on each plate, spread out on organic, natural, no preservatives, no antibiotics, etc. The "truth in labeling" for chickens is going to be the issue for poultry in the future. The sections of "smart chicken", and "free of everything bad chicken" continue to expand.

*What about the rest?* You have **hams**, which tend to peak either around Christmas and Easter, and then the next most popular times are related to being cold out and maybe hosting many guests- like Super Bowl. **Turkeys**, just one time a year. That's it. You know, turkeys for .19/lb. or even .49/lb. are the *best protein deal* in the store. The amount of time to prep a turkey is the reason they haven't caught on for occasions other than Thanksgiving, but they are a great value.

Where can you make a difference in sales and margin in the meat department? Frozen. Think specialty **frozen burgers, appetizers, meal kits, chicken breasts**, etc. Good growth areas. Another area? Meat bundles. I love meat bundles! Where you have the clientele receiving money once or twice a month from the government, bundling meat packs into $50 bundles, $75 bundles, and even $150 bundles can sell a ton of meat to people who feel the need to stock up for a month. A pack focused on affordable meats to feed your family for two weeks to a month is a great way to help families in inflationary periods.

**Service meat cases**, where a customer can speak to a meat associate and pick out his or her own meat cuts? Yes, there is still a place for service meat counters. That is a high demographic, though. Most customers assume the service meat case products are *better quality and more expensive.* On one hand (price), they are correct. On the other (quality), they *had better be* correct. Make it known the service meat case is not for re-conditioning product that did not sell in the self-serve case.

One other area, **meat grinds**. Make sure the quality control and integrity are maintained in the process. Labeling something 80/20 ground beef, and it's not- that's a bad idea. Customers are quite tuned in to meat fat content, chuck, sirloin, etc. Plus, the government would like you to sell what you say you are selling.

**Lunch meat, bacon, sausages, hot dogs, bratwurst** and the perimeter areas of the meat department have grown in importance. For one (and not a great reason), they are highly preserved, so last a while at home.  And second, they're mostly affordable.  If you're looking to feed your kids, a hot dog or some bologna is just right.  Unfortunately, though, *there is a still a major price gap between the healthier packs and the unhealthier packs*.  Closing that gap could shift customers into a better for them product.

Meat is an integral reason customers shop stores and should be thought of as an *identity department*.  Fresh, well-culled, well-rotated, full assortment, full seasonal offering, it's part of the reason people will choose your store.  When you do this, you meat their demands every day.

# *Refrigerated*

Let's talk **dairy** and refrigerated. What a cool department in which to differentiate your store! Please do not just call it a **dairy** anymore. How's that for step one? There are *so many* people looking for dairy options, just call it the **refrigerated section**- because that's what it is. Let's go through a few sections and see what we can find.

Start with **yogurt**. Probably the hottest refrigerated category the last few years. The health benefits are enormous, and most people are recognizing the value of the *positive bacteria* in your gut (see kombucha), and yogurt tastes great (don't see kombucha). The same benefits are also seen in **cottage cheese**, where fruit-added cottage cheese is trying to make its presence known.

Danone's Activia was the pioneer in pointing out the connection between yogurt and a healthy gut. Now look at everything Danone offers, from Two Good to Oikos to the regular Dannon products. Then, there's **Greek yogurt**. Started by a non-Greek company in Upstate New York (Chobani), it's is about as Greek as a pickle. But, it *does* have extra protein, *does* provide health benefits, and there *are* some packages that try to limit the sugar. All in all, the benefits outweigh the sugar.

With growth comes competition, so along comes Icelandic **skyr**. Skyr describes the process which makes the product *even thicker* and *even better* for you. It's skyr, not yogurt. A slew of skyrs have seen success! Add additional methods of producing a cultured dairy cheese or milk product, like Australian yogurt, etc., and you have a growth category.

The category is a force to be reckoned with. One area to watch, which we've discussed in most categories, is *plant-based*. Technically, **almond, soy, hemp**, and the other dairy alternatives are plant-based; so, they will continue to grow in all areas of the store, mostly dairy and meat.

Then you have **kefir, drinkable yogurts**, anything **fermented**, etc., to round out a smokin' hot category. Everything is being turned into drinkable form, plus a distinction between adults and children is also becoming prevalent in this section. Strangely enough, organic and grass fed are not as highly accentuated in this section. They are available but are not the drivers of consumption. The drivers of the consumer decision tree are sugar (lack of) and protein content.

Next in line with growth is the explosion of **milk options**. Soy milk (*beverage*, it's not really milk) used to be fringy, but now soy is front and center, and joined by hemp and almond and a whole bunch of ways to make something *taste like milk without being milk*. The poor little cow has been squeezed out to about 50% of the category it invented. It's not your job to singlehandedly save the dairy farmers. The customers vote, and you want to win their vote. One thing to keep in mind, both in the stores and at home- ***"Don't give milk a warm welcome!"***- get it into the refrigerator as it comes off the truck!

**Cheese** is next in line. Cheese is having its moment! Not that it was ever *not* popular, but now everyone is adding more flavors to the already massive lineup of singles, strings, shreds, blocks, snack sizes, etc. Cheese is continuing its growth in the specialty section, and that has now made its way to the back of store refrigerated section. Customers cannot get enough of cheese!

We grocers need to decide how *not to have cheese in multiple locations*. The best way to get a customer to trade up is to put the unique items next to the top sellers. At this point, the *unique items* are handled by the deli, while the *top sellers* are handled by the dairy department. But, having said that, the hottest segment in cheese follows the trend everywhere else, look for healthier products like grass-fed, organic.

**Eggs**, the best growth in eggs is….say it with me….yup, *organic, cage free, healthy, omega added*, etc. If you get anything out of this book, it's that we are becoming a healthy world (notwithstanding mukbangers and those who make money on social media for overeating). It's a great trend, and we should embrace it. A growth area in eggs? **Hard boiled and peeled eggs.** Once again, customer-first focus. Customers love hard boiled eggs! They are convenient and you can just pop 'em in your mouth, cut them up in salads, add them to your ramen, etc. They are difficult to boil and peel correctly. Such a simple, but highly frustrating, process. Then someone comes along with boiled and peeled. Magic! Watch these things. They are hot!

The rest of the refrigerated section has been stable. **Butter** is trying to be healthy, with grass fed, real butter, taking the yellow coloring out, etc. Kerrygold has a super following and is one of the true grass fed butters. **Cookie dough** was hot for a while (but eaten cold), went through a bit of an issue with bacteria, and now there's a whole line of "edible cold" cookie dough. Many retailers shelve the **refrigerated bagels** in the refrigerated section, near **cream cheese**. This makes a ton of sense to customers. Shows you are focused on customers and solves the issue of where to put the bagels.

One of the worst trending major sections in the refrigerated case would be **fruit juice**, led by orange. Had a great run, with an aura of healthiness, until somebody analyzed it and found a pile of sugar, found that processing fruits takes most of the goodness out of them, found that companies were taking sub-par juice from Chile and mixing it with a little Florida, etc. *This section will continue to shrink over time*, just like the shelf-stable juice section. It's a sign of the times.

There is a growth trend in juice around mixed lemonades, anything Newman's Own, pomegranate juice, and anything related to superberries. If you read the ingredients, you could have the same issue as with orange juice, but it doesn't seem to make the connection with the customer.

One of the hottest trends in the refrigerated section is making a **breakfast section**, consisting of **ready to eat breakfast packs** (there are eight foot sections in some stores!), **refrigerated bagels and biscuits, microwave hash browns and shredded potatoes**, KraftHeinz's Just Add an Egg etc. What a neat and….customer-first section! Watch this section, as ready to eat packs are showing up all over the store. Included in this area would be **canned RTD coffee**. It's showing up in almost all refrigerated sections and deserves a seat at the table.

Two more hot, hot, hot sections: coffee creamers and RTD coffees. These things are on fire! You can get a **coffee creamer** in any flavor, and co-brand combination, any base (milk, cream, oat, soy, plant), and can come back next week and find ten more new items! Americans cannot get enough of coffee creamer. Add to that, **Ready to Drink Coffee**. Stok, Colombe, Califia, Chobani, everyone is in the RTD coffee game! It's a fun category to watch and shows just how much this world loves coffee.

The refrigerated category is an interesting one and demands the need to flex in and out of categories as they trend up and down. One way to add flexibility is to make a **cheese section** in a *separate area of your store*. Combining the cheese you'd normally find in the refrigerated section with the cheese you find in the deli section, and the cheese you find in the meat department, may come across as a robust and bountiful "cheese world", and allow you to cut some cheese redundancies at the same time.

# *Frozen*

Let's talk about **frozen**. Almost everything in the freezer is a replication of something you can find elsewhere in the store, so the frozen section reflects the same trends as the rest of the store. What holds true for *shelf-stable* desserts, holds true for *frozen* desserts. What holds true for *shelf-stable* juice, holds true for *frozen* juice. You get it.

Frozen is having a moment! As shoppers are considering how to feed their family with wholesome foods, throw away less spoiled foods, and offer a variety of dishes that make life exciting, *frozen foods are right there with them*!

Let's talk about the two major categories that are the most popular in the frozen food section: **pizza and ice cream**! Yeah! Say pizza and ice cream, and you've got a party! Let's talk about pizza first. Pizza has been, and remains, an all-around everlastingly popular food, snack, breakfast, hangover remedy. You name it. **Pizza rocks!**

On this one, the big challenge is to make sure customers buy enough to *always have some on hand*. If they don't have it on hand when the pizza monster rears its big purple head? Yup, they order it from that big bad delivery spot that takes $3 worth of ingredients, cooks it for you in eight minutes, and charges you $12, a service charge, delivery charge, and driver tip! Or they make it a little bigger, pair it with a Coke and some wings, and ding you for $50. And why do we do it? *Because everyone loves the pizza person!*

Make sure you constantly have stock-up sales on pizza, so it's in the freezer when the customers want it. Plus, you know what I'm going to say....make sure you are in business on the healthy brands or versions, like **Amy's Organic Pizzas, Newman's Own**, thin-sliced, clean ingredients, etc. It's a trend. You're not trying to alienate places like Domino's, but a frozen pizza is the ultimate fun food for all occasions. I cannot see where pizza will ever die in popularity. Just not going to happen. *Not as long as I'm around!*

What about **ice cream**? We offer every form and flavor of ice cream possible, and volume keeps growing! Sure, we might look at healthier versions occasionally, but you don't eat ice cream as a health food. *It's indulgent, it's fun, it's a kid favorite, it's an adult favorite!*

Big buckets of ice cream for parties, little containers for when you break up, imported products for "high end" nights, regular containers for after dinner, novelties to have around during the summer, it's all there. Everyone knows ice cream is mostly unhealthy and they don't care. If you want to be healthy, don't eat it. One thing to keep in mind- ***"If you're out of vanilla, you're out of ice cream!"***- keep vanilla in stock. Make sure vanilla has plenty of room!

The other trends in frozen food? The **frozen berry** section took off at the same time as the slushie blender craze took off, so that was a nice bump in sales. For the most part, frozen berries still maintain their healthy goodness and are an excellent healthy choice, and sales are still strong.

**Appetizers**, sure they have a nice niche around the holidays, but most people see them as a salt-laden junk food. Well, except **pizza rolls**....pizza rolls! The popularity of pizza lives in appetizers. Anything handheld and pizza-related is popular. Pizza rolls will live forever!

**Frozen vegetables** are on a tear! First, have you ever tried to push a peapod out of a fresh pea? Yeah, it kind of sucks as an activity, and *peas are so good for you*! Enter the frozen pea! Now, translate that scenario to broccoli, corn, etc. and you can see why frozen vegetables are having a fun time! Make sure you have a mix of "cook in bag" and larger bags that are apportioned as you are cooking. They both have a place in the customer's freezer.

The rest of the sections that could make up a meal, including **fish sticks, fish fillets, frozen breaded chicken and chicken sandwiches, pierogies, frozen waffles and biscuits, plant-based frozen products**, etc.? Remember, the trends in *non-frozen* reflect the trends in *frozen*. Salty frozen chicken is now being replaced by *natural, antibiotic free*, chicken. Egg biscuits are now partnering with plant-based biscuits. It's all there, and it's all customer-focused!

Let's talk **de-sku'ing** of healthy lines. Not getting rid of them, but de-sku'ing. Certainly, the brands will tell you differently, but the customers have their own way of choosing switchability versus walkability (if you're out of an item, will you switch or walk (leave)). We have entire aisles of quite similar healthy brands, and there is always pressure on assortment in frozen. This is the area I'd look to first.

One key area in frozen is showing how you waste so much less food when you buy frozen, <u>and</u> add variety to your life at the same time. Buying a fresh fish fillet or fresh berries means you have started your countdown clock towards spoiling. You don't use it, it goes in the trash or compost. For frozen, that problem is solved for you. *The more we can get the message out about the sustainability of frozen foods, the more we can help the customers.*

# *Alcohol*

For the next three sections, we're going to talk **alcohol**. I'm giving each of the "traditional" sections their own spot; but, if you're in this business, you know *it's all merging in the eyes of the consumer*. The most interesting part of the store right now is watching what's going on with alcohol.

This book is sold all over the country, so I must note many of you *cannot sell* **all three types of alcohol** in your stores. We have federal, state, and county laws in the United States about only being able to choose one alcohol (usually beer), being able to sell two (beer and wine), all three (beer, wine, spirits), beer and wine (but only wine under 14% abv (yes, it's a law), being able to sell it all 24 hours of every day, being able to sell it on every day except Sunday, being able to sell it only after noon on Sunday, etc. Being an alcohol buyer for a retailer is a testament to how many rules you can memorize about all your operating areas.

Then, you have the mandated three-tier distribution system, and cannot sell directly. Or can you? Sometimes you can go to a retailer, sometimes you can't. *Let's talk about some of the trends going on in alcohol.*

**Blending of barriers.** The first trend is the blurring of the three "types", for the consumer. What were previously clear and distinct differences between the types of alcohol have been blurred to an almost indiscernible point. Is it a **hard seltzer** or a **wine spritzer**? Is it a ready to drink **Moscow Mule** or a **Mule flavored malt beverage**? Why is the 4-pack of **Ketel One** cans $11.99 and the 12-pack of **High Noon** also $11.99? We're confusing the heck out of consumers! But, to defend the industry, *everyone is in everyone's shorts*; so, what are you supposed to do? You can't sit there and let someone take your business!

The best thing about the blending of the barriers is **everyone is trying everything**. The *trial and experiment* feel that was brought on by craft beer is now all over the alcohol section! It's a great time to be in alcohol, for both consumers and for the companies diversified enough to operate in all areas of alcohol.

**Flavor is a barrier breaker.** When you add flavors to traditionally unflavored items, it makes them more accessible. That's not such a bad thing, unless you only operate in one arena. Alcohol is expandable consumable, so you're always looking to make one more sale.

**Trial is everywhere.** As I just mentioned, everyone is trying everything. Especially in spirits, where mixing a drink might have been difficult to master, or maybe you didn't want 750ml of that spirit sitting around for months, or you wanted to go on a boat and not bring a massive bottle of **Deep Eddy**. Flavors have made everything approachable.

It's a **double-edged sword**. Trial and lower *barriers to trial* also translate into difficult to obtain brand loyalty. It's fun, right? Put odd combinations and mixes out there and they keep selling. Then, as soon as you ramp up production, the customers *move on and try something else*. The term used lately to describe customer behavior in alcohol has been **brand promiscuity**. They move around and are loyal to very few brands.

What about the **non-alcohol trend**? Well, I don't know. Mocktails are cool, and NA items are necessary, but I wouldn't jump headfirst into this trend. Carry it, acknowledge it, and move on. Alcohol without alcohol is juice.

Where is the next source of growth in this industry?  At this point, we've flavorized everything, mixed all sorts of various concoctions, had significant trial of everything, and now the market is flooded with products.  There needs to be some falling out of brands, or there will be some massive deflation, whether in regular retail prices or being able to only sell product on promotion.  Keep these over-arching themes in mind as we head into discussing beer, wine, and spirits.

# *Refrigerated RTD*

It used to be quite simple, **beer** is sold refrigerated and non-refrigerated, and all the other alcohols stayed in their own spot. Except for some chilled white wines, everything in the refrigerated alcohol section was malt-based. Fast forward to today, and the case is roughly 10% refrigerated wine-based or non-vodka drinks, then 25% are vodka-based drinks, then 20% flavored malt beverage (seltzers), then 40% beer products.

One solution could be to continue expanding <u>refrigeration</u> in alcohol. Another solution is to start de-SKU'ing items that have no differentiation. The solution is possibly a *mix of both*. Even if beer has tapered off a bit, the refrigerated alcohol section is still one of the most popular sections in the stores. The variety needs to be curated, though, to maximize your connection with the customers. And what do customers want in this section? Everything.

They want *variety.*

They want *treasure hunt.*

They practice *brand promiscuity.*

They want *healthy.*

They want *taste.*

They want convenience of *cans.*

They want taste of *bottles.*

They want *pre-mixed* spirits and soda.

They want *everything* from this section!

First, stop calling it the beer section. Seltzers and spritzers and ready to drink spirits have blurred the lines. Call it the **refrigerated alcohol** section. The switchability is high here. *If you're out of what I want, I'll just try something else.* As you can imagine, being in-stock is a *big deal.* Planogram placement and spacing is paramount to a successful brand in alcohol, and right now *all brands are fighting for the refrigerated space.* Ready to drink means….**ready to drink!** No one wants to wait for their new vodka soda to chill down. I'm. Ready. Now!

We need to talk about **craft beer** first. Cool names, local appeal, limited time only, in and out seasonality- *craft beer has it all.* Craft should be roughly 40% of your beer space allocation. It needs to be cold and ready for consumption, full of variety and offer a multitude of "in and out" seasonal items. If you are carrying items for variety, and they don't sell as quickly as other items, those are the ones to keep on the non-refrigerated shelf. Refrigerated items need to be "paying the rent", as that's the most valuable space in the section.

The most visible trend has been the **lowering of alcohol by volume (abv)**. I know what you're saying, *give you the high test 11% and let you roam free!* Not always. You need a mix. Where everything previously was heading to high abv, we're seeing some settling. And, to put it in perspective (so you don't think I'm crazy), I'm talking 4.5% abv. If you can think back to when the "ice beers" came out, they were hovering around 4.5%, and were touted as *high alcohol content*. We've come a long way since then!

The beer types that put craft on the map have been **India Pale Ales** (or IPA's), and double IPA's and American Pale Ales (APA's). *They connected.* Sometimes, something just connects, and those styles did. IPA's are significantly slowing down, and the abv's are taking a turn down to something a little more handleable. We have the "juice bomb", or New England IPA, or hazy IPA's, or even unfiltered, and anything with fruit added. You put a bunch of hops in a drink, and then work your tail off to infuse the hops with citrusy flavors. Inside the fruit genre, we have sours, wheats with fruit, etc. *This area is really slowing down in sales!*

It needs to be noted, brewmasters have been saying this for years: an IPA is one of the *least refined* ways of making beer. The massive amount of hops and alcohol can be used to cover up impurities. To a brewmaster, a perfectly brewed lager or pilsner, with reasonable alcohol content, is how you prove your craftmanship.

One of the trendiest areas in beer now is the return of **imports** and certain **domestic mainstream** beers, primarily Modelo, Corona, Pacifico, Heineken, and even Miller Genuine Draft. Yup, MGD is back! Enjoy the high life! Of all of them, Modelo has rocketed to number one!! *An absolute monster of a beer.*

Quick review: most beers are either **lagers or ales**. Lagers are produced with yeast that ferments at the *bottom* of the barrel, and ales are produced with yeast that ferments at the *top* of the barrel.

**Top fermenting ales** are a bit less sensitive, more tolerant of alcohol, and brew at a higher temperature. **Stouts, wheat beers, and IPA's** are made with top fermenting. In ales, you find *American amber ales, American pale ales, American IPA's, Imperial IPA's (or double IPA's),* etc.

**Bottom fermenting lagers** are more fragile and need to ferment at a slower pace. A lager is how you show you know how to brew beer. Most **Oktoberfest** beers are lagers, same with **bocks**, and **pilsners**. Pilsner is a type of lager with a different yeast used and with hops added to it, making it hop forward. In lagers, you find *American lagers, German Helles, all pilsners, amber beers, the various bocks (doppelbock, weizenbock, maibock),* etc.

Don't forget to pay homage to the great low bitterness **Belgian beers** that put beer on the map, the super wheat beers, the beautiful porters, etc. Then, you have all the various beers with chocolate added, coffee added, fruit added, bacteria added (good bacteria), aged in wine or bourbon barrels, etc. *There is so much history in beer.*

Just remember, the craft beer customer is a *fickle and experimental* customer. They like to buy beer by the *type* they drink and not necessarily by the *brand*, so keep that in mind in your assortment. As soon as they like a brand, they move to another brand. Keep assortment moving in and out, so the experimenters can move around and try new things. Oh, and craft beer drinkers love *samples, events, meeting the brewers, beer shows,* etc. Be involved where these drinkers are, and you win.

And if you were wondering, *Budweiser and Coors are American lagers, Miller Lite is a pilsner, Yuengling and Sam Adams are lagers, Shiner is a bock lager (bock is German for ram, if you wanted to know why there's a ram on the label), Dos Equis is an amber lager, Pliny the Elder is an Imperial IPA, Blue Moon is a wheat beer, and on and on.* Sometimes, walk the beer section and read the labels, it's interesting the creativity and alchemy that comes from brewmasters.

Now what? Well, we've gone crazy in two areas: **healthy and spiked "anything"**, including *seltzers and spiked teas and lemonades.* For health, once customers saw how many calories were in IPA's (some were up to 300 calories), there's been a move towards the "under 100 calories and 2.5 carbs) alternatives. *This segment just took off!* Everyone got in the game! Corona Light and then Premiere, Michelob Light then Ultra then Premier, etc. A new sub-segment was born, and it's still going.

As this healthy segment was bumping up against the need to ensure females could feel as bonded to beer as males, the **hard seltzers** hit the market and took off. **White Claw** and **Truly** were market leaders. **Mike's Hard** was there before them both, and now has re-invented itself after this craze took off! Today, we have **spiked everything!** Not to be outdone, we have the traditional domestic beers in the game: **Bud Light Seltzer, Natty Seltzer**, and on and on. This has truly become a cluttered section of alcoholic options! You can summarize all of the above mentioned as **flavored malt beverages (FMB's)**, as they are made by adding flavors to a malt base (same base as beer).

And, as we mentioned earlier, ready to drink spirits and ready to drink wine spritzers (like seltzers, but made with actual wine) deserve their spot in the cold case, so make sure the spacing reflects the....*customer demand.*

You can see all brands expanding into **vodka-based drinks**, including vodka in 750ml from both White Claw and Truly. The seltzer trend may be down, but the expansion of drinking options is not! Look for RTD gin to be trending this year.

The malt beverage section is due for some fallout, as a crowded section, after a while, becomes just too much. Too many choices usually equate to **brain freeze** by customers, then they head towards simplification. Some reduction in assortment, some clarity in malt-based beverages, spirits-based, and wine-based would be good here. *Customers like simplicity.*

# *Wine*

Other than playing in the ready to drink trend, **wine** is having a *tough time keeping customers locked in*! It's a super section, with a ton of loyalty to drinking a glass (or two or a bottle) a night, but this category needs to find a way to appeal to the next generation. A point of interest, the next generation of consumers is the *first generation that will consume more THC than alcohol.* Yes, read that one again. The next generation becoming "of age" is the first generation that will **opt for a cannabis product over an alcohol product**. And the first category being knocked out is wine.

So, yes, some re-invention is necessary here! Lock in on the **4-pack spritzer** business first. A *wine-based* 4-pack is more expensive than a *malt-based* one, but price is still a secondary concern. Make it fun and exciting, and it'll gain the attraction of the younger generation. And, yes, *you're going to need to add flavors*. I know, a winemaker will faint when reading that line. Sorry, in this book we're....*customer-focused*. The next generation wants flavor forward beverages.

**Rosé** was a super start! Yes, I know it's been going on for years, but it showed some spunk and some excitement. Keep it going. Like white zinfandel and sangria decided to have a child. Add some rosé's with fruit in them, and make them stronger than sangria. We'll need a combination of flavor, energy and excitement, but still have an abv over 13.5%. **Flavor** is winning today. Expand on flavor and **sweetness**. Blame it on the flavor trend, if you'd like, but sweet wines are trending quite well.

**Package.** Yes, *package type* is a consideration by a consumer. Besides the 4-packs mentioned, there is *high acceptance* of **boxed wines**, canned wines, and handheld little boxed wines. This trend, reflecting the improved quality of the wine in this type of packaging, the convenience of having wine available on the go, and the freshness of having individual cans, has spurred a major real estate expansion in the category.

Not only should the section of canned and boxed wines be more elaborate than in previous years, but there needs to be a refrigerated component for the white and rosé offerings- not all of them, but a good selection. This is also where you would place the wine spritzers in 4-packs that are made with real wine.

**Handheld boxes!** What a convenient little item to carry with you. And, it's resealable. That's the issue sometimes when we're so focused on what *we* know, we rarely ask the customer what *they* want us to know. A handheld little box of wine, where you can put the cap back on, is a great little item! Play it up!

**Wine varietals** haven't changed much in years, neither has the merchandising of wine. When the wine is *inexpensive* (say, less than $15 for a 750ml), consumers appreciate the value of a *familiar brand*; so, we place all the brands together. A consumer can safely move within the brand with confidence.

As the wine drinker develops a palate for more *expensive* bottles (> $15 for a 750ml), they turn into more of a treasure hunt customer within their *favorite varietals* (sauvignon blanc, pinot grigio, chardonnay in whites and pinot noir, merlot, cabernet sauvignon, red zinfandel, grenache, syrah in reds (plus some variations and blends in both)). So, we focus more on a varietal set and move labels in and out.

If you choked on your grape when **flavor** was mentioned, then hopefully you cleared your throat by now. A *customer-focused* company looks at trends and talks with customers about what *they* want. Right now, the customer wants fun, flavor, convenience, and a little bit of zippiness to their drinking experience. Somewhere there is a gin or vodka master distiller who sat back and thought *"hey, no way will I add flavors to my product! There's no way I will go down that road. I'm a purist!"*.

You know what that person is doing today? *I don't either.* Customers have a funny way of asking you to come along. They're going a certain direction no matter what, you can come along or watch the caboose as it fades into the sunset.

# *Spirits*

As the last of the three major types of alcohol, **spirits** have done a fantastic job re-inventing themselves! Honestly, this category had been left in the boneyard with the armadillos and tumbleweed. No longer the "old person pouring scotch at 5:00 before going to bed at 7:00" category, we now have *vibrant colors, flavors, small batches, large batches, hot locations, and a slew of new ready to drink options.* Like the phoenix, spirits have come back to life! Let's talk about a few areas.

**Vodka and Gin.** Good ole vodka and gin. Like the siblings that grow up and are "same, but different". Both are fermented, then distilled. Both can be made with potatoes, rye, corn, even grapes and carrots. It's the flavor and the *water* setting them apart. In *gin's* case, you then add juniper and flavors. In *vodka's* case, you're trying for the neutral template, so it can be used as a mixer with whatever flavor you choose. Once distilled multiple times, you add water back in to bring the abv to 40%. *Water quality becomes the distinguishing factor in the tastes.*

Some spirits, like vodka, were *already trending up.* Vodka has a slew of new botanical-infused offers, but then also has the "Tito's effect", where Tito's became ubiquitous in recent years, then Deep Eddy, and on and on. This is where vodka and gin separate on the railroad tracks. **Vodka** seems to have the upper-hand in uniqueness and innovation, as well as playing up location-specific differences. Remember, this isn't like a grape that must be grown in a region, *you can make vodka and gin anywhere*; so, it's all in the marketing. Tell your story better, and you win. Tito's uses corn from Indiana, they just don't talk about it. The message of "handmade in Texas" is what works. Defining "handmade" is like defining bottled water's "bottled at the source". What does that really mean?

The additional trend here is in the **mixers**, especially **ginger beer**. Holy cow, ginger beer has exploded in popularity! It seems everyone is making some sort of Moscow Mule, and might not even know it. Make a section with **ginger beer, lime juice, triple sec, soda water, alcohol-infused olives**, etc. This is a fun addition to the category and elicits the alchemist in all of us. And it's ginger, it must be healthy!

**Whiskey!** Adding to the vodka trend is whiskey. Or should I say "whisky"? Whiskey (and whisky) are on fire, both figuratively and literally! Yes, adding *cinnamon* to whiskey is hot, and it started with **Fireball** (whisky). **Jack Daniels** (whiskey, *or is it Kentucky Bourbon*) didn't want to miss the craze, so there's Jack Fire (plus honey, apple, etc.). What a fun category! Flavors, single batch, single barrel, multi barrel, etc. This category has everything going for it. *Fuel the fire* in whiskey.

Closely related, **bourbon** is also rising, but is still partially seen as an "older person" drink, so some re-invention needs to happen here. The issue with bourbon is the good stuff costs *so darn much.* The price makes it either inaccessible to a large portion of the population, or too risky to try at that price. Put **scotch** in this slot, too. Tell me the last time you heard any young person ask for a scotch? I'll wait.

**Tequila and mezcal.** Another "same, but different" pair of siblings. Both come from the core of the *agave plant*, but tequila is produced by steaming the agave in *industrial ovens*, while mezcal is traditionally cooked in *earthen pits*- although it's difficult to produce a lot of product by earthen pit cooking, so this is becoming more industrialized. *Tequila* has three types (blanco, reposado, and anejo), which represent length of aging time. *Mezcal* took the same route, except uses joven in place of blanco. Both, though, have a reputation for low calories and are seen as "healthy". They're a healthier choice *in alcohol*, maybe not necessarily healthy. **Honestly, the healthiest alcohol is still red wine, if pesticides aren't coming along for the ride.**

As we discussed earlier, **ready to drink (RTD) spirits** are where it's at! These days, you can find any mixture of spirits already mixed in a can and ready to drink (thus, the name). And it's highly appealing to customers to see these high abv RTD spirits sitting in <u>refrigeration</u>. Being able to drink a **Moscow Mule** or a **lemon vodka**, without needing to bring out the bottle of vodka, lime juice, lemon juice, ginger beer, etc. is a time utility provided by RTD's. Keep focusing on this segment, and the customer will continue rewarding you with sales.

We do not see alcohol trending down any time soon. In fact, the biggest trend that could hurt alcohol sales? **THC legalization**. As we discussed, legalizing marijuana has shown an impact on alcohol sales, primarily due to the younger generation of consumers finding THC as a viable choice for relaxation. Just something to watch.

Overall, *alcohol is on a tear!* Keep up with, and stay ahead of, the customers! They're fickle, treasure-hunt oriented, and are showing signs of continuing the upward trend for the foreseeable future.

# *Center Store*

We've been walking the perimeter of the store, and now let's head to the center of the store. We usually call this area the....**center store** (we're simple folk here!). For overall image of freshness and abundance, the fresh departments we just covered are the drivers. For overall reputation of *assortment and fulfilling the needs of every shopper* to feed themselves and/or their families, center store is the center of attention.

All areas of the store feed off each other, so to speak. Where a store that sold only meat and produce would be fun to stop by *occasionally*, it wouldn't fulfill all your needs. Vice versa, a center store without super fresh departments, also will not fulfill all your needs. It's why you go to the farmers market and walk around, but *still need to go shopping for "regular" food later.*

There are a few overall keys here that apply to the entire center store. Understand the **traffic flow** (which way the customers normally traverse your store) and ensure you have an opinion on traffic flow and adjacencies by category. In general, though, your *upsell* and *higher margin rate* items should be eye level and first in traffic flow. The higher volume items should be on the bottom shelf for inventory holding power, where you'll have a better chance of being in stock throughout the day. The **higher volume items**, since they need to be competitively priced (and less margin rate), aren't necessarily the first items you want a customer to consider. They'll find the ketchup on their list; they won't always find the locally made special sauce- let them see the unique item first.

You should try to consider the **consumer decision tree** (CDT) for each category, as in which decision is most important to most of the customers (price? brand? flavor?), then second decision, and so on. For example, coffee, most customers know the form they want first (Keurig machines versus other coffee machines, or wanting whole beans, etc.), then decaf or caffeinated, then flavor. As they scan the shelf, you can make it easier for them to find what they want if you attempt to follow *their decision-making process*. The CDT is one of the most important aspects of relating your shelving and assortment to the customer's expectation.

As always, remember customer first and you'll be okay. Let's go up and down the aisles.

One point here, I'm going to focus on *trends*, and break them up by **beverages** and **food**. Not all categories have changed much in the last few years, where other categories have had an *unbelievable amount of change*. All of it customer driven. That's where we'll focus. You don't need a book to tell you to put syrup next to pancake mix. Hopefully.

# *Beverages*

We're going to start in the **beverage aisle**. The beverage aisle has exploded into "everything in liquid form" over the last few years. There is no end in sight. Of course, you still need **carbonated soft drinks**. They're not on a positive trend, but they're not going away either. The shelving of Coke and Pepsi and all their usual line-up of diet and yellow (Mountain Dew) and green (Sprite) and everything in between makes sense, and the customers expect it to be organized in this manner. The little cans, the Coke from Mexico with real sugar, etc. are all part of the normal offer.

One magical item is the *24-pack cube of soft drinks*. As a rule, I'd suggest you always keep cubes of soft drinks on the sales floor. They are magical. Even when two 12-packs would be cheaper, customers *still buy the cubes*. Not sure why, but whatever makes them happy.

Where beverages *have* split off, though, is in the **everything else** category, which includes….everything else. You need to take control of this explosion of products and help the customer make some sense of it all. And, to make it even more complicated you have "real" and "fake" products. You have real tea, like from **Ito En**, and you have sugary tea from **Arnold Palmer**. Then, you have "energy" drinks like **Red Bull** and you have "energy plus" drinks like **Monster** or **Bang** or any of those power sounding drinks.

And what do you do with **Celsius, Bubly, Zevia, Bubbl'r, Bai**, etc.? These are alternatively tea-based, water-based, guarana filled, juice-based drinks that tout their DBA's (distinctive brand attributes) as healthy and/or effective.

In case you were starting to make sense of it all, many of these products are great for **instant consumption** (so they need refrigeration) and many are for **stock-up** at home. What do you do with all this confusion? The jury is still out, especially when you have mass confusion, like **Starbuck's** brand on items that *look like* coffee and items like **Super Coffee** that *are* actual coffee sweetened with MCT oil. The best suggestion is let it play out for a while. Stick with the "Red Bull-like" products near the Coke and Pepsi, and try to make some organization between **fruit drinks, superberry drinks, real tea drinks, sugar drinks**, and oh yeah….**bottled water**.

**Water** needs to be near these other drinks, but it has multiple uses that must be acknowledged. Some cities simply have bad water. In those areas, a 24-pack of single-use bottled water is not the solution. You need larger packs, and larger sizes in those packs, including a water machine. In other areas, like resort areas or anywhere in the south, you have heavy consumption of bottled water for individual hydration. No one said this was going to be easy, did they?

*What's new in this aisle, though?* Here's a question for you, what's **Pedialyte** used for? If you answered something about babies, you're only partially correct. Go to Walgreens in Las Vegas and look at the endcaps of Pedialyte. Now, look around at all the babies….*there aren't any*. Re-purposing electrolyte drinks as a *hangover cure* is one of the more brilliant re-branding initiatives of the last few years. And now **Gatorade** (including **Gatorlyte**) has introduced new products, mainly because they were first on the electrolyte market, and need to protect their turf! There are so many versions of Gatorade available in the store, including caffeine enhanced

Fast Twitch and Gatorade Water (next to Propel, also by Gatorade).

A suggestion, a radical suggestion....either *move the Pedialyte products into the beverage aisle*, or at least place them in both Health and Beauty Care (HBC) *and* the beverage aisle. Or, place them near the alcohol section. Remember, customer-focus first. Like red Solo cups and ping pong balls in the alcohol section. There's no need to act like we don't know what customers are doing.

**Coffee** is trending like crazy, in all areas: ready to drink, drink in store, drive-through, make at home, frozen drinks, even added to beer. If you want to make an impact in a category, this one is a sure bet to reward your efforts. Like pizza, there is always demand for coffee, you just need to *take the customers from someone else*. Plus, also like pizza, customers have shown an amazing ability to consume everything you put in front of them. People see a Starbuck's and they start to salivate (for real), **so why not offer coffee bars in the stores, and go big**?

Make *coffee and tea bars*, stock your coffee and tea aisle adjacent to the coffee and tea bar, give some outside or inside seating, make sure your wi-fi is strong, *really play this up*! And, if you can locate the coffee and tea bar near the perimeter of the store, then you can offer drive-through and pick-up. The coffee trend shows no signs of slowing. And if you don't have room, try **coffee kiosks** in your parking lot. You have got to make sure you capture as much coffee business as possible.

Speaking of **tea**, the same trends in coffee are even stronger in tea. *Ready to drink, make at home, experimental, trial*, they are all showing solid trends. Yup, another healthy item on fire. The variety seems to have no end. Think of how informed the customers are today. Most people previously only knew black tea. Now, they look for green, white, chai green, matcha, chai white, orange, Pu-erh, and on and on. Keep a special eye on anything with **lemon and ginger**. They are rocking flavors right now!

**How do you organize all this?** If you step back and look at all the non-alcoholic beverages in the store, you can come to some sort of categorization, in the sense you have **soft drinks and energy drinks**- with a blurry line between them (made even more blurry with Coke Energy); then you have juice-based drinks- which may or may not be related to superberries; then you have **coffee and tea**-based drinks- which may or may not contain coffee or tea; then you have the other varieties- like **aloe drinks**; then you have the **fermented drinks**- like kombucha; and you have the **meal substitute** drinks- like Carnation Breakfast and Ensure; and you have **drinkable yogurt and kefir**; then you have drinks that *caffeinate* you to the sky and drinks that put you to *sleep*. It keeps expanding exponentially. At least acknowledge drinks have some sort of "base" ingredient, so you can help the customer make decisions.

The customers are showing they love beverages, so don't back off. Customers shift preferences constantly, look at how much cranberry and grape juice has *shrunk* the last five years, but the space for beverages has *expanded*. This is like squeezing a balloon. As one area declines in popularity, another expands. The point is, customers lead the way, and we're here to take care of them.

# *Center Store Food*

We'll talk about a selection of the center store **food** areas. Like I said at the beginning, the focus will be more on *trendy* areas, and less on categories that are stable. Technically, this section is anything in the center store you *don't drink*.

Okay, here's a question for you? **Where's the bar?** No, not that one. Where do you find **protein bars**? Where do you find **meal replacement bars**? What if you want **Rx Bars**? What about **Atkins**? The answer to all these questions remains....*I have no idea*. Yes, we have totally confused the customer on this one. You can find Quest, Pure Protein, Atkins, WW, etc. in the *HBC aisle*. You can find Rx Bars, Luna, Kind, etc. in the *center store*. And what about the OG granola bars? Are they candy or protein? And what to do with Belvita? Been asking that for years!

I'd suggest the customer would appreciate **one spot with all bars**. Stop letting how you *procure* the product dictate where you *shelve* the product. Unless you have a dietitian on staff who will evaluate every bar you offer in the store and categorize by health benefits, the best bet is to let the customers decide. **But!** But, *put them all in one spot*. And, make sure you offer a competitive value on multi-packs.

Here's a secret, the customer isn't telling you they're confused. *They're just going somewhere else.* Try typing in pureprotein.com, and you'll see some great offers for multi-packs; plus, reduced prices on continuous *subscriptions* of product. Every customer who signs up for a subscription directly from the manufacturer is gone from your store. *Forever.* When it comes to protecting your turf, the only choice is to come out swinging!

**Snacking packs.** Like bar proliferation, snacking packs are *everywhere*. I'm purposely calling them *snacking packs*, not *snack packs*. I want to reflect the broader purpose of these packs. As opposed to protein bars, I'm not suggesting these should be combined, solely suggesting they be *acknowledged as a trend*. There are snacking packs in refrigerated, as we already discussed; but there are also snacking packs in the snack section, packs in the jerky section, snacking packs in cereal, snacking packs in breakfast, etc. Just monitor them, and make sure to understand where the customer is going.

To add to snacking packs, let's talk about traditional **snacks**. I'm going to combine **salty snacks** and **cookies and crackers** and include **jerky**. The primary utility provided by all these items is to snack, *right*? And switchability? It's high amongst sub-categories. You cannot substitute an **Oreo** for a **Tostito**, but you could potentially substitute a **Chips Ahoy** for an Oreo, or a different corn salty item for a Tostito.

Let's add **multi-packs** to the trend, as we discussed earlier. In fact, multi-packs of snack packs are where it started, before multi-packs took off everywhere! Join the multi-pack revolution.

Once again, if you look at these categories from the customer's perspective, you have categories that can be organized in a few different ways: **salty snacks**, with corn tortilla base or potato base or cheese base; then **pretzels**, with a million different ways to form a pretzel; then the **vegetable-based** products, which may or may not contain vegetables; and then those perfectly shaped potato products called **Pringle's** (and Lay's Stax). Watch for **chicken skins** to join **pork skins** in this section.

Then, on the cookie and cracker side, you have the thousand different ways to make a **chocolate chip cookie**, then the **Nilla Wafer** section, then the various types of **crackers**- some (like graham) to be eaten straight, and some to be used as carriers of cheese, spreads, or whatever you can place on them. A Ritz can do both.

Then there's the hot one- **jerky**. Oh boy, everything is in jerky form now! *Salmon, beef, turkey, buffalo, mushrooms, pork, plant-based*, etc. Everything can be "jerkied", and it's all selling. The *inflation tip* here is jerky tends to be expensive. Smaller packs of jerky can help the customers. The convenience of an item that doesn't need refrigeration, can last forever (figuratively) is what's making it attractive to consumers. Take care of this section and continue to expand the space.

Look for **sea floss, kelp, seaweed, yuzu, and ube** flavors to trend in the snacking section this year.

For snacking, *think like a customer*, and understand your definition of brand loyalty may not equate to the customer's definition of utility and value provided by snacks. Focus on being in-stock, then allow for a "better for you" section of organics, plant-based, etc. Humans will always snack. It happens. Be there for them and offer a large variety.

One other area exploding is the **snacking nuts** section. There are so many ways to package a nut, and a ton of different levels of roasting and salting them, and there seems to be a customer for *every level and every mixture*. Almost every customer is trained to look for the nuts they are searching for in the snack section first; then, if they cannot find them, they go to the baking nuts section to look for them. It's possible we could eliminate some confusion by having a "nut world" somewhere in between the snacking aisle and the baking aisle. One hot trend are the **shelled pistachios**. What was previously a fun thing to do, shell each pistachio, is now a pain in the arse. Along come shelled pistachios. They really are hot! In the nuts section, I'd suggest trying packs of nuts mixed with pretzels, buts mixed with melba toast, etc. If this takes off, and it probably will, then you'll want to combine these items with the assortment in the Chex Mix aisle. Let this take off, and here are your incremental sales for you. Make them in your store brand, and have some fun!

While we're in a snacking mood, let's talk **chocolate and candy**. Think of these as two separate areas, and two distinct customers. On one hand, you have the "normal" candy sections of **peanut-based, non-peanut, chocolate-enrobed everything, non-chocolate**, etc. This area shows innovation by using the same known name brand item and adding new spring flavors, fall flavors, etc. Hey, why not? You know **M&M's**, so why not try caramel M&M's? And **Reese's**, oh my goodness! The candy section is almost all "Reese's orange" these days! Also, why not? *How can you not love Reese's?* I'd pick Reese's for breakfast and lunch, with pizza for dinner. *The perfect day.*

In addition, you have the explosion of **dark chocolate** as a healthy item in most diets. And, because it's attracted a health-oriented crowd, you have a gushing fountain of *organic, free trade, various levels of cacao, varying levels of sweet and bitter, addition of all types of fruit flavors, and then various forms*. You have the traditional bars, like **Lily's** and **Justin's**, you have the on-the-go snack bags, like **Brookfield,** and then any variety you can think of **enrobing a nut with a chocolate**. Give me dark chocolate raspberry covered almonds any day of the week!

All snack and candy items are *expandable consumable*, as in "the more you have at home, the more you consume". It's going to be difficult to corral and channel the growth in innovation and variety in candy and chocolate, but improved organization to the sets would make sense, and help the customers make decisions.

Now that we've had our dessert first, let's talk about the meal. *Affordable eating and stretching meals* are the top actions in inflationary times, and the center store is perfectly situated. Let's talk **pasta, noodles, ramen, rice**, etc. You may think it sounds like Depression Era eating, because it kind of is, you know? When you're tight on money in inflationary times, or a college student, *ramen and pasta are your best friend!*

If there are any items that stretch a budget, it's a **carb** that can feed many people. Think of most meals in this world, they consist of putting some type of protein in/on/or surrounded by a carb. It's the way the world works. Not suggesting anything new for this section except keep it in-stock and keep trying new things. New **soba or udon** noodles from Japan, **bronze cut pasta** from Italy, **sweet potato pasta**, even higher quality **ramen** than the college-staple ramen, really anything you can do to help customers make it through inflation.

Speaking of inflation, **canned meats** are still hot. **Canned fish** had quite a trend as a clean way to introduce small fish with high omega-3's into your diet, like **mackerel and sardines**. Still some of the best fish for you, but the trend has leveled. And remember snacking packs, *tuna is still the leader in canned fish, when you consider snacking packs*. In the "other meat", well, you've got **SPAM**. SPAM enjoyed a nice resurgence the last few years, and it's not slowing down. It's SPAM. *A tradition like no other.* SPAM musubis are so much fun to try at home, it's worth it to talk them up in your stores.

**Baking!** Talk about a category left to die that came back to life in a big way! So many people renewed their joy, or discovered a new joy, for cooking and baking the last few years! As the chefs say, *"be creative while cooking, stick to the rules in baking"*. The rigidity of baking is appealing to people. The fact you must follow the directions is kind of relaxing. And when you get that *one perfect loaf of bread*? *Magic!* There are a few areas in this section that have seen the most impact- **yeast and flour, spices, healthy coatings, and nature-based sugar alternatives, like monkfruit and MCT oil.**

**Spices** are on fire! All of them. As part of the health and cooking kick, customers have realized that spices are *pretty darn good for you*. An informed customer is using **turmeric** for anti-inflammation, using **cloves** for digestion, using **cayenne** for metabolism, **cinnamon** for everything, **garlic** for vampires, etc. And the list goes on. The beauty of the spice category is there is *so much variety*. So, keep up with variety, keep up with health food sites, keep up with social media where people talk about how they cook, and this category is going to be on fire for a while!

There is also an intermix here between **spices and sauces**. Especially, as you might imagine, *sauces made with spices*. We've talked about **turmeric** several times, the star of the last few years. We also need to understand how Asian spices and broths play into what people are buying in this section. **Piri Piri sauce, Lao Gan Ma, Za'atar, sriracha, and gochujang** are seriously coming into their own in Western diets. And, while you're at it, don't forget all the various forms of **curry**, almost all including....turmeric.

And **broths**? Another area where baking and broths and cultures are combining beautifully. **Bone broth** is much more expensive than "regular" broths and is *significantly better* *for you*. Adding spices to bone broths is a way to seem like you are preparing a "homemade broth", but much easier. It, of course, brings up another question: where do you put the **sipping bone broths**? Sipping bone broth is a trend. The best place for the broths is to have them all together in the baking aisle, and adjacent to the soup aisle. The broth section is now almost 24 feet in most stores.

*What else is going on in center store?* How about everything **Truff**? Hot last year, dead this year. That's how trends go. You ride them while you can. Anything by **Momofuku** is hot. A testament to the power of a restaurant name, and how it pervades consumer goods on the shelf. **Fancy mustards** have had a comeback, led by anything with Dijon or whole grain and whole seed. **Prebiotic** and anything probiotic. Say *microbiome*, and you catch the attention of most shoppers. I'd say cauliflower pastas and crusts, but....*I just can't stand cauliflower*. I've yet to find anything made with cauliflower that tastes good....including cauliflower. If you're a cauliflower grower and are offended. *Sorry*. It's my book, and I have an opinion.

**Cereal**. This aisle is crazy. As I pick up my new Little Debbie Oatmeal Pie cereal, I'd have to wonder why we need all this assortment. Once again, if you look at it from the customer's point of view, you have **healthy** and **not healthy**, and in many forms and sizes. This is not to say innovation is bad. It *is* to say, though, we may not need five different sizes of Cheerios and eight different flavors. And, if you're going to get rid of either sizes or flavors, make it the sizes.

A radical idea, how about a **breakfast solution** area in the store, so all breakfast options can be explored by the customers? And, instead of a *cereal* CDT, how about a *breakfast* CDT? That way, a customer can pick and choose based upon their circumstances. As retailers and consumer packaged goods companies, you need to choose the customer first over what you might need for your current assortment. If in the end the customer does not want your current offering, develop (or buy) what they want.

For the most part, the large companies in this space have done an excellent job expanding into breakfast bars and other solutions- they just forgot to suggest which items in boxed cereal *need to be deleted*. That is why we do not have enough variety in healthy oatmeal, overnight oat prep areas, keto products, healthy pancake solutions. We need room. When one segment needs almost two sides of an entire aisle for its assortment, *it has too much assortment*. Customers want your help! When Aldi can carry forty cereal items and their stores are expanding like crazy, do you really think you need four to five hundred SKU's of cereal? And this is not to hurt the major manufacturers of cereal. In fact, it would help efficiencies if the volume could be pumped into fewer items.

And **Pop Tarts**! You know, there are *very few items* where no one has been able to put up a good fight against them, and you can count them on one hand: Gatorade, Pringles (yes, I like Stax, but still), Totino's pizza rolls, Dorito's, and Pop Tarts. *No one can touch Pop Tarts*. You have got to respect the power of Pop Tarts and ride any new trends they bring. You really have no choice.

How about **bread**? I'm not a big fan of the bread aisle being combined into the bakery, as some stores have done. Customers do not think that way, and you just confuse them. When you do have the bread aisle in the *regular aisles* of the store, you can have the same bountiful selection of types of breads, varying levels of healthiness, dinner rolls, tortillas, hamburger and hot dog buns, and even pita breads.

An area to look for here is ensuring the **healthy breads**, the ones that *are healthy*, have a prominent spot in the aisle. Make sure the ones called healthy, but still loaded with sugar, salt, and high fructose corn syrup, are in the traffic flow by the snack cakes. That's what they are. **Thin sliced, whole grain breads** are having their moment, and are sometimes squeezed out by the white breads. If you were to find a picture of the bread aisle ten or fifteen years ago, it would have been dominated by white bread. No longer!

And, yes, the age-old question of where to house the **peanut butter and jelly** should be answered here. Right here, next to their best friend- *bread*. PB&J as an adjacency to bread is expected by the customer. And, inside PB&J, keep in mind the need for *organics, natural, real peanut butter and jelly*. Peanut butter, especially, has been morphed and altered so many ways! *Sometimes actual peanuts are not even the top listed ingredient!* Bread, and its close friends PB&J and snack cakes, have a super connection in the eyes of the customer. They are family. Keep the family together.

There are new trends and food segments popping up continuously, like anything **keto, healthy popcorns, salts from around the world, immunity shots, restaurant pastas (think tagliatelle), anything microbiome, anything containing ginger and turmeric, and anything around health and immune system boosting**. Environmental scanning is the key to knowing where the customer is going and getting there ahead of them *and* ahead of the competition.

# *Nonfoods*

The **nonfoods** section of the center store has been the story of the last few years, due to the ability to *clean things*, or because the *supply chain couldn't keep up*. Other than that, we do have a few categories to discuss, but it'll be short.

     **Antibacterial wipes**. The story of the last few years. We seem to be back to normal in this area. In fact, it's seeming like "back to normal" means no one cleans anything anymore. Even the **Seventh Generation** product is selling again.

     **Paper Towels and Bath Tissue and Laundry Detergent.** Other than keeping them in stock and having a variety of one-ply all the way to four-ply, this category needs *organization*. But how? Who really knows? The different pricing and sizing and "sheets per roll" have made it an incredibly confusing category for customers to shop and compute value. Customers have adjusted and just trust that anything on display is a value. Not sure that's such a bad thing.

     I included **laundry detergent** in here for the same reason as towels and tissue. The customer is so confused by number of loads and ultra versus premium versus regular, they tend to trust *anything on display is a value*. The focus has returned to how detergents and cleaners impact our health and the earth, so eliminating harmful chemicals has become the *re-focus*.

     Other than those main areas, nonfood is stable, in the sense that not much has changed in twenty years. You still need **storage bags** that can withstand the freezer, and **storage bags** that can hold a sandwich. You need **aluminum foil** that can withstand a grill and **plastic wrap** that can *not wrap the first time and frustrate you to no end!!!!* And, yes, it's good when **disposable plates and cups** hold drinks and food.

     **Brooms and mops and Swiffer products, buckets and sponges and cleaning accessories**. All essential, all necessary, and all have at least three tiers of quality: opening price point, national brand, and value added (or high end).

     Let's move on to *drugs*....

# Beauty and Drugs

As we finish our walk of the store, we round the corner into the **health and beauty care (HBC)** section. If there were ever a confusing section of the store, it would be this one! *This is cereal times 1,000!* Have you ever had a horrible headache and stood in front of the pain relievers and *your headache got worse* as you tried to figure them out? Do I need a tension or a migraine solution? Do I want caffeine in it, or not? Will the store brand work as well as the name brand? Did I read acetaminophen was good for me or bad for me? Did I hear I should not mix ibuprofen and aspirin? Is this going to put me to sleep or make me jittery? Why do they sell ibuprofen in 1,000 tablet jars? Does that mean it must be safe for my stomach? **I'm. So. Confused!**

I know what I'll do, I'll just brush my teeth and go to bed. I just need **toothpaste**. Let me head over there…. Ahhhhhhhhh!!!!!!!!! *Why are there so many toothpastes?* And, while we're at it, why are there so many mouthwashes and shampoos and conditioners and body washes and soap *for men* and soap *for women* and soft toothbrushes and hard toothbrushes and a whole bunch of products in case I feel incontinent right here in the aisle? *If I weren't incontinent before I entered this aisle, that's changed.*

The main idea in this area of the store is these items are usually an **immediate necessity** (my head!), a **personal and private choice** (do I want Trojan or Durex?) or are for **someone else** (you were the only one healthy enough to go to the store). Organize it all in a way that you are over-communicating the uses and the types to the customer. If you think of it as we do specialty wines or cheeses, you'd be thinking *customer-first*. Plus, if you reminded the customer they could order online (even give them a QR code in-aisle) and the personal and private products would arrive in a little brown box at their front door, you could stop the sales erosion to online ordering from Amazon and Walmart. *Do you really think anyone wants to stand in line at the front checkout with a big box of **Depends** and risk a price check?*

De-SKU, communicate the differences in the products, make it private and personal, and offer online options in a simple manner.

One note, items proclaiming they are **immunity boosters** are going to be popular for quite a while. Emergen-C and all those vitamin C's and D's make sense, if the product works. Since you are not in the efficacy testing business, just carry them. And newness? **Mushroom extracts, chlorophyll tablets**, etc. *Trends are constantly flowing through this section like flax.*

Health and beauty care is an interesting section, driven by immediate need, most of the time. Matching up the *customer's need* with *simplifying their shopping experience* could pay out in spades. You will need to decide, though, on *where to shelve nutrition powders, nutrition bars*, etc. Target has them split, with bars in the snack aisle and powders in the pharmacy area. Walmart has them all together in health and beauty care. *Just decide and stick with it.* Not sure the first thought when about to head to the gym and needing a protein powder is to walk to the pharmacy.

# *Should you carry CBD?*

I've written three books on **Cannabidiol (CBD)** and the other cannabinoids from the cannabis plant, including up and comers **Cannabigerol (CBG) and Cannabinol (CBN)**. By most indications, the stigma that might have been present with these products has vanished in favor of the fact *they tend to work*.

Then, you have the federal legalization of the big dog, **Tetrahydrocannabinol (THC)**, or the cannabinoid coming from the cannabis plant that connects with the CB1 connector in your Endocannabinoid System (ECS), and sometimes impairs motor skills (CBD comes from hemp, has less than .3% THC, and blocks any connections to the CB1 connector, only bonding with the CB2). For the purposes of the grocery stores, we are only talking about **CBD** products, and the other cannabinoids that are *not THC*. Unless you open your own dispensary, you cannot carry THC.

But you *can* carry CBD, and I'd suggest you get into it in a big way. It's showing no signs of slowing and is becoming a go-to natural solution for inflammation, insomnia, and assorted pain (remember that bottle of 1,000 ibuprofen pills?).

That's all I'll say about CBD. I have three other books you can read about CBD, including the latest *The ABC's of THC and CBD*, available on Amazon in over 25 countries☺

# *Pricing*

We've walked this big, beautiful place we call the grocery store, we've talked about trends and customers and assortment, and now one more thing: **pricing**.

A number of years ago, we published a strategy in the *Journal of Food Products Marketing* that covered the topic of traditional food stores using their store brands program for an **everyday low price** component, to enhance their service and customer engagement strengths. To read the entire article, see Everyday Low Pricing: A Private Brand Growth Strategy in Traditional Food Retailers in *Journal of Food Products Marketing*, 24(10), pp. 1-19. To summarize some key findings, though, here is what we found. If you are struggling to find a way to compete against the price operators, this is a proven strategy that is affordable for most traditional retailers.

**The idea:** *If we move the pricing of our store brands program to everyday low price, and then communicate those prices, we will see a sales increase at a higher rate than the national brands versus last year.*

The store brands EDLP test was to address the needs for a traditional food retailer to have a viable strategy versus everyday low price operators, without diminishing its identity as a promotional retailer. In addition, the intrinsic benefits that come from store brands growth should increase customer loyalty and repeat visits, without a nice bump to margin rate- ostensibly building a barrier to entry around the retailer versus the competition.

The study aimed to expand the domain of store brands strategies by including a broader sales growth role than is normally found in the branding literature, particularly using store brands as a centerpiece of growth and not solely as a less expensive option to national brands.

The results prompted program adoption. *The results were significant enough for the retailer in the study to adopt the pricing model permanently.* It suggests that successful food retailers explore pricing models different from their preferred format to enhance sales growth. The study also suggests a link between traditional "mass merchant categories" (those categories offered at everyday low price in mass merchants- household, paper goods, cereal) and growth through everyday low pricing.

Even considering the various unknowns, we believe we can suggest specific inferences for store brand pricing in highly promotional food retailers. **"Mass merchant" categories may show a positive increase in sales through an everyday low price component being added to the marketing mix.** Paper goods, household, detergent, and staple everyday categories can benefit from a consistently low price available the entire month on certain SKU's. **Heavily promoted categories could react favorably to an everyday low price component.** In this specific study, cold cereal responded extremely well (best in the study) to an everyday low price grouping of SKU's being "brand blocked" in the cereal aisle.

This study showed traditional retailers can win the price game in a highly competitive market, while maintaining what makes them special- their service and engagement- their people. Do it! Your customers will love you for it!

# *Store Walk*

There you have it, a walk through a store today, in today's environment of treasure hunt versus inflation, commodity needs versus the need for experiences, health and wellness needs versus affordability; combined with the hottest trends in the food industry. The beauty of the grocery store is **it's all here**! Inside these four walls is a beautiful and bountiful offering of the greatest food assortment our world has to offer.

We're fortunate to be involved in this industry! An industry that feeds people, helps them celebrate, commemorates graduations and deaths, brings people together for weddings, and provides the ice cream and margaritas for the divorces. We're there every step of the way. The fortunate few who grow up in this business are the lucky ones!

*From one lucky one to another, I hope you've enjoyed this book!*

*~ Dr. Z*

# A Little Story

It all started when I was fourteen. I can remember the day like it was yesterday. I received a call on the phone that was connected to the wall, and picked up the receiver that was connected by a cord to the phone connected to the wall- giving you a little insight into the timing and my age. And, surprise to anyone under twenty years of age, we did _not_ know who was calling. That little bit of technology would come later. It was my brother on the other line. He was calling from Fogle's Food City in West Columbia, South Carolina. My brother worked in the produce department, and wanted to know if I could come down and work a few shifts while the older teenagers went to the beach. He had gotten his job because our oldest brother had referred him. In fact, pretty much everyone working at Fogle's Food City had gotten the job because someone in their family had previously worked there. It's what you did in the small independent operators, much like still happens today in IGA stores all over the world. The job? Bag groceries, take them to the customers' cars, and pocket the tips. I would work for tips plus $2.25 per hour, paid with cash from the register. I was underage, after all.

So, that started what was going to be a neat career in the food industry; but, I didn't know it at the time. In fact, once I became of "legal age" and took my rightful place replacing my brother as the "assistant produce clerk," in a department of two of us, the industry was already changing rapidly. Looking back now, the industry has always been changing rapidly. My Produce Manager at the time, Forrest, taught me one of my first lessons in food. When I asked him how to pick out the best watermelon, he told me simply- "tap three and pick the middle one". That little tidbit of wisdom had deeper meaning, and was more prescient, than Forrest probably even knew.

First, **customers are constantly searching for knowledge and insight into what they should eat**. Second, **they seem to trust anyone who acts like they know what they are doing**. The responsibility to take food nutritional guidelines, safety procedures, contamination control, etc. seriously weighs on the merchant or the food purveyor. There is an inherent trust in those who hand us our food. Whatever life lessons I learned, they didn't matter, I was going to the University of South Carolina and majoring in Engineering. I would keep the job until I graduated and would then get a "real job". After a semester in Engineering, I realized quickly that I needed to find another major. Choosing Psychology as my major, I still had plans to graduate and get the heck out of this grocery business.

One more lesson from Fogle's Food City before we move on. A lesson in consolidation and just how **tight the margins** are in food retail. Fogle's, owned by Bobby Fogle in Neese's, South Carolina (home of the best liver mush in the world....if you like that kind of stuff), was supplied by Thomas and Howard. Thomas and Howard, like many voluntary wholesalers (a term used to describe the supplier relationship between the retailer and the wholesaler) had an inherent desire to want to be paid when they shipped goods to retailers like Fogle's. The basis of marketing is exchange, remember? Two parties exchange something of value so that both parties are better off after the transaction. Well, in this case, Fogle's was running out of their side of the exchange equation- the cash side.

Wholesalers exist because small independents, like Fogle's Food City at the time, are not large enough to buy the goods they sell at the best price on their own. They need a wholesaler to link them together and buy for them. In exchange for a fee, the wholesaler buys the goods from the major consumer packaged goods companies at the best bracket price, holds those goods in inventory, and ships them to the retailers when the retailer needs them. Over time, though, independents sometimes run short of cash, cannot pay their supplier, and then either must sell the operation to someone else, go bankrupt, or be bought by their supplier.

Fogle's was eventually bought by Thomas and Howard, became a Giant Food World, then became a furniture store, and is now well- I have no idea what is there. It wasn't the best area of town. The Fogle's Store Manager through most of my time there, Keith, had a saying, "Ain't nothing but a thing". I never was quite sure what he meant by that,